THE INDUSTRIAL DEMOCRATS

Other books by the Author

DEMOCRATIC SOCIALISM, Longman, 1965.

MORE POWER TO THE PEOPLE, Longman, 1968. Co-edited with Brian Lapping.

WILL THORNE: CONSTRUCTIVE MILITANT, Allen and Unwin, 1974. With Lisanne Radice.

The Industrial Democrats

*Trade unions in an
uncertain world*

GILES RADICE

London
GEORGE ALLEN & UNWIN
Boston   Sydney

First published in 1978

GEORGE ALLEN & UNWIN LTD
40 Museum Street, London WC1A 1LU

British Library Cataloguing in Publication Data

Radice, Giles
   The industrial democrats.
   1. Employees' representation in management –
Great Britain
   2. Trade-unions – Great Britain
   I. Title
331.89'14   HD5660.G7   78-40222

ISBN 0-04-331073-7

Typeset in 10 on 12 point Times by Trade Linotype Ltd.
and printed in Great Britain
by Biddles Ltd, Guildford, Surrey

To my wife

Acknowledgements

I owe a debt of gratitude to my union, the General and Municipal Workers, for teaching me about trade unionism. The comments of David Lea, William McCarthy and David Winchester have significantly improved the book. Victor Thorpe (formerly of Allen & Unwin) and John Churchill, my publisher, have both helped me considerably. My thanks to Hilary Allen for ironing out inconsistencies and infelicities in the text, to the House of Commons library for checking some references, to John Kirkwood for assistance with the index, and to Sheila Kapila, Jackie Kirk and Mrs Somes for their typing assistance. My wife has corrected successive drafts. I hope she feels that the final result justifies her hard work.

GILES RADICE

Contents

Introduction

Few institutions (with the possible exception of parliament) are more constantly criticised than British trade unions. They are said to be the cause of strikes and the main reason for inflation. They are accused of being largely responsible for our poor economic performance. They are even alleged to be a threat to individual liberty and parliamentary democracy. *The Times* of 14 September 1977 came to the conclusion that 'the unions are the biggest national problem'. This book, by attempting to define the purpose and objectives of trade unionism against the background of late twentieth century industrial society, seeks to restore some balance to the debate.

However, I am not attempting to write an apologia for the trade unions. Indeed, my main theme is that, if they are to represent their members effectively in the conditions of today, they need to develop a more ambitious and constructive approach. A large part of the book is, therefore, devoted to a discussion of a modern trade union strategy. In particular, I argue that a major objective of British trade unionism must be the extension of industrial democracy.

There are now overwhelming arguments for more industrial democracy. In human terms, it is widely recognised that the deeper the involvement the greater the satisfaction. Work can and should be a major source of fulfilment and growth for the individual and not merely a means of meeting his basic needs. Yet, for most employees, the design, organisation and control of their work allows little room for development. Morally, the democratic case within industry has the same basis as democratic arguments elsewhere – that every individual should have a say in those decisions which affect his life. And when democratic values (if not always their practice) are broadly accepted throughout the rest of society, it is all the more difficult to deny their validity within the shop, factory or office. A younger generation of employees question management quite as much as other kinds of authority; so much so that it is becoming increasingly hard to run industry in the traditional way. What is now required is nothing less than a new basis for industrial consent.

There is a further powerful argument for more industrial democracy. When I first began the planning of this book at the beginning of the 1970s, the weakness of the British economy was already apparent. Despite the efforts of the Wilson administrations of the 1960s, our rate of growth was sluggish and our inflation rate higher than our competitors. Then, in the autumn of 1973, came the quadrupling of oil prices by the OPEC countries which not only set back the unprecedented expansion which the western industrial countries had enjoyed since 1945, but also dealt its less dynamic economies, particularly Britain, a more severe blow in terms of inflation and unemployment. Although North Sea oil has given the United Kingdom a new opportunity to improve its economic performance, it is obvious that, in many companies and industries, it will simply not be possible to carry through the necessary re-equipment and reorganisation programmes unless the employees and their representatives are fully involved. Indeed, it is no exaggeration to say that, in the exceptional times in which we now live, the strategic industrial decisions are too important to be left to management alone. As in wartime, the consequences of failure have become too appalling to contemplate.

The book recommends that the principle of joint regulation (by which trade unions and employers act as joint authors of rules governing employment) should now be applied to all those issues within industry which have a major impact on employees; and that, in order to ensure the development of this concept, the trade unions should participate in strength. It is argued that a broader democratic role for trade unions is quite consistent with their traditional objectives. Indeed their main purpose has always been a democratic one – to change a system of authoritarian decision-making into one in which management and unions decide jointly. If trade union representation is to be fully effective in modern conditions, then joint regulation should be extended to all strategic decisions.

I attach importance to the political and social side of trade unionism. But while emphasising this aspect, I argue that this wider role should be derived mainly from the industrial interests and objectives of trade unionists. The strength and major purpose of trade unionism is industrial representation which alone ensures that the voice of employees is heeded in the running of industry. However, in a modern industrial democracy trade unions have the right to be heard on the wider economic and social issues affecting their members.

I also examine the impact of an extension of industrial democracy on the rest of the community. I argue that it should make management's task easier rather than harder; and that an increase of trade union involvement will strengthen rather than weaken democracy, provided it is accompanied by trade union awareness of their new responsibilities and by safeguards both for individuals and for the community as a whole.

The book is divided into three parts. After an opening chapter which states the case for modern trade unionism, the first part examines the environment within which trade unions operate and analyses their response to that environment. My argument is that they are faced by new developments both from the managerial side and from the shopfloor to which they must respond. Government intervention in collective bargaining creates further problems. So only a strategy which takes full account of these factors will enable the trade unions to represent and protect their members effectively.

The second part seeks to outline the objectives which are necessary if the trade unions are to move away from a defensive towards a more positive approach. It covers the extension of collective bargaining, the development of industrial democracy, and their broader social and economic aims.

The third part considers the implications of this approach. It looks at trade union internal democracy, trade union structure and services, and the role of the TUC and the Labour Party. It also discusses the trade union movement's relationship with the rest of the community, including the impact of industrial democracy on management and an assessment of the new obligations implied by the extension of trade union rights. There is a short concluding chapter which summarises the book's main themes and proposals.

I declare my bias at the outset. I write as a former head of the research department of Britain's third largest union, the General Municipal Workers' Union, and as a Labour member of parliament sponsored by that union. I am also deeply committed to democratic socialist values. However, within those limits, I have tried to write as fairly and objectively as possible.

Chapter 1

Trade unions as industrial democrats

Trade unions give workers the possibility, through the strength of their combination, of influencing industrial decisions in their favour. Individually, employees are no match for employers. An employer's ability to hire and fire, to promote and downgrade, to deploy labour, and to draw on a wide range of skills and resources (wider today than ever before) stacks the cards on his side. By forcing employers to recognise that, on many issues, employees have a different approach which must be taken into account if the enterprise or industry is to survive, prosper and expand, trade unions bring an element of democracy into an environment which would otherwise be almost totally authoritarian.

Trade unionism is, as it always has been, the collective assertion that workers in industry are human beings, with the right to be treated as such. The workers of today are not over impressed by the fact that they are better off than any previous generation. They judge things in the light, not of their fathers' or grandfathers' aspirations, but of their own. They are often acutely aware of their fate as cogs in an industrial machine run by others; and, in an age of increasing technological change, of giant corporations, of persistent government intervention in collective bargaining, and of considerable uncertainty, they feel that they need organisations to represent their interests just as much, if in a different way, as their forbears.

Independent trade unions are, in truth, an essential part of a democratic society. Not only do they act as buffers against the Leviathan of the modern state; they are also the major source of democratic change within industry. Managers, even if individually enlightened, are committed by their function to put economic objectives first. Though governments are able to influence the industrial power balance, they, like managements, need the constant pressure of organised labour if the battle for a humanised and democratic industry is ever to be won.

Thus, to adapt Voltaire, if they did not exist, trade unions would have now to be invented.

WHY TRADE UNIONS ARE NECESSARY

There are those who will agree with John Kenneth Galbraith, the American political economist, when he says that modern industrial society has changed so dramatically that trade unions are now largely redundant. In the 1950s, Galbraith took the view that trade unionism was an effective source of countervailing power. But, by the end of the 1960s, he had come to believe that the large corporations were now so powerful that they had effectively 'drawn the teeth' of the American unions. His conclusion was that 'the industrial society is unfavourable to the union. Power passes to the technostructure and this lessens the conflict of interest between employer and employee which gave the union much of its reason for existence . . . The conclusion seems inevitable. The union belongs to a particular stage in the development of the industrial system. When that stage passes so does the union in anything like its original position of power.'[1]

Trade unionism is, of course, no exception to the general rule that organisations and their utility can only be assessed against the background of the environment in which they operate. It is, indeed, impossible to understand trade unions, without taking into account that they came into being as defensive organisations to try and improve the appalling conditions of industrial employees and prevent their exploitation by oppressive employers. As V. L. Allen has put it, 'trade unions from the very beginning were devised to protect their members from the exigencies of capitalism'.[2] It is, however, one thing to accept the validity of Galbraith's approach; quite another to accept without question his analysis of social and industrial developments.

It is undeniable that there have been significant changes in the Western industrial nations, especially since the end of the second world war. Under the impact of full employment policies and accelerating technological change, economic growth was – at least until the 1970s – both more steady and rapid. Affluence became relatively widespread. The rising demand for labour enabled it to 'push up' its share of national income[3], while the development of various social benefits allowed other, weaker groups to have a share in the growing prosperity.

There were changes within industry as well. Most Western economies, including Britain's, have developed large public sectors, whilst since the war governments of all parties have followed interventionist policies. In some respects, private industry has changed too. In many of the most important sectors of industry, ownership has become divorced from management, with the shareholders leaving managers very much to their own devices, except in moments of extreme crisis.

A new type of manager has, therefore, emerged, different in many ways from the nineteenth century entrepreneur. Like the worker, the modern manager gets his rewards (except at boardroom level) almost entirely from his salary, and, again like the worker, he is an employee of the company. The increasingly large scale of modern enterprise, whether public or private, and the demands of changing technology have also led to the growth of professionalism. Managers, particularly of the younger generation, tend to have some knowledge not only of business techniques but also increasingly of the social sciences. Among the more progressive managements, there is a growing, if sometimes grudging, recognition of trade unionism and of the legitimacy of workers' rights.

Yet, despite these important changes, British industrial society, in particular, is still characterised by considerable inequality and by underlying conflicts, and, in the less favourable conditions of the 1970s, these blemishes have become more apparent.

Our inequalities are well documented. In Britain, over a hundred years after the creation of the Trades Union Congress and over seventy-five years after the founding of the Labour Party, 1 per cent of the population owns at least a quarter and 5 per cent owns at least a half of total personal wealth.[4] This inequality of wealth exists side by side with considerable deprivation. While 2½ million people officially subsist below the supplementary benefit line, a further 2 million have incomes that are on or below that level.

Although there have been major improvements over the last forty years (see chapter 8), opportunities also remain unequal. This is not only so in the provision of essential services like health and housing and in the spread of social benefits, sick pay and pensions; inequality is also perpetuated through differential educational chances. For example, only a quarter of men and one-fifth of women university undergraduates come from families with fathers in manual occupations.[5] Recruitment to positions of power and influence in society (such as management, the civil service, the media, the judiciary and the government) still tends to be drawn mainly from children with non-manual backgrounds. As far as management is concerned, the effect of the growth of professionalism has actually been to make it more difficult for those with manual backgrounds to become managers.[6]

Lastly, and perhaps most important of all, the power to influence decisions is available only to a minority. As a result, despite the hard won right to choose a government and to form associations to defend and promote their interests, many people feel that over wide areas of their lives (at work and in their local communities) they do not control their own destinies. Again and again, they seem to be on the receiving end of decisions that they have had no chance of influencing beforehand and no opportunity of changing afterwards. Those without organisations to speak for them feel helpless before the power (to act or sometimes not to act) possessed by central government or local authority departments, private or nationalised firms, professional or technical experts. Even those with organisations to represent them (like trade unionists) feel that their power is limited. For many people the traditional 'them and us' division still holds good.

Nowhere are disparities revealed more starkly than at work. For most managers (in common with other professional people) work 'is an opportunity and a challenge'.[7] Their job engages their interest and allows them to develop their potential. They are constantly learning, able to exercise responsibility and have a considerable degree of control over their own – and other people's – working lives. By contrast, for most manual workers and for large numbers of white collar workers, work is a boring, monotonous and (for manual workers) sometimes a dangerous experience. The majority have little control over their environment. They have few opportunities to enjoy responsibility, to exercise judgement, to enlarge their knowledge, or to enjoy the experience of achievement and recognition. Production is often designed so that workers are simply part of the technology. This alienation is not confined to the factory floor. Many office jobs are now so routine that white collar employees justifiably feel themselves to be mere cogs in the bureaucratic machine. In a number of industries there has been a further development: the increase in capital intensity and the consequent growth in shift and overtime working to make maximum use of plant tends to restrict the private lives of growing numbers of workers. Yet the rewards (in terms of wages, fringe benefits, status and security) which employees receive for work which is too often frustratingly routine and restrictive are very much less than managers receive for carrying out more satisfying tasks. And the lack of promotion prospects gives them little opportunity to escape. In the laconic judgement of Alan Fox, 'some forms of work enable man to grow to what their societies define as full human stature. Many others do not.'[8]

These inequalities of autonomy, control and responsibility shape the differing attitudes of managers and workers in industry. Managers naturally stress growth and profits. Workers, as naturally, put their own interests first. Their relative lack of commitment to managerial objectives and to the company as a organisation – even when that company is under threat – is a marked characteristic of the British industrial system. Thus, throughout our industry, there is a conflict of perception between managers and workers about many issues. Managers lay stress on investment and, in private industry, on the distribution of profit to shareholders; workers, without any real commitment to their jobs, will naturally demand that a greater share of the cake should go to wages. Managers consider the introduction of new technology as an essential means of ensuring the growth of a firm; workers often see it as disturbing present pay and working arrangements and also as a possible threat to their job security. Managers proclaim their belief in efficiency and in the 'rational' use of resources; workers suspect that efficiency implies redundancy which can still mean an unforgettable period of insecurity.

The consequent rejection of managerial values and the lack of employee commitment to the enterprise is shown in a number of ways; individually, through absence, sickness, labour turnover or bad work, or collectively, through strikes, go-slows, working-to-rule, resistance to technical or organisational change, manipulation of the payment system, exploitation of overtime, or by higher wage demands than can be justified by extra productivity or by comparison with rates for comparable jobs in other industries. Loyalty, however, cannot be bought by higher wages alone. Though a worker may be prepared to do a boring job provided he is adequately rewarded, this by no means implies a commitment to the firm. On the contrary, it is very often the higher paid workers who show the most open resistance to management. Throughout industry, the sacrifice of human needs to the requirements of the enterprise in the design, organisation and control of work has led to a widespread alienation that is sometimes compensated for but can never be entirely removed by higher rewards.

British trade unions have survived from the nineteenth century essentially because they represent a deep seated and enduring assertion of human values. If trade unions were merely a defensive reaction to an old style capitalist system, they would have disappeared long ago. But trade unionism has always been more than this. Because of its representative character, it has provided, and continues to provide, a democratic challenge to an industrial system which, despite the development of collective bargaining, remains far too authoritarian. The main argument of this book is that, if the trade unions of today are to represent their members' needs and aspirations in today's uncertain conditions, they will have to give a high priority to the creation of an industrial structure which ensures that employees and their representatives have a greater say in the running of industry.

TRADE UNION PURPOSE

What is now required is a definition of trade union objectives which sufficiently emphasises the broader humanistic and democratic aspects. The Webbs, writing when trade unionism was more or less in its infancy and its economic function most apparent, defined a trade union as 'a continuous association of wage-earners for the purpose of maintaining or improving the conditions of their employment';[9] and they distinguished three main methods – unilateral trade union regulation, collective bargaining and statutory regulation. Seventy years later, Allan Flanders, the defender *par excellence* of collective bargaining at a time when it was under attack, broadened the Webbs' mainly economic definition by stressing the democratic side of trade unionism. Thus, according to Flanders, one of the principal objectives of trade union involvement in collective bargaining is the establishment of a system of industrial rights for workers.[10]

Flanders' definition is a decided improvement on that of the Webbs' in that it shows that the purpose of trade unions is more than economic. But for modern purposes, its emphasis on collective bargaining is unnecessarily limiting. For, though it has achieved a substantial measure of joint control over pay and conditions, collective bargaining has not really challenged management's control of industry. As Hyman puts it, trade union involvement in collective bargaining 'permits debate around the terms of workers' obedience; it does not challenge the fact of their subordination'.[11] So a wider view of trade unionism is now required.

The fundamental trade union purpose has always been – and must continue to be – that of democratising and humanising industry. And, in achieving these objectives, a wide range of instruments will be needed. Joint regulation of wages and conditions – a basic democratic right – is and must remain a major trade union function. But, if trade unions are to influence other issues (such as investment, technological change, closures and mergers, location of plant) which are equally vital to working lives, then they must recognise that democracy in industry means more than joint control over wages and conditions. It implies nothing less than joint regulation of *all* the strategic decisions in industry. And, if a democratic industrial society is to be created, then trade unions must also have a say in those general economic and social decisions which also help to shape their environment.

The broad definition of trade union objectives which is advocated in this book would be regarded by Marxists as Utopian. The distinguished American sociologist, C. Wright Mills, highlighted the limitations and ambivalence of the trade union function in his well known description of the trade union leader as a 'manager of discontent' who organises discontent and then sits on it.[12] Perry Anderson put a Marxist position with some elegance when he wrote that as 'institutions, trade unions do not *challenge* the existence of society based on a division of classes, they merely *express* it. Thus trade unions can never be viable vehicles of advance towards Socialism in themselves; by their very nature, they are tied to capitalism. They can bargain within society, but not transform it.'[13]

How valid are these objections? Admittedly there *is* a sense in which trade union activity is confined – and rightly so. For the primary trade union objective must be industrial. This is not to say that trade unions should not also have political and social objectives. Any argument about power, whether within or outside industry, has political implications. It should also be remembered that trade unionists are not only workers, but also consumers, tenants, or householders, parents and potential old age pensioners. Organised labour, therefore, remains the only effective base from which any attempt to create a more democratic and more just society can be made. And, if trade unions are to achieve their industrial aims, they must also have a significant influence on national economic and social policy. But, for the implementation though not for the formulation of their political and social objectives, trade unions must rely on other organisations. Once they forget their industrial role and become primarily political, they are in danger of betraying their members. The strength of trade unionism is industrial representation – to ensure that human values are not ignored and that the workers' voice is heard in the running and control of industry. A predominantly political strategy, an approach which concentrated the whole of trade union energy and resources on objectives other than industrial ones, would risk diluting trade union strength in the area where it is most effectively deployed – and most urgently needed.

It is also the case that there is an ambivalence in the trade union function. But there is nothing in this of which trade unionists need feel ashamed. Trade unions, by their very existence, are a challenge to industrial authoritarianism; and yet, in order to gain benefits for their members in the here and now, they have to reach accommodation with management. There is no way trade unions can escape from this dilemma. As *democratic* organisations representing the views of their members, they have to secure and be seen to secure short term gains. If they were to neglect this side of their job, they would lose the force which enables them to pursue broader objectives. Indeed, the tension derived from this ambivalence of roles has contributed substantially to trade union power and achievement. They have managed both to remain close to their members, while acting as the main force for democratic industrial change.

It is a strange paradox that, despite their different standpoints many managers should take a view of trade unionism which, in its insistence on trade union limitations, is very similar to the Marxist one. The managerial belief that trade unions are industry's 'junior partners' is largely shaped by management's traditional conception of its own role – a conception which is, however, in process of substantial modification. The classic justification for managerial prerogative in terms of property has been undermined by the extension of the public sector and the divorce between ownership and control in many of the largest privately owned companies. But some managers now legitimise their position by reference to their superior technical expertise.

In an industrial system which is growing more complex, so the argument runs, managerial prerogative is more than ever necessary, because management alone possesses the necessary skills. Now of course, there are specialised skills (accounting, economic forecasting, data processing, legal expertise and so on) to which management needs access. Indeed Galbraith has claimed that the development of these specialisms are an important and even decisive constraint on management.[14] But the *strategic* decisions on such vital matters as investment, location, mergers and closures, and the development of corporate policy are still made by managerial generalists (even if it is on the basis of the evidence supplied by the specialists); it is surely difficult to argue that trade unionists are incapable of making a contribution to decision-making at this level when trade union representatives, through collective bargaining, are already participating in strategic decision-making in such crucial, if limited, areas as pay and conditions. Is it seriously maintained that, even if they receive the appropriate training, these representatives will remain unable to become meaningfully involved in decisions on other, equally important matters? The fact that management is increasingly anxious to attract shop stewards to take up junior management positions and to recruit trade union officials into managerial jobs at higher levels, including the boardroom, casts doubt on this type of assertion.[15]

The unease about their position felt by managers is reflected in the following statement by a former director general of the CBI: 'Managers do not – if they ever had – have a divine right to manage. There is no automatic prerogative to make decisions and expect them to be carried out. The process of decision-making will have to be more and more justified and demonstrated to be right in order to command the respect not only of the people working in the company but the community as a whole.'[16] Many managers now accept that there must be a different basis for authority – that of consent.

Of course, there can be very different meanings attached to 'consent'. The slave may be said to 'consent' to his exploitation – but that is because he has no alternative. In the same way, the worker may 'consent' to managerial domination in many areas, because through social and cultural 'blindness' he cannot 'see' any other alternative. But consent in the widest sense, as the best managers recognise, implies full acceptance of the rights of employees.

It is, therefore, not possible, once the broad meaning of 'consent' has been accepted, to draw distinctions between those issues which are to be the subject of discussion, negotiation and agreement, and those issues which must remain exclusively the prerogative of management. Management decisions are indivisible. One cannot in logic say: 'Yes, I am prepared to discuss wages and conditions with trade unions, but all the rest – job design, hiring and firing, managerial appointments, investment, corporate planning – these are my business, even if, as I admit, they are an important influence on wages and conditions.' For decisions about wages and conditions *are* connected with and often shaped by earlier decisions on other even more fundamental matters. So within industry, as elsewhere, authority based on consent implies an extension of democracy to matters which are now decided by management alone.

Management and government have also to accept that an effective strategy to increase industrial democracy must be based on trade union organisation and built on existing trade union achievements in negotiation and representation. A meaningful industrial democracy must give employees a real say and not merely provide a facade for an otherwise authoritarian structure; and the only real guarantee that managers will not manipulate any new constitutional forms for their own purposes is if these are supported by the existing source of collective power. Thus, if there is to be any democratic advance within industry, it can only come if the trade unions themselves are fully involved.

TRADE UNION POWER

There is, however, a widely held belief that trade unions already have *too much* power. In the eyes of the critics, the trade unions are the 'overmighty subjects' of British society, the modern equivalents of the feudal barons, wielding *excessive* power in an *irresponsible* fashion. The Conservative Government's Industrial Relations Act of 1971 was, in part, based on this assumption. But the belief that trade unions are too powerful is not confined to Conservative politicians alone. Large sections of the professional and administrative classes, of the mass media, and, judging from the public opinion polls, of a fluctuating but still significant proportion of trade unionists themselves agree that, in the community's interest, trade unions need to be restrained.

How strong are the unions? In any assessment, some basic points about the nature of trade union power need to be made at the outset. People often speak as though trade unions and management were the same kinds of organisation, doing the same sort of job. They seem to forget that, whilst management's command over a firm's resources and its power to act, is, except in certain areas and in certain circumstances, relatively unfettered, trade union initiative is both extremely limited in scope and also at least partially circumscribed by democratic checks.

As has been mentioned already, the ability of trade unions to influence management has traditionally been confined to the relatively narrow limits of the determination of the terms and conditions of employment. Over most areas of decision-making (production, investment, mergers, marketing and so on), there is no joint regulation at all. Even in those areas in which trade unions are strongest, their power is often expressed negatively, as a defensive reaction to management rather than as a positive initiative of their own. It is true that, in negotiations, it is the union side which normally presents its case first. But, as W. E. J. McCarthy and N. D. Ellis have pointed out, collective bargaining is usually an attempt by trade unions to redress past grievances and complaints rather than to decide on the future.[17] Thus, despite all the complaints about the 'overmighty' trade unions, their power of initiative is often extremely limited. It is management, not the trade unions, which holds the reins of command in industry.

Management's freedom of action is increased by the fact that, outside the collective bargaining arena and in ordinary circumstances, it does not have to justify its actions. The legal obligation to shareholders in private industry is only of importance in crisis situations – for example when there is a prospect of a takeover or when the firm runs into serious financial difficulties. True, there is more effective control by government in nationalised industries; but, even here, a large degree of discretion is still left in management's hands. Of course, trade unions must not forget that there are increasingly powerful pressures on management. Fierce competition in the product market (often expressed internationally), the pace and complexity of technological change, the effect of government decisions, the impact of rapid inflation, the demands of industrial relations, all these are pressures which management has to take into account.[18] But these are different from the self-regulating checks on managerial effectiveness envisaged in the models of classical economists. After all, large parts of the British economy are either dominated by a few giant firms or to some extent insulated from outside influences. So, despite growing pressures, an alert management can still retain considerable autonomy.

Contrast the position of the trade unions. Trade unions not only have, in most cases, to react to management decisions; they must also respond to internal demands, for, unlike business corporations, they are basically democratic organisations. Thus trade union leaders, if they are to be effective, must gain the support of their members. The real democratic check on trade union leadership is not so much the rule book or even periodic elections (though these are important) but the possibility that the membership will act independently. In any situation, the leadership has to be looking over its shoulder to see if it has membership support. So the autonomy of trade union leadership is circumscribed in a way that is quite outside the experience of management.

Bearing in mind this fundamental difference between management and unions, there are a number of factors which are relevant in assessing the balance of power between the two parties at the bargaining table. The most important is the strength of trade union *organisation*, for, unless workers are organised into unions, they are not able to exert their power consistently and effectively on management. Yet a large part of the labour force in this country still remains unorganised. Total trade union membership as a percentage of the labour force has only moved forward marginally since the 1940s – from 46 per cent to just under 51 per cent. Indeed, had it not been for a marked increase in trade union membership (particularly amongst white collar public service and female workers) which began in the late 1960s and is still continuing, the percentage organised would have remained stagnant or even fallen.

Studies of trade union organisation show that formidable obstacles remain in many areas of potential recruitment.[19] Membership gains have been concentrated primarily in large public and private enterprises; in manufacturing establishments employing more than 200 workers, union density is as high as 90 per cent. However, in construction, distribution, hotel and catering and other parts of the private services sector (now a growing source of employment), trade union membership is still extremely weak. Small work units, seasonal or casual employment, and a high labour turnover of female, immigrant or unskilled labour, present great problems to union organisers. When these are compounded by hostile management, recognition of unions becomes even more difficult. As a result, management continues to decide most issues unilaterally; workers can only take it or leave it.

In considering economic factors, it is undeniable that relatively full employment gave organised workers far more power. The disappearance of large pools of unemployed labour in most areas after the war enabled workers and their representatives to extend the effectiveness of collective bargaining and to establish their influence over a number of important shopfloor issues, including control of overtime, discipline, redundancy, manning, promotion and working conditions.

However, following the events of the autumn of 1973, the

British economy moved into a serious recession, with average unemployment levels of over 5 per cent. Naturally, this had an impact on union bargaining power. But even before that the effect of full employment on trade unions was often exaggerated. It should be remembered that the British economy since the war has expanded only slowly and has been frequently interrupted by recessions which have been growing deeper; while higher regional unemployment levels have existed alongside lower average levels of unemployment. A high level of unemployment obviously acts as a constraint on the use of worker sanctions – particularly the final sanction of striking. And, contrary to the view often put forward in the popular press, the vast majority of trade union officials and shop stewards usually think twice, even in the most favourable circumstances, before bringing their members (who are seldom in a position to bear the substantial reduction of earnings involved for any length of time) out on strike. In bad conditions, they are even more hesitant. Indeed, there are times (particularly if demand for their product is slack) when employers can contemplate a strike with far more equanimity than trade unionists.

In any case, the increase in power created by full employment has very often gone not to the national trade union centres but to the shopfloor. In a number of key industries in the private sector, particularly engineering, shopfloor bargaining has become more important than negotiations at industry level. In the pre-war period, industry-wide bargaining had been established and administered by trade unions so that, in favourable conditions, the power of stronger groups of workers could be used to shore up wages as a whole. The growth of shopfloor bargaining was a largely autonomous post-war phenomenon generated *within* the plant or factory by work groups independent of existing trade union organisation. Thus, in large areas of private industry, the increase in power has benefited not so much the national trade union centres but the work groups and their shopfloor representatives.

Trade unions in the public sector (which now employs nearly a third of the total workforce) have greater power. In the first place, the nationalisation acts have all given full recognition to trade unions. Even more important, the centralised nature of the state owned monopolies makes bargaining at industry level far more significant than in the private sector. Although there was a big increase in the number of incentive and payment by results schemes during the 1960s, national settlements still determine the major proportion of workers' pay in the public sector and the efforts of trade unions at national level are, therefore, more important than in much of the private sector. There is the additional point that, in contrast to much of the private sector, trade unionists in the public sector are well aware that the government cannot allow their industries to go bankrupt.

Yet the paradox is that, at least until the end of the 1960s, there were many more strikes in private industry. One of the main reasons for this difference was that trade unions in the public sector were highly conscious of the effect of a strike in their industries on the community as a whole. Even during the industrial unrest in this sector in the early 1970s, trade union consciousness of the extent of their power often acted as a brake on their use of it. Certainly the miners' strikes of 1972 and 1974 provided classic examples of a public sector union determinedly and successfully using an increase in power to gain very substantial increases for its members. But, in both the electricity dispute of 1971 and the gas dispute of 1972–73, the trade unions involved were inhibited by their concern for the community – in the first case by the possible effect of the strike on the sick and the old and, in the second case, by safety considerations as well.

Thus, while relatively full employment has substantially increased the power of organised labour, the situation is more complex than the critics of the trade union movement will admit.

The danger of making superficial judgements is confirmed when we focus more closely on the balance of power between management and workers. It is true that from certain kinds of work employees acquire great potential power. The nature of the jobs of craftsmen and other key workers like cranemen or internal transport workers, for example, enables them to bring a whole plant to a halt more easily and, thus, gives them more bargaining power than is available to other groups of workers. There are also certain industries where, because of the type of product, employers are in a highly vulnerable position. In this category, one must include the newspaper industry (where a stoppage of any length can lead to an irretrievable loss of readership) and the docks (where shippers with perishable goods invariably bring pressure on the stevedoring companies to settle). In some companies and industries, the interlocking nature of operations gives power to workers in key plants; for example, in the British motor industry, a strike by a small group in a component factory can bring the whole industry to a standstill. Capital intensive industries, because of their need to keep their plant in perpetual use, are also particularly vulnerable to shopfloor pressure. However, the technology of some of these industries (like chemicals and oil-refining) can also prevent the formation of effective work groups, by separating workers off from each other.

There are, in any case, other factors which may tip the scales towards management. The sheer size and importance in the economy of the large company often gives managers considerable power. Nearly forty-five per cent of the labour force in manufacturing now work for the 186 companies which employ 5,000 or more workers.[20] As a result, a single management decision within a giant firm can affect as many people as the action of a pre-twentieth century government. Sometimes this concentration of power can be exploited by organised workers. But, in its negotiations with the unions, management has an incomparably larger pool of skills and resources upon which it can call. Even if negotiations break down, the wide range of products often produced by such companies enables it to resist for a long time a stoppage of production in any single plant or in a group of plants making a single product. On occasions, a giant company is even able to direct (or to threaten to direct) production elsewhere. The growth of the multinational firm (about fifteen per cent of British manufacturing industry is now foreign-owned, employing over a million British workers[21]) makes the position more difficult for a union. The ability, which the multinational often possesses, to stockpile or channel investment into other countries increases management's power to resist union demands in a single country. The confidence of a trade union official can be seriously undermined by threats to direct future investment into a country where trade unions are more docile – the more so if he is uncertain whether decisions are made by the manager with whom he is talking or by some Olympian board of directors far away in the company's country of origin.

This brief analysis of the relative power position of management and trade unions shows that, though the power of organised workers has increased very substantially since the war, it is quite wrong to claim that trade unions, in any real sense, run industry. Many employees are still not in unions. Where workers are organised, the scope of trade union influence remains restricted. Trade unions are still mainly reactive bodies, responding to management initiatives. So to a large extent, trade union power is still of a blocking, rather than of an initiating kind.

It is certainly true that, when acting together, the trade union movement is able to exert considerable influence on government. The withdrawal of the Labour Government's industrial relations legislation of 1969, the concerted resistance to the Conservative Government's 1971 Industrial Relations Act, and the development of the 'social contract' between the Labour Government and the TUC since 1974 are all examples of effective use of trade union power. But it is power exercised at the *political* rather than the *industrial* level. And, once again, it is – with the important exception of the social contract – power to stop things happening (industrial relations legislation, a statutory incomes policy and so on) rather than power to help start things off.

RESPONSIBILITY AND IRRESPONSIBILITY

The other question that has to be answered is how far trade unions use the power they possess in a responsible fashion. Charges of trade union 'irresponsibility' are made far too readily on the basis of flimsy reportage by the mass media whose bias is frequently evident.[22] The media too often represents pay claims or stoppages of work as the fault of the trade unions. So much so that a reader or viewer could not be blamed if he received the impression that, in the eyes of most editors, *any* use of union power was to be considered irresponsible. And it is unfortunately the case that the only definition of responsibility that some critics of trade unions would accept would be that of a tame do-nothing trade unionism which provided little more than a democratic facade to the unfettered use of management prerogative. Trade unions cannot accept the strictly limited role which most of those who charge them with irresponsibility would ascribe to them. However trade unions have to recognise their obligations to the community. It is in this respect that it is legitimate to assess trade union responsibility.

There are three main issues about which trade unions are said to be irresponsible – strikes, inflation, and productivity. As far as strikes are concerned the Royal Commission on Trade Unions and Employers' Associations chaired by Lord Donovan which reported in 1968 noted that in terms of strike-days in relation to the size of the labour force 'the United Kingdom's recent record has been about average compared with other countries'.[23] In the number of stoppages per thousand employees this country was the sixth highest out of the fifteen countries listed by the Royal Commission; but, in the number of working days lost per thousand employees, the United Kingdom was lower down – ninth out of the sixteen countries listed. More recent surveys broadly confirm this picture. A study of the comparative performance of different countries in terms of the number of days lost per thousand employees over the ten year period 1966–75 showed that, out of the eighteen countries listed in order of the number of days lost, the United Kingdom came eighth.[24]

It is, however, true that the number of working days lost in this country increased substantially at the end of the 1960s. Whereas the typical strike in the 1950s and 1960s was short and almost always unofficial, a larger proportion of strikes in the early 1970s were both official and longer in duration. One is tempted to the conclusion that the Conservative Government of 1970–74 gave a new life to the long-drawn-out official strike. Their incomes policies certainly appeared to discriminate against workers in the public sector in which there were a number of industry-wide official strikes. Trade unions also believed that the Industrial Relations Act of 1971 was anti-trade union. Thus the Conservative Government exacerbated an already explosive situation in which workers felt that a rapidly increasing rate of inflation was threatening to undermine their living standards. It should be noted that, with the adoption by the incoming Labour Government of a new approach, based on conciliation and arbitration and the extension of collective bargaining, the number of working days lost through strikes declined significantly, despite the persistence of a high rate of inflation.

Much has been written about the cost of strikes, particularly of unofficial strikes. Indeed, it was argued by employers, and broadly accepted by the Donovan Commission, that the unpredictability of British strikes made them peculiarly expensive. Yet the unofficial strike is by no means confined only to Britain – in both the United States and France, for example, there is a large and growing number of 'wildcat' strikes. And evidence about the cost of unpredictability is sparse. For one thing, unofficial strikes are not always unpredictable (an alert management should know when trouble is brewing). Even when they are unpredictable, there is little evidence that they are any more costly than official strikes – particularly when, as is usually the case, the latter involve many more working days lost. There is more to be said for the other Donovan argument about the effect on management behaviour (for example, on the introduction of more efficient methods) of the threat of unofficial strikes. But it was the Commission's own research director, W. E. J. McCarthy, who said 'I have always thought that the Donovan Report grossly overdid the psychological deterrent effect of strikes; it has always seemed to me a managerial excuse, the first refuge of the lazy and the last ditch of the cowardly.'[25] In any case, estimating the cost of a strike, whether official or unofficial, is always very difficult. A fair assessment has not only to include the effect on other factories and industries but has also to take account of the production made good after a strike and of the possible beneficial effects on productivity, once work is resumed, of the workers' involvement in a strike (often noted by sociologists as well as by trade unionists). There is also the point that some strikes are merely substitutes for curtailments of work that would have taken place anyway through lay-offs – which is the reason why strikes are not always unwelcome to management. In short, though strikes are often economically damaging, there are times when their cost can be over rated.

To sum up, the British strike record, if viewed in perspective and if the improvements since 1974 are taken into account, is (with the exception of Germany, the Netherlands, Denmark and Sweden) no worse than other industrial countries. Yet, even if it were substantially inferior, this would not necessarily be solely the fault of trade unions. Indeed, research carried out on the causes of strikes shows that these include such diverse factors as inadequate disputes machinery, unfair payments system, technological pressures, employee insecurity, the reaction of a better educated labour force to a paternalistic management – and sometimes the basic conflicts between management and workers which lie at the heart of the way modern industry is governed and organised.[26] There is also evidence (which I can substantiate from my personal experience) that most trade unions, most trade union officials and most shop stewards do everything they can to avoid a strike. Mention has already been made of the behaviour of trade unions in the public sector. And all recent surveys of industrial relations show that shop stewards, so far from being the irresponsible agitators portrayed by the popular press, are the lynchpins of the industrial relations system, performing an essential negotiating and conciliatory role and only taking strike action as a last resort.[27] Certainly there are still too many strikes – and some industries have a major strike problem.[28] But the charge of trade union irresponsibility, as far as strikes are concerned, is by no means proven.

A more plausible case for the irresponsibility charge is that trade unions are the only or at least the major cause of inflation – an assertion which is too often made by politicians, by journalists, and by some economists. At first glance the argument seems persuasive: 'Trade unions put in wage claims and prices rise. Surely the one is the cause of the other?' Consumers and housewives cannot be blamed if they swallow the editorials in the popular press and harken to the comments made by TV pundits that the trade unions are *always* the villains of the piece.

Yet the causes of inflation are more complex than such a simplistic view allows. Objective appraisal reveals there are other factors involved, including rises in food prices and raw materials, the effects of government policies, the capital requirements of the large corporations, as well as the actions of trade unions.

In a country like Great Britain, which imports much of its food and raw materials, price rises in many essential items are obviously entirely unrelated to the wage claims of British trade unions. The dramatic upsurge in the price of raw materials, particularly oil, which began in 1973 was not the responsibility of trade unionists; it was the result of movements in world prices outside national control. It is true, of course, that increases in the cost of items like food have an influence on the size of union wage claims. Every trade union official has to take into account the rise in the retail price index when deciding on the size of his claim. If he did not, his members (as research on attitudes to inflation shows[29]) would consider that he was failing in his duty as a trade union official. But accepting the influence of price increases on the level of union wage claims is quite different from saying that they are *caused* by union wage claims.

Another important element in inflation is government. A study by Jackson, Turner & Wilkinson has convincingly argued that the sharp rise in inflationary pressure in Britain at the end of the 1960s was, in part, connected with the impact on wages of government tax policies.[30] The rise was not only influenced by changes in taxation rates but also (and perhaps more importantly) by the psychological effect on workers of seeing their wage increases being almost automatically eroded by a taxation system within which increases of income were taxed at successively higher rates. Other economists have pointed to the role of the money supply in the creation of inflation. Without giving it the overriding importance that Milton Friedman and his disciples have attached to it[31], the money supply is also undoubtedly an influential factor (as we saw in 1972–73) which governments alone can control. There is also the effect of exchange rate depreciation on import prices – whether it is caused by moving to a new parity (as in 1967) or by 'floating' (as successive British governments allowed the pound to do after 1972). A particularly dramatic example of the latter was the rise in prices in the first half of 1977, following the sharp fall in the value of the pound during 1976. Lastly, there are the charges of the public sector; undoubtedly increases in nationalised industries prices was a significant element in inflation during 1975.

There is another quarter from which inflation can come. Charles Levinson, general secretary of the International Federation of Chemical and General Workers' Union, has suggested that price rises in many capital intensive industries are increasingly unrelated to wage increases. As he put it, 'there is now a growing pressure arising out of the long term capital plans and expenditure of major national and multinational corporations which has become a pre-dominant parameter in the inflation equation and relegates all other considerations to lesser levels of importance'.[32] Capital intensive industries like chemicals, electronics and oil rely mainly on retained earnings to finance their continued expansion. Capital projects are based on long term plans and any shortfall in profits which could hold back investment can sometimes, in unfavourable conditions, be met by raising prices. So the capital requirements of these firms may also be a significant factor in inflation.

But, though there are many causes of inflation, wage increases *are* undoubtedly an important and, on occasion, the predominant factor in its generation. Any British trade unionist who denies this ignores the disastrous effect of abnormally high settlements during the wage round of 1974–75 and also the beneficial impact on prices of incomes policy in following years.

However, before condemning trade unions out of hand for causing inflation, it should be recalled that trade unions are basically democratic organisations which respond to pressure from their members. Aubrey Jones, drawing on his experience as the chairman of the National Board for Prices and Incomes until its dissolution in 1970, highlighted the difficulties which confront trade unions when he wrote that 'in a society which is accustomed to constantly rising living standards and which seeks to imitate the largest increase in earnings that it sees around it, the tendency will be for earnings to exceed the rate of increase in the gross national product and for labour costs per unit of output to rise'.[33] And the study of trade unions and inflation already quoted concluded 'not merely that unions are far from being the only significant factor in the infla-tionary situation, but they are not generally an independent factor in it'.[34] Despite these difficulties, on at least three occasions since the war and for long periods of time, trade unions have participated in incomes policies which have for a time controlled the level of wage increases.

British inflation needs, in any case, to be put into perspective. If this country had had a better economic record since the war, our rate of inflation would not have been so fast or so damaging. In fact, there is a strong case for arguing that, over the long term, our main problem compared with our industrial rivals has not been that wages have risen faster but that the rate of investment and the use made of both investment and manpower has been inadequate to sustain a satisfactory growth in national output.[35]

For this failure, governments and management must assume at least as great a responsibility as trade unions. It is certainly true that trade unionists at shopfloor level have sometimes resisted changes (either in technology, machinery or working arrangements) which were essential for the health of the enterprise. Such industrial conservatism is highly regrettable and, in the longer run, self-defeating. But to blame trade unionists exclusively for this behaviour overlooks the basic point that managers, not trade unionists, hold the reins of command within industry. Indeed, it was his recognition of this truth that led Allan Flanders to conclude that 'the changing of restrictive union practices is a managerial responsibility'.[36]

The preceding paragraphs have sought to show that charges of trade union irresponsibility over strikes, inflation, and productivity, are often greatly exaggerated. Trade unions and their activities must be viewed more objectively and in the context in which they operate. As things stand, they are mainly defensive oragnisations, reacting to outside events. If they are to be held responsible, then they must be given more responsibility. This is not to say that trade unionists can be absolved from their obligations either to fellow workers or to the community as a whole. Powerful groups of employees *have* a responsibility to the less powerful. Trade unionists *must* take account of the effect their actions have on the rest of the community – a community which includes their own families. So, as is argued in chapter 12, the trade union movement should have a clear understanding about its obligations as well as its rights. It is also essential that trade unions should not only act responsibly – but explain to the rest of the community that they are so doing. They cannot afford to let their case go by default.

The argument of this chapter has been that, because of the inequalities of autonomy, responsibility and control at work, trade unionism – and its underlying democratic purpose – is more than ever relevant. But, to carry out their role in modern conditions, they will need to have more and not, as their critics wrongly argue, less industrial power. This additional power must, however, be used creatively for the extension of industrial democracy.

What is important now is for trade unions to realise their potential. They must not allow themselves to remain trapped in a negative posture, prisoners of the collective bargaining routine and, in some cases, of outdated ideology, usually reacting in a defensive and, sometimes self-defeating, way to events. They have to adopt a positive approach. They must define clearly their strategic objectives, construct a programme around them, and act upon them. Their primary task should be to create an industry 'with a human face'. But their commitment to humanistic, democratic values also implies that they cannot concern themselves solely with industrial questions; these have also to be considered in a wider context. So trade unions must not only be allies of progress within industry but also claim their proper share in the process of national decision-making.

In short, major democratic changes both in industry and in society as a whole will only take place if organised labour is able to realise its underlying *raison d'être*. The remaining chapters of this book examine the context and the conditions for such a development.

REFERENCES

1 J. K. Galbraith *The new industrial state* Hamish Hamilton 1967 p. 274. For his earlier view, see *American capitalism* Pelican edition 1963, and for a qualification of his later view see *Economics and the public purpose* Pelican edition 1975 p. 275.

2 V. L. Allen *The sociology of industrial relations* Longmans 1971 pp. 46–47.

3 For a convincing discussion of labour's share of national income see Jan Pen *Income distribution* Allen Lane 1971 pp. 158–233; also C. Feinstein *National income expenditure and output of the United Kingdom 1855–1966* CUP 1972.

4 *Royal Commission on the Distribution of Income and Wealth* HMSO report no. 1 1975 pp. 139–45.

5 See the Sheffield University study reported in *The Times Higher Educational Supplement* 25 February 1972.

6 See Howard Glennester's essay 'Democracy and class' in *More power to the people* Young Fabian Essays Longmans 1968.

7 Roy Jenkins *What matters now* Collins-Fontana 1972 p. 82.

8 Alan Fox *A sociology of work in industry* Collier-Macmillan 1971 p. 13.

9 Sidney and Beatrice Webb *History of trade unionism* Longmans 1894 p. 1.

10 Allan Flanders *Management and unions* Faber 1970 pp. 41–42.

11 Richard Hyman *Strikes* Fontana 1972 p. 96.

12 C. Wright Mills *The new men of power* Harcourt Brace 1948 p. 9.

13 Perry Anderson 'The limits and possibilities of trade union action' in *The incompatibles* Penguin 1967 pp. 264–65.
14 *The new industrial state* pp. 58–59.
15 This and the next four paragraphs are drawn from the Fabian pamphlet *Working power*, published in 1974, which I edited for a Fabian working group on industrial democracy.
16 W. C. Adamson 'CBI director general's inaugural letter to members 1970' quoted in W. W. Daniel and Neil McIntosh *The right to manage* PEP 1972 p. 114.
17 W. E. J. McCarthy and N. D. Ellis *Management by agreement* Hutchinson 1973 pp. 102–3.
18 *Management by agreement* pp. 92–94.
19 See studies by Professor G. S. Bain: for example, 'Trade union growth and recognition' *Royal Commission on Trade Unions and Employers' Associations Research Paper no. 6*; and R. Price and G. S. Bain 'Union growth revisited: 1948–74' in *British Journal of Industrial Relations* November 1976 pp. 339–55.
20 Report on the census of production: summary tables *Business Monitor* PA 1002 1972.
21 *International companies* TUC pamphlet 1970 p. 4.
22 See ACCT Television Commission's survey *Our week* 1971.
23 *Royal Commission on Trade Unions and Employers' Associations* HMSO 1968 para. 363.
24 *Department of Employment Gazette* December 1976.
25 W. E. J. McCarthy 'The nature of Britain's strike problem' *British Journal of Industrial Relations* July 1970 pp. 224–36.
26 See *Strikes* pp. 106–39.
27 See 'Workplace relations' in *Government social survey* 1968; and Stanley Parker *Workplace industrial relations 1972* HMSO 1974.
28 *Department of Employment Gazette* November and December 1976 and February 1977.
29 Hilda Behrend 'Public acceptability and a workable incomes policy' in *A workable incomes policy* ed. Frank Blackaby Heinemann 1972 pp. 186–214.
30 D. Jackson, H. A. Turner and F. Wilkinson *Do trade unions cause inflation?* CUP 1972.
31 See Milton Friedman *Unemployment versus inflation* Institute of Economic Affairs 1975.
32 Charles Levinson *International trade unionism* Allen and Unwin 1972 p. 32.
33 Aubrey Jones *The new inflation* Penguin 1973 p. 25.
34 *Do trade unions cause inflation?* p. 113.
35 For a discussion of Britain's economic problems and productivity, see *Britain's economic problems* Brookings Institute 1968; D. T. Jones 'Output, employment and labour productivity in Europe since 1955' *National Institute Economic Review* August 1976; *The U.K. and West German manufacturing industry 1954–72* National Economic Development Office 1976; *Industrial efficiency and the role of government* HMSO 1977.
36 *Management and unions* p. 58.

Part One

The Trade Union Environment

Chapter 2

Management and industrial change

There is a need, as has been argued, for a more positive trade union approach. But, if it is to be effective, it must take account of the realities of modern industrial life. The next section, therefore, analyses the environment within which trade unions work and the trade union response to that environment. In particular, it highlights the three main challenges facing the trade unions within industry – the developments on the management side, the changes in employee attitudes and the increasing tendency of governments to intervene in collective bargaining.

MANAGEMENT'S CRUCIAL ROLE

The crucial role in the shaping of the working environment is still played by management. Peter Drucker has written that, 'the manager is the dynamic, life-giving element in every business. Without his leadership, the "resources of production" remain resources and never become production.'[1] This chapter describes how many of the major decisions affecting lives of working people are made by management without reference to them or their representatives. It also considers the way in which the pace of technological change, the size of firms, and the spread of the multinational corporation not only affect employees but make the task of trade union organisation and representation more difficult.

However, if we are to comprehend the environment within which trade unions operate, it is important to realise that during the 1970s British management has itself been under greater pressure than at any time since the war. Faced both by falling or stagnant demand for their products *and* by dramatically rising costs, some firms, including those (like British Leyland, Rolls Royce and Alfred Herbert) of vital importance to our economy, have gone bankrupt, whilst many more have had to struggle to survive. In these deteriorating conditions, rapid and unpalatable decisions have often had to be made, sometimes with only an imperfect knowledge of the relevant facts. In order to compete, managements have been forced to reduce their labour force or to merge with other firms. In view of these external threats, and the need to respond quickly, it is understandable that many managers should continue to be less than enthusiastic about sharing decisions which they now make unilaterally.

It is certainly still the case that, despite the changes described in the previous chapter, in most of the crucial areas of industrial decision-making the modern manager still retains the unilateral prerogative of his nineteenth century predecessor. Anthony Crosland, writing in 1962, claimed that 'the trade unions, skilfully exploiting the existence of a sellers' market for labour, have established a remarkable degree of control over those management decisions which directly affect the day-to-day life of the worker'.[2] It is true that where trade union organisation is strong, collective bargaining and its shopfloor relation 'custom and practice' have established a say for employees not only over pay and conditions but also over such issues as the organisation of work, hiring and firing and even promotion. But in most of the major decisions on such critical issues as production, purchasing of materials, capital investment, marketing, personnel policy, organisational structure and (perhaps most important of all) the determination of overall corporate strategy, workers have no say at all. It may be possible to claim that workers do not wish to influence these major decisions. What it is not legitimate to argue is that these decisions do not affect workers' lives. On the contrary, they shape the environment within which employees work.

It goes almost without saying that the process of production and its effectiveness is of vital importance to employees. On it will depend not only a worker's remuneration and job security but also the quality of his work experience. It has often been demonstrated how work groups have used their power to control output and establish their own interpretation as to how work ought to be carried out.[3] However there are obvious limits to worker influence. The purchasing of materials and their provision at the right time (obviously crucial for effective production) will continue to depend upon a managerial decision. The ability of work groups to influence their own environment will in part be determined by technology – again a management decision. In assembly line technology, for example, workers have minimal control over the pace of work or even of its quality. The formation of work groups is also limited by the design of the assembly line and by physical conditions (such as noise level). Process technology generally gives individual employees more autonomy and responsibility. But here also the relative isolation of many process workers prevents the formation of work groups.' Thus technology and its utilisation are key constraints on both the quality of work experience and the development of worker influence over production. Yet, in this area and in the purchasing and provision of raw materials, management makes the decisions which are vital to production without reference to the workers concerned.

One would expect employees to have more influence over those manpower issues which concern them more intimately. Certainly, in a number of companies and industries, work groups and their representatives have established rules governing procedure over vital matters like hiring and firing and promotion. But the most important manpower decisions – which affect the security of employment of large numbers of workers – are those which are made when management decides on its investment programme, its marketing policies and the direction of its overall company strategy.

Investment is a central influence on the lives of employees. The preservation and growth of employment depends primarily on the quality of investment decisions. A failure to invest in the right machinery at the right time can lead to a drop in sales which, in its turn, can result in men and women losing their jobs. Even a successful investment decision can have a profound impact. A decision to introduce new machinery or to change the technology is bound to have its effect on existing work habits and relations. It can often necessitate adaption to new patterns of work and the acquisition of new skills. It sometimes means redundancy. Yet whether the investment decision is good or bad, the workers have no say in the process of decision-making. At best, they are able to object when they become aware of its effects – by which time it is almost always too late. Such protests can only be expressed negatively and usually in a self-defeating way – by refusing to work with the new machinery. Workers will however have had no influence at the critical stage before the investment decision is made, when it is still possible to consider alternatives.

Marketing decisions (which are concerned with matters like forecasting, pricing, promotion, distribution, and servicing) seem the most remote from the shopfloor. Yet, as workers often discover to their cost, an incorrect demand forecast, an uncompetitive pricing policy, a weak distribution system or an inadequate after-sales service, can throw thousands out of work, although neither the workers nor their representatives have had any share at all in the shaping of that marketing strategy.

Management can usually select and deploy its own personnel as it wills. It is often said by senior managers that the most important decisions they make are those concerned with the appointment and development of their potential successors – the junior managers. If what might be called personnel policy is important to management, it is also of concern to workers. This is not only because the future of the organisation lies in the hands of junior managers; it is also because they represent the level of management with which workers come most in contact. Yet employees have no say in the choice of their rulers.

Nor do they have a formal voice in deciding the structure of the organisation or the level at which decisions are made. Management theorists often argue about what kind of structure business organisation ought to have.[5] Questions are raised as to whether decision-making should be centralised or decentralised. The 'management by objectives' school stresses the freedom of management to choose what kind of structure it likes. Social scientists have, however, pointed to the structural constraints imposed by technology. Whatever the truth, it is clear that the ability to set up a relevant organisational structure, which can be crucial to the success of the firm, rests with management – not the employees.

Perhaps most vital of all to the future of workers is the direction and shape of company strategy. Is the company going to expand or contract? And where? Is it going to diversify its operations or specialise? And in what direction? Is it going to embark on a policy of takeovers or mergers? Or is it going to allow itself to be taken over? All these are crucial questions which are bound to affect the workers' future in one way or another – yet on which they have no say at all. Sometimes, too often in the British economy, the company itself does not have a clear idea of its future. Such a state of affairs should also be a matter of concern to the workers – but, because they have no say, neither they nor their representatives will be in a position to know one way or another.

Thus, with the possible exception of parts of the public sector, management takes nearly all the strategic decisions affecting the workers without reference to their views. It is no exaggeration to say that British industry is organised on largely authoritarian lines, with decision-making power concentrated in the hands of management.

This authoritarian power structure is buttressed by a managerial ideology which asserts that management can be trusted to take unilateral decisions on matters which are of importance to the workers because the interest of managers and workers are always the same. In addition, some managers emphasise their legal responsibilities to the shareholders – and use this legal fiction (as it now is) as justification for the preservation of managerial prerogative. It is true that younger managers often question whether managerial ideology still reflects industrial realities. They can see that, though there is obviously a common interest between workers and management in the survival of the enterprise, on many questions the interests of management and workers are in conflict; and, faced by increasingly assertive behaviour by employees, they are becoming increasingly aware of the need to give workers a greater say in the running of the enterprise. But in much of British industry, the traditional ideology is still dominant, while even those managers who question the orthodox way of managing an enterprise have not always fully worked out the implications of running industry more democratically.

Meanwhile, recent industrial developments have not only had a significant impact on working lives but, in a number of ways, have also made it more difficult for employees and their representatives to influence management decisions. These developments include the increasing pace of technological change, the growing size of firms and of the resources on which they are able to call, and lastly, the spread of multinational firms.

THE PACE OF TECHNOLOGICAL CHANGE

Technology is not something which comes into being by itself – it is devised, introduced and organised by men. As Hyman notes, 'Whether the consequences of technology are in fact liberating or enslaving depends on how it is decided to use the machines and on who makes the decisions. To attribute unpleasant social consequences to inanimate machinery is to evade examining those human actions which, deliberately or by default, are in fact responsible.'[6] It is legitimate to point out that technological change is introduced by managers. It is only fair to add that, in a competitive world of national and international trade, the introduction of new technology not only brings with it material benefits but is often also the only way to protect the future of the company concerned. And those trade unionists and politicians who demand new investment have also to face up to its implications. In popular mythology 'automation' is often used as a shorthand to describe the present stage of technological change, but, as a GMWU report on technological change pointed out,[7] this is far too narrow a definition. Besides automation, there have been rapid advances in mechanisation, further developments in new materials and new production techniques, and a faster growth in the reorganisation of firms and the adoption of new work methods, coupled with the introduction of new management techniques and skills. Partly as a result of these changes, there have also been dramatic shifts in demand.

Technological change has always been a characteristic of industrial society. What distinguishes modern industry is the pace of the change. One striking illustration of this obvious truth is the reduction in the length of time taken to develop new techniques. It has been estimated that it took thirty-six years (1820–76) for the development of the telephone, thirty-five years (1867–1902) for radio and fourteen years (1923–36) for television. The development of transistors took only five years (1948–53).[8] Another example of the increased pace is the speed-up in the process of technological obsolescence. ICI, for example, has reduced the period of depreciation from twenty years before the war to between five and seven years today.[9] Though the impact of this accelerated rate of change is patchy, most industries have been influenced by it to some degree. The effect of this on working lives has been profound and is likely to continue to be so.

The threat to employment is the most immediate. The basic purpose of introducing new machinery is to reduce the number of jobs required to produce a given amount of output and, therefore, to increase output per man. The degree to which the threat of unemployment is realised will depend mainly on what happens to the total output of a firm or industry. The only way that it is possible for employment to keep pace with the increased productivity resulting from labour-saving machinery is by increased production. In fact, technological change, combined with other factors such as shifts in demand and expansion of state services, has had a considerable effect on employment.

Jobs in some of the older industries like agriculture, cotton, coal mining, shipbuilding and railways have disappeared very fast. Employment in the newer industries – synthetic fibres, motor vehicles, chemicals and oil – has either remained static or, through greatly increased production, actually expanded. As a result of increasing affluence and government intervention, service industries and public administration have expanded enormously.[10]

Employment is also growing far quicker in some areas of the country than in others. For the last twenty years, expansion of employment has been much faster in the south-east than in the north. Between 1958 and 1973, the traditional industries of the Northern Region (agriculture, coal mining, shipbuilding, iron and steel, marine engineering and transport) lost over 210,000 jobs. So, despite the regional policies of successive governments which created some 50,000 new manufacturing jobs in the decade up to 1973, the level of unemployment in the north has remained well above the national average and substantially above the level in the south-east.[11]

In addition, there have been changes in occupational structure. In manufacturing, the demand for unskilled labour has tended to decline, though this has been partly offset by the expansion of the private and public service sectors. In the case of skilled workers, technological change has undermined some skills but created a demand for others, particularly on the maintenance side. Perhaps the most significant change of all is the growth in the number of white collar jobs, both absolutely and also relative to manual grades. By the end of the century, it is likely that there will be considerably more white collar than manual workers in the labour force. Another development, which has implications quite as important as changes in occupational structure, is the increase (both absolute and also relative to the increase in male employment) in the numbers of working women.

These shifts in employment obviously have a considerable effect on working people. According to the model of the classical economists, the employee who loses his job in one industry is able, through the working of the market economy, to find a job in another industry. The real world is different. The redundant Durham miner, for example, often finds that job vacancies occur at the wrong time and in the wrong place – and for a skill which he does not possess. However necessary technological change may be for the survival of enterprise, for the worker in the position of the out of work miner it can be a terrible sword of Damocles threatening him with permanent unemployment.

It is true that since the war the worker in the south-east has been reasonably certain (at least until the recession of the 1970s) that, if anything happened to his present job, he was likely to find another one fairly easily. But, even in the south-east, it is far easier to find a new job if one is either a skilled or a white collar worker. Changes in the pattern of employment are likely to continue. The probability is that workers entering the labour market now will have to change jobs at least three times during their lifetime. This implies that, unless workers receive not only retraining in new skills but also the initial educational foundation to enable them to equip themselves for change, high levels of unemployment will continue in the future. With the limited training and educational facilities at present available, it is not surprising that many workers regard with suspicion any technological changes introduced by management, however strong the economic arguments.

For trade unions, these developments present additional problems. Trade union organisation has been strongest traditionally among manual workers in those industries which, like coal mining, cotton textiles, shipbuilding and railways, are now losing jobs fastest; employment is growing fastest in those industries, in those occupations, in those areas of the country, and in that sex in which trade union organisation has been weakest. So, unless the trade union movement can continue to organise effectively where employment is expanding at its fastest rate, the power of management to act unilaterally will grow.

Technological change not only has an impact on employment; it can also affect pay determination. By transforming existing job definitions, it undermines wage structures. The process of readjustment often leads to considerable strains between different groups of workers. In the case of the technologically advanced industries, the relative importance of production and maintenance work changes as the numbers and responsibilities of maintenance workers increase. Maintenance workers then try to improve their relative position – a move which is usually resented by production workers. Often these resentments lead to disputes with management at a time when the workers' cohesion has been undermined.

The wage system also comes under pressure in another way. In automated plants, the level of output ceases to be under the control of the production worker and it therefore becomes impossible to measure his work. Conventional payment by results schemes become irrelevant and management changes either to group incentive schemes or some form of measured day-work. As trade unions are only too well aware, the changeover from payment by results to another payment system almost always causes trouble, particularly amongst those workers who have benefited most from the existing system.

In addition, technological change affects differentials between industries. Capital intensive industries, whose labour costs are also a small and (usually) a declining proportion of total costs, can afford to pay higher wages than can labour intensive industries. But the less well-paid workers naturally resent the resulting widening of differentials. They feel, with some justice, that it is unfair that, through no fault of their own, their wages should fall behind those of workers fortunate enough to work in industries where the opportunities for expansion are so much greater for purely technical reasons. This feeling of injustice was one of the main driving forces behind the 'revolt of the low paid' during the late 1960s and early 1970s.

As far as working conditions and work experience are concerned, technological change also involves considerable readjustment. In the process of change from individual or craft production to mechanisation, the worker loses control over his work. When job operations are characterised by the repetition of a sequence of simple tasks with the pace dictated by machinery, the worker becomes little more than a machine minder. At higher levels of technology, the problem is different. Here machines take on many decision-making functions and the worker's job becomes mainly one of inspecting or supervising an automatically controlled operating system. In this situation, the worker combines social isolation with a relatively high degree of responsibility for expensive and often dangerous plant. The strains imposed by the shiftwork often involved with this type of production can also be considerable. Shiftwork itself involves disruption of domestic and social life and can mean additional expense. There is no clear indication that it has a bad effect on work, but common complaints are loss of health and sleeplessness. Digestive disorders, especially ulcers, and psychological strains are frequently observed among shiftworkers. The difficulties are usually more severe during the period of adjustment when shiftwork is first introduced.

It is not blue collar workers alone who suffer from technological change. The introduction of mechanisation, accompanied by rationalisation has transformed the job of many office workers from one which brought them into close association with their employers into one which is 'extremely like that of the factory operative'.[12]

To sum up. The introduction of new technology, usually vital to the future of the firm, can have a significant effect on the jobs, pay and work experience of employees; it also creates considerable organisational and representational difficulties for trade unions.

THE GROWTH OF THE LARGE FIRM

A notable characteristic of the British economy over the last twenty years has been the growing dominance of the large firm. This section considers the implications of this development for workers and trade unions.

Briefly, the facts are as follows: whereas the 320 largest companies held 62 per cent of total net assets at the end of 1957, by the beginning of 1968 (the latest figures available) they held 87 per cent, with the top eighty companies alone holding 63 per cent. In addition, the size of the large company is growing. In the eleven years to 1968, the number of large companies in British industry and commerce fell by nearly two-fifths, from 2,024 to 1,253; out of these, the forty largest companies, which in 1957 had accounted for 35 per cent of net assets of all such large companies, had by 1968 increased their share to 49 per cent.[13] In terms of output, in 1953 the 100 largest manufacturing enterprises in the United Kingdom accounted for 26 per cent of the total net output. In 1972 the corresponding figure was 39 per cent.[14] The Committee of Inquiry on Industrial Democracy, chaired by Lord Bullock, estimated that more than a quarter of the total workforce are now employed by big companies in the private sector.[15]

The reasons for the importance of the large firm in our economy are complex; they include the persistent weakness of our industrial structure and the pressure of overseas competition, the high cost of technological innovation, the desire to spread corporate risk by diversification, public ownership and government intervention, and, during the takeover spree of the late 1960s, sheer speculative greed. It is perhaps significant that the increasing dominance of the giant enterprise came mainly from takeover and merger rather than internal growth. The spending on takeovers, which was dominated by big firms, increased enormously from £300 million in 1957 to a high point of over £2,500 million in 1972.[16] Though the number of takeovers has decreased, the difficult conditions of the 1970s have also led to further concentration and mergers.

From the employees' point of view, size is a mixed blessing. Large companies tend to survive better, pay more, and devote more resources to industrial relations. On the other hand, the process of becoming bigger by takeover and merger often leads to redundancies, which may be economically justified but which certainly affect many workers. (Despite the implications for employees, at no stage of the merger process are their interests ever fully discussed. An Acton Study Report showed that many managers considered a projected takeover of no importance to the workers. Nine successful bids were studied; only two companies made an attempt to inform staff that a change of ownership was imminent.)[17] Working for a giant corporation can have other disadvantages. Workers in smaller firms tend to identify more with the firm, as absentee records show. Indeed, some experts argue that there is a correlation between size and higher labour turnover, more strikes and lower job satisfaction.[18] And the larger the company, the more momentous the effects of their decisions. A wrong decision by a giant corporation can throw thousands out of work, and threaten the livelihood of a whole community.

In its relationship with trade unions, the management of a large company has a number of advantages. If work groups gain in bargaining power in some circumstances, the resources of the big company helps it to sit out a strike. And, when it possesses, as do many large corporations, a large number of plants or operations in other industries, it may not be so disrupted by a stoppage in any single plant or in any group of plants specialising in one particular product. The ability of management to call upon a wide range of resources and skills to justify its position during negotiations obviously gives it a further advantage. Consider the powerful position of the management side; it will be able to employ industrial relations and personnel specialists, work study, job evaluation and productivity experts, economists and accountants, lawyers and publicists – a battery of expertise which far outstrips that of any trade union.

Size also permits a shift in the locus of decision-making. Managements of large companies have at their disposal a variety of administrative aids, including computers and new advanced mathematical and statistical methods for the collection of data and the analysis of administrative and technical problems. As a Swedish trade union report commented 'the new methods give management previously undreamed of opportunities to rationalise the systems of information and decision-taking in the firm'.[19] They increase management's 'span of control', considerably widening the scope of decision-making both in space and time. The way is thus open for more centralised decision-making. If trade unions wish to influence this new concentration of power, they have to develop representation at the appropriate level. Their response is complicated by the way that large industry is organised into holding and subsidiary companies. Though representation at the level of the holding company is essential for influence over strategic decisions, in some companies subsidiaries retain considerable autonomy.

So, despite the undoubted benefits of size, the speed of concentration in British industry has led to uncertainty amongst employees; there is also some evidence that it increases the sense of alienation which is such a marked feature of parts of our industrial system. As far as trade unions are concerned, they have to respond to this development by building up representation where important decisions are made and by improving their own services and organisation.

THE RISE OF THE MULTINATIONAL COMPANY

The multinational corporation has been called 'perhaps the most rapidly expanding institution of our time'.[20] It has been estimated that the value of the turnover and sales of international and multinational companies exceeds the gross national product of the entire world outside the United States and the Soviet Union. The budgets of some of the giant multinationals (many of them American) are greater than that of many countries.[21] About 25 per cent of all the exports of the United Kingdom are accounted for by foreign companies and, if the exports of British-based companies to their overseas affiliates are added, the proportion amounts to almost half. The rate of growth in the sales of multinational companies is much faster than the rate of growth in all world sales – 10 per cent compared to 4 per cent. Indeed, it has been estimated that if their growth continues unchecked, by the turn of the century the 200 largest multinational firms will be supplying something like half the world's total output of goods and services.[22]

Multinational companies are a dynamic force in the world economy – and in terms of investment, jobs and living standards have brought considerable benefits. However, their size and spread has other implications which need also to be considered. The TUC has argued that, with the growing dependence of world trade and technological development on multinational companies, their decisions are already beginning to determine the pattern of industrial development up to the end of the century. Yet, for the exercise of their power, they are ultimately responsible to nobody except the parent board. Assisted by the use of new information techniques, the decision-making process is increasingly concentrated at head office, so that the high command can direct the activities of its subsidiaries throughout the world. The structure and power of the multinationals present a real challenge to those who argue for more industrial democracy; they may even affect a country's ability to direct its own affairs.

Multinationals can have an impact on the national community in a number of ways. Companies with foreign subsidiaries can avoid tax obligations through transfer-pricing arrangements and by basing their operations in tax havens. The extensive inter-relations between multinationals also makes it difficult to apply anti-trust and anti-cartel policies. Their vast resources and their ability to switch such resources across national frontiers can be a threat to the stability of national exchange rates. The trend for multinationals to reach overseas customers through direct production and sales in their markets rather than by the shipment of products produced domestically can have balance of payments consequences. The last two attributes of the multinationals are of particular importance to this country. It is possible that speculative runs against sterling have in the past been in part precipitated by multinationals understandably protecting their position against a possible change in the exchange rate, while observers have noted the tendency for many of the major British exporters to penetrate overseas markets by direct investment rather than by exporting, to the detriment of the balance of trade figures.

Yet the ability of the multinationals to direct investment to more attractive countries inhibits national governments from protesting too vigourously. Governments are well aware that a successful multinational, with access to capital, technology and expertise from outside, is often in a position to create more and better paid jobs than the equivalent purely national firm. Initially, a foreign firm investing in Britain brings in a job-creating capital inflow which is as important for workers and trade unions as it is for governments. In addition, a multinational is more likely to be persuaded to locate plant in a high unemployment area. There are a number of reasons for this. There is little doubt that the detailed discussions with government departments which usually precede such an investment lay stress on the financial incentives available in development areas. If the venture is completely new, there is no offsetting cost of the kind which a company already established in another part of the country will have to take into account. There is also some evidence that American companies, in particular, are often happier to go to areas where they can create their own conventions in the labour market.

Despite their advantages, employees often feel a sense of insecurity – at any rate initially. They believe that there is likely to
be a greater threat to the workers' job security because decisions
about employment are now being taken from outside the country
and within a different context. Clearly employment in a subsidiary
of a multinational is as dependent on the global performance of the
corporation as on the performance of the subsidiary; this can be
both a strength and a weakness. The strength comes from its ability
to spread both its profits and losses. However, in the case of many
American firms, the largest part of the market for the subsidiaries'
goods will be in the United States and demand for the product will
depend largely on conditions in that market; the TUC noted that
'American companies have provided considerable additional jobs
in Scotland, but their dependence on the American market means
that some of these jobs are less than secure'.[23] There is always a
possibility that, in a crisis, it will be the subsidiaries that will be
sacrificed first – though the public outcry that followed two notor-
ious mass sackings in France in the early sixties (by General Motors
and Remington Rand) has, in the judgement of one commentator,
'convinced most of the major US multinationals that they have little
freedom in the area of redundancies'.[24]

More serious, in the long run, may well be the effect on employment patterns. For integration increasingly implies some specialisation of labour between nationally-based subsidiaries. As the TUC
has pointed out, 'there is already a tendency for American companies to use the engineering skills of European countries for the
"second grade" technical aspects of production, and more notice-
ably, of research' and that 'trade unions need to seek ways of
influencing these decisions to ensure that an adequate skill mix is
retained in the United Kingdom towards the end of the century'.[25]

It must not be forgotten that, as well as American, there are also
British (and partly British) owned multinationals, like ICI, BP, Shell
and Unilever. From the viewpoint of the British worker, the increasing overseas investment of British multinationals may mean
less jobs in this country. The most extreme case is, of course, that
of the 'runaway company' – a phenomenon which is a feature of a
number of American industries, in particular the electronics, foot-
wear and textiles industries. Higher American wages have tempted
American firms to construct plants in cheap labour areas in order
to compete not only in overseas markets but also in the American
market with their foreign rivals, thus reducing the number of
production jobs available to American workers. Such a tendency

has been less noticeable so far in Britain, owing partly to its distance from cheap labour areas (though this may no longer be such a barrier); the problem for British workers is the low relative rate of investment by British multinationals in this country and their high rate of investment abroad. Though overseas investment can help their jobs by encouraging exports, it is not surprising that British employees are sometimes concerned less the lack of investment here may affect their living standards.

The ability of workers to make their voice heard in the decision-making process of the multinationals depends on the effectiveness of trade union organisation. The spread of the multinational corporation, however, raises serious difficulties for the trade unions in meeting this organisational challenge.

Many international companies are prepared to accept trade unions and the collective bargaining and labour practices of the different countries in which they operate. Some like Esso, Alcan, Mobil Oil and Shell have in fact acted as innovators in industrial relations in Britain. These firms, while recognising British trade unions and respecting British collective bargaining practices, have used the system as a way of deploying their labour force more effectively.

However, there have also been other firms which have behaved less well. For example, powerful American firms like IBM, Kodak and Gillette held out against *bona fide* trade unions in most of their operations. In the 1960s four famous foreign firms (International Harvester, Standard Telephones, Hoover Ltd., and Electrolux) were referred to the Commission on Industrial Relations because, at one or other of their plants, they had either refused to recognise trade unions fully or had other industrial relations problems. One of the most spectacular British strikes since the war took place in 1967 over the withdrawal of union recognition by an American company which had taken over a British textile machinery firm, Roberts-Arundel. When the company dismissed all union members and replaced them with non-union female workers the union involved (the giant Amalgamated Union of Engineering and Foundry Workers) called a strike which lasted for a year until the company capitulated. The company, however, had the last word. It closed down the factory and withdrew to the United States.

Where a multinational corporation is prepared to accept the trade union role, its greater freedom of action can give it a number of advantages over a national company. The ability of a multinational to move profits around, through transfer-pricing policies, to the country whose tax laws suit it best makes it more difficult for a trade union to establish a rational case for wage increases based on a company's overall ability to pay, whilst making it correspondingly easier for a company to claim local 'poverty' as a reason for blocking wage increases. The obscurity surrounding the accounts of the multinationals can contribute to the atmosphere of distrust through which the activities of the multinationals are sometimes viewed by their employees.

If it comes to a dispute, the multinational has a number of weapons at its disposal. First, the confidence of the workers can be damaged by threats to direct production or investment elsewhere. During the 1969 Ford strike in Britain, it was rumoured that Ford's large commitment in the United Kingdom would be withdrawn to Germany or Belgium. During the 1971 strike, Henry Ford overtly threatened to withdraw investment elsewhere. However, in 1977 Fords announced its intention of building a new engine plant in South Wales. In the Chrysler dispute in 1973, that company not only threatened to withdraw investment but actually to shut down the plant – a threat which in view of the poor results of the company was taken seriously. In 1975, only the employees' agreement to a reduction of a third in the labour force and the grant of considerable sums of public money persuaded Chrysler to continue its operations in the United Kingdom. The then Prime Minister's comment that Chrysler had put 'a pistol to our heads' was a frank acknowledgement of multinational power. Though a multinational is usually unlikely to close down a profitable existing investment, its multinational character does mean, however, that threats to direct future investment to countries with a more congenial industrial relations climate have to be taken seriously.

With forward planning, a multinational can also undermine a strike threat by stock-piling. During 1966, Goodyear, which has plants in the United States, Sweden and Germany, encouraged its Swedish subsidiary to stock-pile in anticipation of a strike in the United States. Not only was this more than enough to check the American union plans that year but it also acted as a deterrent to German union strategy in the year following. Karl Casserini, research director of the International Metalworkers' Federation, described how the United States copper companies, 'despite the fact that their main production facilities were in the U.S., were able to resist a national bargaining coalition of twenty-six American unions for $8\frac{1}{2}$ months by increasing production in their foreign subsidiaries and by the compensation of high prices on the London

Metal Exchange'.[26] Obviously, the smaller the proportion of its output in any one country, the longer the company can afford to resist a strike in that country. The ability to resist is far greater, however, when the technical process involved is similar in different countries than when there is technical specialisation – though, even in the latter case, such resistance will depend partly on the relative size and strategic importance of the plant or group of plants involved.

Underlying these difficulties there can also be a more fundamental clash between the multinational corporations and the trade unions. Trade unions sometimes complain that they are never able to find out at which level and in which country real decisions are taken. The management of subsidiary companies claim that key decisions are made at the centre, whilst central management says that it leaves such decisions to its subsidiary management. The obscurity about who really takes decisions, in fact, masks a process of increasing centralisation which includes industrial relations as well as other major management decisions such as investment. A dramatic example of this concentration of decision-making is the persistent interference in motor industry disputes by American head offices; even in other industries, with less obvious industrial relations problems, policy guidelines are decided at headquarters. The main reason for this centralisation is the desire by multinationals to create a secure environment for further investment by 'forward planning'. The watchword of Mr. Geneen, then Chairman of ITT, was 'no surprises'.[27] Other top multinational executives may express themselves in more sophisticated terms but they share the same objective – to increase control over key aspects of multinational operations, including industrial relations. So it is natural that they should stress employee loyalty to the company; and it is understandable, if short-sighted, that they should sometimes consider that trade unions, by introducing divided loyalties, are a challenge to them.

This chapter has described how the major decisions affecting employees are made without their voice being heard. It has also considered the impact on the workers of the pace of technological change, of the growing importance of the large firm and of the spread of the multinational firms. There must now be an effective trade union response to these developments. Unless trade unions can organise where employment is growing fastest, and ensure that their representation reflects the problems raised by change, their influence will decline. They also need to build up their organisation and services to act as a countervailing force to the large native and multinational firms. Above all, they must ensure that they are represented in force at the level at which the strategic decisions are made.

REFERENCES

1 P. F. Drucker *The practice of management* Pan 1968 p. 13.
2 Anthony Crosland *The conservative enemy* Cape 1962 p. 218.
3 See L. Sayles *Behaviour of industrial work groups* Wiley 1958, and Tom Lupton *On the shop floor* Pergammon 1963.
4 Tom Lupton *Management and the social services* Penguin 1971 p. 53.
5 *Management and the social services* pp. 116–41.
6 *Strikes* p. 101.
7 *GMWU Congress Report* 1965.
8 These estimates are quoted in Andrew Shonfield *Modern capitalism* Oxford 1965 p. 41.
9 *Modern capitalism* p. 42.
10 See estimates by Vivian Woodward in *Department of Employment Gazette* May and July 1975.
11 See the Northern Regional Strategy Team's *Main Report* 1977 chp. 2.
12 D. Lockwood *The black-coated worker* Allen and Unwin 1958 p. 92.
13 Monopolies Commission *A survey of mergers 1958–1968* HMSO 1970 p. 8 and Appendix 9.
14 For 1953 figures see S. J. Prais *A new look at the growth of industrial concentration* Oxford Economic Papers July 1974 p. 283; for 1972 figures see *Economic trends* August 1976 p. 91, and *Business Monitor* PA 1002 1972 Tables 1 and 2.
15 *Report of the Committee of Inquiry on Industrial Democracy* 1977 p. 6.
16 *Business Monitor* M7 1st quarter 1975. There are, however, signs that, partly because of the recession of the 1970s, the merger explosion is over.
17 Acton Society Trust *Mergers: the impact on the shop floor* 1966.
18 See Geoffrey K. Ingham *Size of industrial organisation and worker behaviour* CUP 1970 for a discussion of the effect of size.
19 *Trade unions and technological change.* A research report submitted to the 1966 Congress of the Swedish Confederation of Trade Unions ed. S. D. Anderman. Allen and Unwin 1967 p. 61.
20 *International trade unionism* p. 39.
21 *International companies* TUC 1970 p. 23 Table 2.
22 *International companies* p. 5.
23 *International companies* p. 13.
24 Louis Turner *Politics and the multinational company* Fabian Research Series 1969 p. 9. See also two other useful Fabian pamphlets for details about multinationals: W. Kennet, L. Whitty and S. Holland *Sovereignty and multi-national companies* Fabian Society 1971 and Carl Wilms-Wright *Transnational corporations: a strategy for control* Fabian Society 1977.
25 *International companies* p. 13.
26 Karl Casserini *OECD trade union seminar paper* 1969.
27 Anthony Sampson *The sovereign state* Hodder and Stoughton 1973 p. 68.

Chapter 3

The revolt of the shopfloor

The second factor which the trade unions have to take into account is the new mood of employees. A better educated, more confident and more powerful workforce has greater expectations than its predecessors. Naturally employees want to raise (or at least maintain) their living standards and, in the uncertain world of the 1970s, to preserve their jobs; but, in addition, they are now demanding a greater say in the decisions which shape their environment. The following chapter looks at different aspects of their attitudes and explores the implications of these for trade unions.

In chapter 1 it was pointed out that in no other sphere of activity are divisions so deep seated as in industry. Yet, so long as they are accepted by employees, it is possible to continue to run industry in the traditional way. The change that has come about is not so much in the facts of the situation but in the workers' perception of these facts. The argument of this chapter is that a qualitative shift in workers' attitudes is now occurring on a far wider scale than before, and that this requires a response by both management and trade unions.

THE NEW CLIMATE

There are three main reasons for this transformation. The first is a pronounced change in attitudes towards those in authority throughout the whole of society; the second is the development of an educational system which has ensured that workers are both more likely and better equipped to want to influence managerial authority; the third is the effect of full employment since the war on the power and self-confidence of workers.

The generation which has grown up since the war is far more intolerant of authority than any previous one. Of course, acceptance of the *status quo* is still a powerful force. But, in many areas of life, attitudes have changed to a remarkable extent. Children no longer accept without challenge. Marriages today are much less likely than formerly to be based on the unquestioned predominance of the male. In politics, the 'revolution of rising expectations', a feeling that government is there not just to govern but actually 'to deliver the goods', indicates both a healthy lack of awe for those in authority and also a new feeling that egalitarian rhetoric should be taken at its face value. The demands that workers are making both reflect and are an important ingredient in a general shift away from a 'deferential' towards an 'assertive' society.

The main impact of education on worker attitudes has been in raising the level of aspiration. Though the educational system has not proved nearly as efficient a channel for social mobility as many had hoped, the more democratic structure now coming into being, in conjunction with the greater resources which have been channelled into primary and secondary education, *is* having some effect. The opportunities opened up by modern teaching methods and facilities stimulate an increasingly wide range of educational ability. School makes its mark even on unwilling pupils.[1] On first leaving school, young workers may enjoy the freedom from school discipline and their new earning power. But, for those whose aspirations are not fulfilled or for those whose ideas of the demands which work would make on them were inaccurate, the feeling of satisfaction often does not last long, particularly when they realise that other employment options are now closed to them. It is, perhaps, significant that dissatisfaction appears to increase with further experience of work. The reality of the work environment fails to meet the expectations formed at school of what work should or could be.

It is also possible that the much expanded (though still sadly insufficient) vocational training schemes for young workers also have an effect on worker attitudes. For even practical down-to-earth day-release courses have social implications. Craftsmen who have learnt a whole range of skills at training schools will inevitably question an industrial system in which those skills are not fully used, while semi-skilled workers, whose training programmes have shown them the possibilities of more fulfilling jobs, will feel frustrated by the limitations of their work experience.

Thus increasingly a better educated workforce, whose horizons have been expanded by school and by subsequent training experience, is beginning to reject, if only passively, a work system in which its members' potential is not fully realised.

If education has provided workers with the inclination and the tools to challenge existing arrangements, full employment has given them the power and self-confidence to make that challenge a formidable one. Since the war, groups of employees have in many industries demanded and attained new rights at shopfloor level, while their spokesmen, the shop stewards, have greatly increased both numerically and in power. The number of shop stewards has grown dramatically. Though other authorities quote lower figures[2], the TUC now estimates that there are about 320,000 shop stewards. Whatever the exact number, it is clear that effective shopfloor organisation now exists in most organised industries.

The inquiries carried out for the Donovan Commission in the late 1960s, and for the Department of Employment in the early 1970s, confirmed that shop stewards have considerable power.[3] The majority negotiate on a wide range of topics, including wages, working conditions, hours of work, discipline and employment issues. Almost all those who negotiate have dealt with some aspect of working conditions as standard practice. Most stewards also settle wage issues and at least one aspect of working hours, such as overtime distribution, and they bargain over employment questions and settle disciplinary issues. The vast majority of stewards believe their work is accepted willingly by management and most managers also consider that stewards are efficient representatives of the employees. So, in most cases, the shift in power at shopfloor level seems to have been accepted by management.

My own judgement is that the growing self-confidence of employees and their representatives has not been undermined by the recession of the 1970s. There is, perhaps, a greater awareness of the effect that big wage increases can have on prices; there is also a determination to preserve the gains that have been won – both in terms of living standards and of job security. But uncertain economic conditions have not led to a noticeable scaling down of aspirations. If anything, it has increased the conviction that employees need a greater say in the way their enterprises are managed.

ATTITUDES TO WORK

The following sections examine in turn employee attitudes to work, to management and industrial democracy, to trade unions, and to society as a whole. At the outset, it is worth emphasising the difficulties of generalising. Like other groups of people, workers will want different things at different times. This is not merely because individuals differ. Equally important, the differing needs and experience of workers, which they bring to and derive from their work, are bound to influence their attitudes.

Thus, younger workers may well put more emphasis on higher wages and less on security than older workers. Those women for whom work provides a second family income may have a different attitude to work and also to management and trade unions than men or women whose pay is the only source of family income. Employees with a white collar family background may be more optimistic about their chances of promotion and, therefore, less concerned with collective action. Workers whose formative experience has been in areas dominated by the mining industry and by the Labour movement (like the north-east, and parts of Scotland and Wales) will tend to have a stronger sense of solidarity than workers in other areas (as, for example, the south of England).

The work experience itself is also an important influence. Those workers who do dangerous and physically demanding work (like miners, dockers and shipyard workers) usually have a greater group cohesiveness than do those whose work is less difficult. Workers in large factories in which the work flow creates meaningful work groups are more likely to take collective action than are workers in small establishments. Skilled craftsmen tend to lay more stress on the need for satisfying work and to maintain solidarity more effectively, even though scattered throughout a plant, than those with more monotonous and routine tasks to perform.

Given all these differences, no one generalisation can be valid for all groups of workers. It does not follow, however, that it is impossible to outline the main trends of worker attitudes and aspirations today. If looked at in relative terms, the views of different groups of workers may seem to differ. But, compared with those who make the important decisions in industry, most workers have a common inability to influence those decisions and a common experience of doing jobs that carry relatively little responsibility, autonomy or control. So, within limits, some generalisation is legitimate. The following paragraphs are based partly on my experience first as research officer for one of the two great general unions and then as a member of parliament representing a northern industrial constituency.

There has been a good deal of academic controversy, which is worth briefly examining, about the employee's attitude to his work.[4] The Herzberg school (which follows the American industrial psychologist, Professor Herzberg) believes that there are needs and satisfactions shared by *all* categories of workers; and distinguishes between the factors (such as money and working conditions) which can cause dissatisfaction and those (like interesting work, responsibility, recognition) which promote positive job satisfaction. Others have, however, underlined the limitations which the system of production imposes on the freedom to change work patterns, attitudes and relationships.[5]

In its turn, the Cambridge University 'Affluent Worker' study (based on a survey of better paid workers at Luton in the early 1960s) emphasised that the response of workers to their work situation could only be fully understood by reference to expectations derived from *outside* the workplace.[6] The attitude of these workers was defined as 'instrumental' – that is to say work was experienced as essentially a means to the pursuit of ends outside work and usually ones relating to standards of domestic living rather than something to be enjoyed for its own sake. Although a majority preferred previous jobs because they had more scope or were more interesting, they were prepared to put up with the monotony, pressure and deprivation of assembly life work because of higher earnings.

The Cambridge study has been criticised from a number of directions. Alan Fox has pointed out that, though workers expect and are resigned to work being instrumental, they wish that it could be enjoyed for its own sake;[7] whilst W. W. Daniel has argued that, though it is the cash return which is the priority when an agreement is first being considered by employees, the intrinsic rewards (increases in job interest and autonomy and improved relationships with workmates and supervisors) become the more important once the agreement is in operation.[8] Daniel has also distinguished between the choice of the job and the actual work situation. In the first, a worker may be forced to decide between unsatisfying work which is better paid and a more interesting, though lower paid job. In the second, he is able, through collective action, 'to maximise on all dimensions' – including higher earnings, a greater sharing of power, and reorganisation of work to make it more interesting.[9]

It is not necessary here to explore further these arguments about the roots of industrial behaviour – important though they are. It is enough for our purposes to isolate the main *developments* in attitude. Putting the debate into perspective, one can accept that, in the past, most industrial workers have had little choice other than to regard work purely as something from which they derived a living. In this sense, an 'instrumental' attitude is nothing new.

However, relatively full employment and economic expansion has meant that, in some enterprising industries at least, the living has become an increasingly good one (though there is still a sizeable proportion of low paid workers scattered throughout industry and high concentrations of the low paid in a number of industries). At a time when there are a wide range of attractive and useful consumer durables which make life easier and more pleasurable, it is not at all surprising that younger workers, eager to see their households established, should be prepared to give priority to increasing living standards. Even for these workers, two important qualifications have to be made. In the difficult conditions of the 1970s, employees are naturally attaching greater importance to job security. And a growing number of workers also want jobs which are more rewarding in human terms.

Indeed, over the last few years, there has been an increasing revolt, particularly among younger employees, against the inhumanity of their work. This revolt is expressed sometimes in strikes, sometimes in absenteeism and sometimes in frequent changes of job. On occasions the only way open for workers to demonstrate a grievance is through wage demands;[10] this is certainly often the case with those dissatisfied with the nature of their work. My own contact with the shopfloor during the sixties and seventies has convinced me of the increasing importance attached by shop stewards and trade unionists, from many differing industries, to job satisfaction. Naturally enough, this is on a different level of priority to money or job security. And the intensity of the demands will vary from industry to industry and among different groups of workers. But, without a doubt, it is now a factor in industrial relations which trade unions, management and governments ignore at their peril.

It would, however, be wrong to suppose that an increase in job satisfaction can bring about instant industrial harmony – particularly if it is introduced at the expense of monetary rewards and job security or as a way of bribing workers into acquiescence, whilst leaving existing power relationships intact. However, managements who continue to believe that higher wages will always compensate for 'dead end' jobs are likely to find themselves deceived. In the the end, the best way forward is, where possible, to make work more satisfying.

INDUSTRIAL RELATIONS AND INDUSTRIAL DEMOCRACY

There has also been a substantial shift in employee attitudes towards management, both as regards their acceptance of managerial authority and their desire to participate in managerial decision-making.

As was mentioned in the last chapter, the classic management view of industrial relations is based on a *unitary* perspective.[11] It assumes an overriding community of interest between employers and employees through which managerial prerogative is legitimised. The employee's role should be that of a loyal member of a team – and any behaviour which contradicts this thesis must be irrational. While many managers insist on the underlying harmony of industrial relations, Marxists argue that the conflicts between workers and management are so fundamental that they cannot be reconciled within the existing structure of industry. According to this analysis, employees can never be other than foot soldiers in the class war – and any behaviour which contradicts their thesis must likewise be irrational.

Neither of these theories provides an adequate explanation of what actually happens. In my experience, workers see their relations with management in different perspectives according to different circumstances. Sometimes they perceive their interests to be in harmony with management, sometimes in conflict. Thus most workers accept that they have a common interest with management in the survival and development of the enterprise. However, when it comes to the division of the cake, workers feel their interests to be in conflict with management. Daniel has pointed out that workers are able to sustain these two quite distinct images of the relationships between management and labour because of the different context in which each is perceived. At work the predominant image is one of teamwork, whilst during negotiations the conflict image becomes more important.[12]

But while the model of industrial relations as a spectrum of attitudes which varies according to context corresponds most closely to reality, there *has* been a change. There is now far more questioning of managerial authority than ever before. Despite the increased importance of wages in an inflationary period, strike figures show a substantial number of disputes which are concerned with other issues such as working arrangements, rules and discipline which, as Professor Turner has argued, 'reflect an implicit pressure for more democracy and individual rights in industry'.[13] Perhaps more significantly, there is unmistakeable evidence that many workers now believe that industry is run without their interests being properly considered.[14] Though this view is expressed most strongly in the division of the industrial cake, it is not confined to this context. Workers also feel that in the design, structure and administration of the work, their views are ignored. Indeed, some commentators have concluded that dissatisfaction with management is now so deep that the industrial relations system itself is on the point of collapse.[15]

Without taking such an apocalyptic approach, my own view is that the rejection of managerial authority is growing in intensity. The new generation of shop stewards are very different from their predecessors. They are tougher, more demanding, and more critical of management. In this, they reflect the changing attitudes towards management of their constituents. There is a very real pressure from below which is making it increasingly difficult to run British industry on the old authoritarian basis.

How far does this growing challenge to managerial authority also imply that workers seek a larger share in decision-making? Attitude surveys show that employees want more participation, particularly in those decisions which appear to be of direct relevance to themselves; thus most employees would like a greater say in the day-to-day running of their own plant. But, in the deteriorating conditions of the late 1960s and 1970s, there was also a significant increase in the number of workers who would like more influence on top level decisions and who would support measures, including the extension of collective bargaining and employee representation at boardroom level, to secure this.[16] So there is growing support for policies to increase involvement at *all* levels of decision-making.

ATTITUDES TO UNIONS

As far as employee attitudes to trade unionism are concerned, workers join trade unions for a number of reasons. The predominant one is probably as an insurance policy against the hazards of industrial life; in particular, in periods of high inflation, employees will become trade unionists in an attempt to defend their standard of living against the threat of rising prices (as the explosion in trade union membership since 1968 indicates).[17] A favourable climate for trade union recognition is also important, as is the impact of closed shop arrangements.

However, if trade unions are to overcome the unfavourable trends which are undermining their traditional strongholds, they will need to pay particular attention to the needs of those groups whose role in the economy is becoming increasingly important. The growth in white collar and female unionism over the last decade shows that the rewards for a specialist approach are likely to be high.

Traditionally women have been far less 'union minded' than men. But changes have occurred which make it likely that most women at work will see the need for collective action in the near future. In the past, working women were by and large merely filling in time before marriage. Today, however, over 60 per cent of all employed women are married. This development has meant that women are increasingly questioning their auxiliary role within industry and demanding equal rewards and opportunities. In the establishment of industrial equality within industry, the Equal Pay and Sex Discrimination Acts have an important role to play. But the backing of effective trade union organisation is also crucial, as more and more women are realising. The percentage of female workers who were trade unionists grew from nearly 26 per cent in 1948 to nearly 37 per cent in 1974.

For a number of reasons, including the hostility of employers and the identification of employees with employers, white collar workers in the private sector have been far less densely organised than manual workers. However, white collar workers are also joining trade unions in increasingly large numbers. Quite apart from inflation the scale of mechanisation and rationalisation is such that many office workers feel that they have become mere cogs in a bureaucratic machine – and that, if their voice is to be heard, they need representation. By 1974, 39 per cent of white collar employees were trade unionists, compared with 30 per cent ten years earlier.

The Donovan inquiry showed that, for most workers familiarity with trade unionism brought with it a clearer appreciation of its benefits.[18] A large majority believed that there were substantial advantages in belonging to a trade union, including improvement of wages and conditions, protection of employment, legal and other services, and democratic representation with the employer; and 82 per cent could see no disadvantages at all. Significantly the vast majority of those affected by closed shop arrangements would continue to belong even if trade union membership was not a condition of employment.

Naturally enough there is far greater support for shopfloor trade unionism than for trade union activities at a higher level. Surveys confirm my own personal impression that the work of shop stewards is generally highly appreciated by trade union members.[19] To most trade unionists, the shop steward *is* the union. They are fully prepared to take part in shop steward elections, to take their problems to their shop steward, and to put their trust in him as their representative. In contrast, most trade unionists are not interested in the work of their union branches, let alone their district, regional or national governing bodies. In fact, to the majority the national union is only relevant when it is giving backing to issues which are of direct relevance to the shopfloor.

There is, however, substantial evidence that a growing number of employees would like their representatives to play a greater part in the running of industry. Obviously, they do not wish to forego the benefits of conventional trade unionism. But the actions of trade unionists in the 1970s (ranging from the defensive sit-in's at the beginning of the decade to the more positive responses in the middle seventies at Meriden, Lucas Aerospace, British Leyland, and Chrysler) as well as opinion surveys indicate that many workers want trade unions to expand their activities beyond the traditional confines.

SOCIAL AND POLITICAL PERSPECTIVES

The predominantly instrumental approach to trade unionism by no means implies that some employees do not have deeply held social attitudes. In the inquest on Labour's third successive election defeat in 1959, it was fashionable to believe that greater affluence was turning an increasing proportion of the working class into members of the middle class. Zweig, for example, argued that large sections of the working class were 'on the move towards new middle class values and middle class existence'.[20]

However, it is now clear that conditions of relative affluence do not necessarily change the perceptions of many industrial workers. They remain employees who gain their livelihood by placing their labour at the disposal of an employer in return for wages. And, though they put a high priority on home and the family, there is no evidence that they are either adopting a middle class life style or have any wish to integrate into middle class society. Even in their hopes for their children their aspirations were expressed in terms not of status but rather of the importance to the child 'as an individual of having work which would be as rewarding as possible to him, whether economically or otherwise'.[21]

The picture is thus of an emerging group of affluent workers which cannot accurately be called 'middle class'. But the attitudes of these workers tend to differ from those of more traditional communities, such as are found in the north and in Scotland and in mining, shipyard and dock areas. The better off worker has far less instinctive loyalty to the Labour movement. He looks at these organisations more in terms of the benefits they can bring to him and his family than from the viewpoint of traditional class solidarity. Butler and Stokes, in their survey of political attitudes in Britain[22] showed that, though workers still vote Labour because they believe it to be a workers' party, their attitude is increasingly one of scepticism; while McKenzie and Silver, in their study of working class Conservatism, also noticed a tendency for younger working class Tories to view the Conservative Party with a less deferential eye. They are more inclined than other, more traditional working class Conservatives to be critical of society and of the power of big business.[23]

The increasingly rational, calculative attitude does not necessarily imply a commitment to the *status quo*. Sometimes it goes hand-in-hand with a considerable degree of dissatisfaction with society as it is. Nearly three in every four of those interviewed for the Cambridge 'affluent worker' study agreed with the view that there was one law for the rich and another for the poor. According to the McKenzie and Silver survey, one in every two of the total sample and two in every three of Labour voters agreed that 'the upper class . . . have always tried to keep the working classes from getting their fair share'.[24] Butler and Stokes showed that seven out of eight of working class supporters saw politics as the representation of class interests and almost half of these regarded such interests as opposed. There is also evidence that inequality in some areas, such as education and housing, is much more sharply perceived. The Cambridge survey showed, for example, that working class parents' aspirations for their children 'appeared to be running well beyond the latters' actual chance of success within the existing system of educational provision'.[25] But, though there is a desire for change, this is not necessarily linked to support for wholesale government intervention or for increases in public expenditure paid for out of increases in taxation.

Indeed, there are doubts both about the relevance of the social and political objectives of the trade unions and also about the effectiveness of the Labour Party. As many as one in every two in the Cambridge survey thought that trade unions should be separate from the Labour Party, while, according to Butler and Stokes, even the majority of trade unionists think that trade unions should stay out of politics. This is, perhaps, partly explained by another finding that even a substantial number of Labour voters consider that it did not make much difference which party wins a general election. Politics is seen as a marginal subject, irrelevant, unlike shopfloor trade unionism, to the personal concerns of the individual worker.

What has been revealed by this chapter is a very solid support amongst an increasingly powerful and confident workforce for the existence and development of trade unionism. It is, however, a trade unionism which is being judged in terms of results and which will have to devote more of its resources and efforts to satisfy shopfloor demands. These are now being expressed in a call for more satisfying jobs and for greater control over the working environment as well as in purely monetary terms. There is little doubt that a trade union movement, committed to democratising and humanising industry, would get widespread backing from the shopfloor. That, in short, is the main message of the workers' revolt.

There is also widespread dissatisfaction with the opportunities afforded by society as it is. There is, therefore, a need for a social and political trade unionism, as well as a purely industrial one. However, the doubts expressed by many workers about the trade union movement's present social and political activities and about the Labour Party in satisfying their needs, indicates that there will continue to be a considerable role for leadership in the co-ordination and articulation of working class views into a coherent and realisable programme of industrial and social change. But though there is likely to be support for some radical changes, there is clearly little backing for revolutionary politics.

REFERENCES

1 For a discussion of this question see E. T. Keil, D. S. Riddell and B. S. R. Green 'Entry into the occupational system' in *The sociology of modern Britain* ed. E. Butterworth and D. Weir Fontana 1970.
2 Apart from the TUC estimate quoted, estimates of shop steward numbers range from 90,000 (H. A. Clegg, A. J. Killick and R. Adams *Trade union officers* Blackwell 1961), to 100,000–120,000 (A. I. Marsh and E. E. Coker 'Shop steward organisation in the engineering industry' *British Journal of Industrial Relations* June 1963), 125,000–133,000 (J. F. B. Goodman and T. J. Whittingham *Shop stewards in British industry* McGraw Hill 1969), and 175,000 (W. E. J. McCarthy and S. R. Parker 'Shop stewards and workshop relations' *Royal Commission on Trade Unions and Employers' Associations Research Paper no. 10*).

3 'Workplace industrial relations' *Government social survey* 1968, and Stanley Parker *Workplace industrial relations 1972* HMSO 1974.
4 There is a useful summary of this debate in the essays by R. Brown and W. W. Daniel in *Man and organisation* ed. J. Child Allen and Unwin 1973.
5 See Joan Woodwood *Management and technology* HMSO 1959, and *Behaviour in industrial work groups.*
6 The relevant volumes are J. H. Goldthorpe, D. Lockwood, F. Bechhofer and J. Platt *The affluent worker: industrial attitudes and behaviour* OUP 1968, and *The affluent worker in the class structure* OUP 1969.
7 *A sociology of work in industry* p. 22.
8 W. W. Daniel *Beyond the wage-work bargain* PEP 1970 pp. 84–85.
9 W. W. Daniel 'Understanding employee behaviour' in *Man and organisation* p. 61.
10 See T. Lane and K. Roberts *Strike at Pilkingtons* Fontana 1971 p. 17.
11 See Alan Fox 'Industrial sociology and industrial relations' *Royal Commission on Trade Unions and Employers' Associations Research Paper no. 3* 1966 for a criticism of the unitary perspective; also his later work *Man mismanagement* Hutchinson 1974.
12 *Man and organisation* pp. 49–50.
13 H. A. Turner *The trend of strikes* Leeds University Press 1963.
14 See the Opinion Research Centre (ORC) survey in *The Times* 14 January 1975.
15 For example Alan Fox 'Is equality a necessity?' *Socialist Commentary* June 1973, and his *Man mismanagement.*
16 The ORC survey in *The Times* 14 January 1975, and the ORC evidence to the Bullock Committee on industrial democracy.
17 See R. Price and G. S. Bain 'Union growth revisited' *British Journal of Industrial Relations* November 1976.
18 *Workplace industrial relations* paras. 6.63–6.67.
19 *Workplace industrial relations* paras. 6.31–6.40.
20 F. Zweig *The worker in an affluent society* Heinemann 1961 p. ix.
21 *The affluent worker in the class structure* p. 133.
22 D. Butler and D. Stokes *Political change in Britain* Macmillan 1969.
23 R. T. McKenzie and A. Silver *Angels in marble* Heinemann 1968.
24 *Angels in marble* pp. 127, 135.
25 *The affluent worker in the class structure* p. 189.

Chapter 4

Government and collective bargaining

The third major challenge facing the trade unions comes from government. Particularly during the last decade, governments of both major political parties have intervened in order to try and influence both the results of collective bargaining and the relationships within it. This chapter examines the growth of government intervention in this area, analyses the reasons for it and discusses its effectiveness. It also shows the difficulties this intervention has created for trades unions and their members.

TRADE UNIONS AND THE LAW

At the outset, it is necessary to point out that the great expansion in the influence and power of governments during the twentieth century has, in other fields, received the backing of trade unions. Trade unionists supported the introduction of a welfare state, including old age pensions, unemployment benefits and family allowances, the creation of the National Health Service, the development of public housing, and a comprehensive state system of education. It was the trade union movement which gave the most enthusiastic welcome to the 1944 White Paper on Employment Policy committing all political parties to the acceptance of government responsibility for the maintenance of full employment after the war. The extension of public ownership, mainly under the Labour administrations of 1945–51 was welcomed by the trade unions, for whom the public ownership of 'the commanding heights of the economy' had become a central part of their policies. They also backed the interventionist policies of later Labour governments. Trade unions supported legislation on training, health and safety, redundancy and sex discrimination as well. In all these areas, trade unions not only supported state intervention; their persistent lobbying was, in part, responsible for the decision to intervene.

But, when governments tried to interfere in collective bargaining, British trades unions were almost uniformly hostile. Their history explains why. The years from 1860 to 1914 can be viewed partly as the struggle of a young trade union movement to remove liabilities imposed upon it by the judgements of the courts (which, under common law principles, had considerable discretion in the application of the law), and to get legislation enacted which would exclude judges from any jurisdiction over collective bargaining.[1]

It was certainly a struggle. So much so that until the first world war, it seemed as if the passing of any pro-union legislation was merely the signal for a counter-attack by the employers through the courts. The historians of the period have pointed out that, for fifteen years after the Conspiracy and Protection of Employment Act of 1875 (which has been called 'the bedrock of British workers' rights to organise and take effective industrial action'[2]) the employers had little need either to seek help from the courts or to agitate for a revision of the Law, because trade unions were so weak.[3] But from 1889 onwards, with the coming of 'new unionism' and the revival of the 'old' unions, the employers turned once again to the courts. A whole series of cases including Lyons v Wilkins (1896), Quinn v Leatham (1901) and Taff Vale Co. v Amalgamated Society of Railway Servants (1901) seemed to undermine the position which trade unions had secured by the legislation of the 1870s. Above all, the *Taff Vale* judgement, which held that the Amalgamated Society of Railway Servants, though not a corporate body, could be sued in a corporate capacity for damages alleged to have been caused by the action of its officials, appeared to threaten a trade union's ability to carry out its normal functions. The eminent lawyer R. B. Haldane, writing in 1903, commented on the effect of these judgements as follows: 'I should be very sorry to be called on to tell a Trade Union Secretary how he could conduct a strike lawfully. The only answer I could give would be that, having regard to the diverging opinion of the judges, I did not know.'[4]

However, the Trade Disputes Act of 1906 (made possible by the Liberal landslide of that year and by the return of a significant number of MPs with strong links with the Labour movement), gave trade unions new protection by ensuring them immunity against any action for damages in tort and by expressly legalising peaceful picketing. Until the 1960s, the 1906 Act, combined with the 1871 and 1875 Acts, created a system of immunities by which trade unions were free to operate *without* the intervention of the courts. Counter-attacks continued. The *Osborne* judgement (1909) restrained unions from spending their funds for political purposes, until a new act was passed in 1913; the Trade Disputes and Trade Unions Act (1927), introduced by a Conservative Government after the 1926 general strike and repealed by the post-war Labour Government, declared illegal (amongst other things) sympathetic strikes in industries other than the industry in which the strikers are engaged and established a 'contracting-in' system for the payment of the political levy to the Labour Party; and, during both world wars, legal restrictions on strike action were imposed. But, in general, the new system of 'non-intervention' by the law was respected by judges who came to accept (at least until the 1960s) that workers' collective interests were as valid as those of employers and, therefore, abstained from intervention, so long as each side pursued self-interest by acts lawful in themselves. Thus protected by certain basic immunities and aided by two world wars and by full employment, the trade union movement grew more powerful until collective bargaining had become, in the words of Professor Wedderburn, 'the most important factor in determining the wages and terms of employment of a majority of workers'.[5]

Insofar as there was any government intervention, it was employed to underpin collective bargaining. Thus official conciliation and arbitration services were used to support bargaining arrangements, and a system of wage councils was developed, one of whose objects was to stimulate collective bargaining. In addition, under the Terms and Conditions of Employment Act (1959), an employer could be obliged to accord terms and conditions of employment no less favourable than those established in a relevant collective agreement; and, by the Fair Wages Resolution of 1946, a similar obligation was put upon government contractors. But, except in the ways just described, governments left collective bargaining to management and trade unions.

INCOMES POLICY

Yet, during the 1960s and 1970s, both Labour and Conservative governments made attempts to control collective bargaining relationships by legislation. What happened to change the minds of governments about 'non-intervention'? The background to this *volte-face* lay in the new situation created when governments, with trade union support, accepted responsibility for maintaining full employment after the second world war. One implication of this decision was that governments had also to deal with the consequences of sustaining a high level of demand. For if internal prices rose faster in Britain than in other countries, this would reduce the competitiveness of her exports and make imported goods more attractive, thus seriously affecting the balance of payments and, in the long run, increasing unemployment. Rapid price increases would also redistribute wealth towards the more powerful and away from the weaker groups. It could also create severe industrial and social dislocation. Thus successive governments since the war have had to grapple with inflation.

There were a number of fiscal and monetary weapons which a government could use. It could reduce its spending, thus decreasing its contribution to demand; it could increase taxes on the income of corporations and of individuals, or increase taxation on goods and services which individuals bought, with the aim of reducing their contribution to total demand; or it could make it more difficult for companies and individuals to obtain credit. But often these kind of measures were either ineffective or had unwelcome consequences in other areas which had not been foreseen. There was, therefore, a constant temptation for governments to try and limit wage settlements negotiated through collective bargaining as an additional and more *direct* way of controlling inflation.

For trade unions, these incomes policies created formidable difficulties. Trade union officials were, of course, quite as aware as anyone else of the effects of price increases on their members' living standards. Most accepted that wage increases, particularly in the more labour intensive industries, were a major factor in price inflation. But, as leaders of democratic organisations, trade union negotiators had also to reflect the views of their members.

Throughout the post war period and particularly since the beginning of the 1960s, we have seen what Aubrey Jones has called 'the assertion in the economic field of rights enjoyed in the political arena'.[6] It has become a familiar pattern of modern British industrial relations that a wage settlement in one firm or industry sets off demands for a comparable increase in another firm or industry, sometimes regardless of the relative levels of productivity. The framework of reference in the search for equality has not always been confined to fellow workers. Occasionally it has ranged wider to include the salaries enjoyed by top management and the professions, the dividends taken from the firm by the shareholders, and the unequal opportunities possessed by a privileged minority in education, housing and wealth.

Thus trade unions have been trapped between two conflicting

pressures; the desire of governments to moderate wage demands and the growing aspirations of their own members. Their problems have been compounded by the failure of the British economy to grow as fast as the economies of other industrial countries, so that incomes policy has seldom been seen by workers as much more than an instrument which has worked against their interests. Given these obstacles, it is not surprising that, viewed historically at least, the various attempts at incomes policy can hardly be considered an unqualified success.[7]

Perhaps the most successful of all British incomes policies was that instituted during the second world war by the coalition government led by Churchill. As a basis for union agreement, the government stabilised the cost of living by a system of food subsidies and rationing. In return, the trade unions made only modest and infrequent pay claims at national levels and acquiesced in severe restraints on their freedom of action, including the direction of labour, the prohibition of strikes and compulsory arbitration. In terms of increases in the standard of living of British workers, trade union acceptance of incomes policy during the war was justified. Between 1938 and 1945 prices rose by only 48 per cent, while average weekly earnings increased by 80 per cent.

What was willingly accepted in wartime was, however, far more difficult to achieve in peacetime – even under Labour governments. In 1948, the Labour Government's appeal to the unions for total restraint was met, at first, with considerable co-operation by the unions. There were no pay increases in some industries for two years and elsewhere the settlements were modest. At plant level, however, earnings continued to rise. Though, from a government viewpoint, the rise in earnings was not as fast as it would have been without the policy, this wage restraint caused considerable resentment amongst those groups of workers whose earnings had fallen behind. The devaluation of 1949 and the price upsurge caused by the Korean war eventually destroyed the policy.

The Labour governments of the 1960s, also convinced that an incomes policy was an essential ingredient of their strategy to promote economic growth, developed a far more comprehensive strategy than any British government had previously attempted. Galvanised by George Brown (the energetic Secretary of State for Economic Affairs) and trading on its historic links with the trade union movement, the Government won the co-operation of the trade union leadership. Brown insisted that the Labour Government's policy was to be more than an incomes policy; it was also to cover productivity and prices. The policy laid down a 3 to $3\frac{1}{2}$ per cent norm on incomes increases with exceptions for extra productivity and low pay, and was backed by a National Board for Prices and Incomes.

Yet, despite the initially ambitious claims for the policy, the results, at least if judged in terms of adherence to the criteria laid down by successive modifications of the policy, were disappointing. Except for the second half of 1966, during the pay standstill, earnings always rose faster than the norm. During 1965 and the first half of 1966, when the norm was 3 to $3\frac{1}{2}$ per cent, weekly earnings were rising at about 8 per cent a year. During 1967, with a zero norm, or no norm at all, the increase was about 6 per cent. In 1968 and 1969, with a ceiling of $3\frac{1}{2}$ per cent, the rate of growth of incomes returned to the 1965 level.

Why was the policy not more effective? Basically because the Government did not deliver its side of the bargain. It had promised that if workers held back, the government would control price increases. Yet it did little to make that side of the policy work. Even during the second half of 1966, when there were no pay increases, the deflationary tax increases of July 1966 pushed up prices. During 1967, tax increases continued to push up prices and, in November 1967, devaluation of the pound sterling raised import prices and led to further price inflation. The Government had also promised that the policy would help the low paid. But, despite the commitment, differentials remained much the same.[8] Perhaps most important of all, the Government had asserted that acceptance of an incomes policy would help produce the conditions for a higher rate of economic growth, and thus make possible the creation of a better society promised in the Labour manifestoes of 1964 and 1966. Yet, in practice, incomes policy during most of this period was used as a means of sustaining the untenable – the bolstering up of an overvalued currency – rather than as an aid to economic growth. Incomes policy, therefore, came to be regarded not as a means of ensuring a faster real growth in living standards but purely as an instrument of wage restraint.

In 1970, the incoming Conservative Government, despite the flirtations with forms of incomes policy by previous Conservative administrations during the 1950s and 1960s, at first set its face firmly against this kind of direct interference. Instead it allowed unemployment to rise to its highest level since the war, apparently believing that, by so doing, it could diminish the capacity of trade unions to negotiate high wage settlements. However, increases in earnings continued at a high level, while prices rose faster than for many years. By the end of 1972, Mr. Heath's administration had been forced to abandon its previous ideas and to return to a prices and incomes policy, with statutory backing including the setting up of official bodies to investigate pay and prices.

This about-turn, however, proved to be the Government's undoing. Whilst there might possibly have been trade union acquiescence in an incomes policy which was part of a more general adjustment in other government policies (particularly those on rents, land prices and industrial relations) the trade union movement was not prepared to support a policy which was far stricter on wages than on prices and which specifically excluded food prices. The Heath policy was also accompanied by excessive monetary expansion. Though a large number of settlements were made within the policy, a dispute between the National Union of Mineworkers and the National Coal Board in the winter of 1973–74 over a pay claim which was above the pay limit was regarded by the Government as a threat to its authority. Instead of either climbing down or of exploring ways out of the *impasse*, the Government gambled on winning an election victory on the issue of: 'Who governs the country – the government or the unions.' Though no party had an overall majority, the Conservative Party won less seats than the Labour Party in the February election of 1974 and, despite overtures to the Liberals, was unable to form a government.

In the light of the failures of the 1960s and the experience of the Heath administration, the Labour Government, which came to power in March 1974 and was confirmed in office by a narrow majority at the general election of October 1974, introduced a new concept – the social contract. The social contract was a wide-ranging agreement between the Labour Government and the TUC which covered many aspects of policy. In return for the repeal of much of the legislation of the previous Conservative administration and for the pursuit of an ambitious programme of social change, the trade union movement agreed to restrict settlements to pay increases in line with increases in the cost of living. But initially the social contract did not succeed in slowing down the rate of inflation. In fact, during the wage round of 1974–75, the level of settlements rose to as much as 30 per cent and pulled prices with them to a rate of increase twice as fast as that of most foreign competitors. Rapid depreciation of sterling during June 1975 led to TUC acceptance of a much tighter incomes policy. Its main features were a £6 flat rate increase, backed by the full authority of government in the public sector and, in the private sector, a ban on price increases caused by settlements above the £6 limit. This second phase was strictly observed and the rate of inflation was halved. It was followed from the middle of 1976 by a third and more stringent phase; but the collapse of sterling during that year pushed up import prices to such an extent that price increases ran significantly ahead of increases in earnings, so undermining trade union support for a further period of income restraint. Even so the rate of inflation fell from the middle of 1977, thus showing that both the third and the following stage had been effective.

It still remains an open question how far it is possible for an incomes policy to be successful over a longer period of time. Each successive phase creates more discontent. In addition strains are created in the labour market of which the subsequent stage has to take account, without, at the same time, being rendered ineffective by its own flexibility. It is, however, plain that British governments, particularly in the uncertain world of today, are likely to continue to try to influence the determination of pay. It is also likely that, unless incomes policies are accompanied by rises in real living standards or by other compensating factors, they will meet with resistance (at least in the longer term) from the shopfloor. Thus, the strains on the trade union movement may increase rather than diminish.

DONOVAN AND 'IN PLACE OF STRIFE'

It was, in part, the lack of success in achieving a viable incomes policy which led governments to try to modify collective bargaining relationships directly by legislation. It is, however, a curious paradox that it should have been the Labour Party, brought into being primarily to ensure that the law be kept out of collective bargaining, which, in government, should have made the first attempt since the 1920s to introduce legislation against strikes. Because of its abiding lessons for Labour politicians, it is worth examining this unhappy episode in some detail.

When Labour came to power in 1964, it was faced with two kinds of pressure. The trade union movement, which, as a consequence of the Rootes v Barnard judgment (1964), believed that the legal immunity established by the 1906 Act was threatened, sought new protective legislation. Meanwhile, if opinion polls were to be taken seriously, there appeared to be a mounting and slightly confused desire for something to be done about the unions and unofficial strikes. To appease the unions the Government introduced the

Trade Disputes Act (1965) which restored the trade unions' legal immunity. At the same time, it yielded to the prevailing view of public opinion by setting up a Royal Commission on Trade Unions and Employers' Associations, under the chairmanship of Lord Donovan and with leading representatives of both sides in industry as members.

But after three years of painstaking work, the Donovan Commission reported in 1968 that the major problem of British industrial relations was its failure to come to terms with the growth in shopfloor power. According to Donovan, in many industries, particularly in the private sector, the influence of industry-wide agreements had declined dramatically; instead of making agreements which would define the status of shopfloor bargaining, management had allowed the authority of industry-wide bargaining to be eroded without replacing it by anything else. The increase in 'unconstitutional strikes', the spread of wages drift, the degeneration of payment by results schemes, and the mushrooming of overtime were, in the view of the Donovan Commission, only symptoms of the chaos that had developed at plant level.

In the words of the Donovan Report, 'the root of the evil is in our present methods of collective bargaining and especially our methods of workshop bargaining, and it is in the absence of speedy, clear and effective disputes procedures'.[9]

Thus, the Donovan Report challenged the myth, so dear to the mass media, that the trade unions were mainly to blame for poor industrial relations. And, though the trade unions were criticised for failing to come to terms with plant bargaining, the report said that the main responsibility for industrial relations must lie with management. If management claimed the right to manage, it could not absolve itself of responsibility for either breakdowns in industrial relations or for helping to change the system.

On balance, the Donovan Commission decided against legal intervention. It was not, in principle, against legal enforcement of collective agreements. However, it considered that, given the inadequacy of most agreements, it would be self-defeating to introduce enforceable contracts unless and until the system itself had been reformed. 'To make the present procedure agreements legally enforceable would be at variance both with our analysis of the causes of the evil and with our proposals for a remedy. It would divert attention from the underlying causes to the symptoms of the disease and might indeed delay or even frustrate the cure we recommend.'[10]

The Donovan Report, therefore, concluded that the major thrust of reform should be to tackle the *causes* of industrial relations problems. To encourage firms to negotiate effective plant agreements, it proposed that companies should be obliged to register collective agreements. In addition, the Donovan Commission suggested that a statutory body, the Commission on Industrial Relations (CIR), should be set up to examine and to give advice on problems arising out of the registration of agreements, of trade union recognition, of deficiencies in factory procedures and of industrial relations generally. But, in line with the Donovan Commission's general approach, the CIR was to rely on persuasion and not on legal backing.

Thus the conclusion of the Donovan Commission was to reject the case for legal sanctions. Believing as it did that the main problem of industrial relations was the system's failure to readjust to the growth in shopfloor power, it proposed instead the development and reform of collective bargaining on a mainly voluntary basis.

Given the lack of enthusiasm that the Donovan Report had so clearly shown for introducing the law into collective bargaining, how was it that the Labour Government then decided in favour of legal restraints on unconstitutional strikes? The answer lies mainly in the appallingly weak economic and political position in which the Wilson administration found itself in 1968. In the period immediately following the devaluation of November 1967 the government was neurotically aware of the effect that strikes in key export industries (for example, shipping, the docks and motor manufacture, amongst others) could have not only on the monthly trade figures but also on overseas confidence in the British economy. And, because the Labour Party was trailing so far behind in the public opinion polls and had suffered an astonishing number of humiliations at by-elections and local elections, it was also over conscious of the possible political attractions of the tough approach to industrial relations adopted by the Conservatives in their policy document *Fair deal at work*, also published that year.

For the most part, the Labour government's controversial White Paper *In place of strife* was based on the Donovan Report (including its proposals on the registration of agreements, on the setting up of a Commission on Industrial Relations (CIR) and on trade union recognition). Much of it would have been of immediate advantage to the trade unions. In particular, the proposals on trade union recognition would have helped to overcome the opposition of hostile employers to union organisation, which had been the major factor in holding back trade union growth. The Government also suggested a scheme for grants and loans to assist trade union mergers, training, research and the employment of management consultants which could have benefitted the trade unions considerably.

But fierce trade union opposition was aroused by a proposal which represented a radical departure from the Donovan approach. Under Labour's legislation, the Secretary of State was to have 'a discretionary reserve power to secure "a conciliation pause" in unconstitutional strikes and in strikes where, because there was no agreed procedure or for other reasons adequate joint discussions have not taken place'. The TUC rightly pointed out that many procedures were often narrow in scope and one-sided in operation. Moreover, agreement on new procedures would be made much more difficult if they were to be coupled with legal sanctions. The trade unions also bitterly opposed the financial penalties which a new industrial court (as proposed by the White Paper) could impose to enforce a 28-day 'conciliation pause' and the proposal for strike ballots in official strikes which, in the opinion of the Secretary of State, 'would involve a serious threat to the economy or public interest'.

Despite TUC criticism, it is just possible that, if the Government had put the whole of *In place of strife* into one Bill, it might have carried the day, since it was well known that some unions were sufficiently attracted by the favourable aspects to tolerate the unfavourable ones. But, on 15 April 1969 the Government utterly destroyed its chances of getting its legislation through Parliament by the mistake of allowing the Chancellor of the Exchequer, in the course of his budget speech, to announce the so-called 'short Bill'. Of the five proposals in the short Bill, two were unpalatable and three were favourable, but the Government compounded its error by describing the Bill as 'an essential component in ensuring the economic success of the Government'.[11] From that point it was strongly opposed by trade union leaders and, equally important, by backbench Labour MPs particularly trade union sponsored members.

Thus the Labour Government was forced to give way. In exchange for a 'solemn and binding undertaking' from the TUC General Council to deal toughly with unconstitutional disputes, the Government dropped the 'panel' clauses. And though the CIR was set up in March 1969, it was easy enough for the Conservatives to say that Labour had done nothing about industrial relations. The trade unions can be blamed for failing to take seriously the possibility that a defeat for the Labour Government (particularly as it could be presented as a climb down in the face of union power) in June 1969 might lead to an electoral victory for the Conservatives in June 1970. But it was the Labour Government's insistence on being seen to take some rapid though almost certainly ineffective action against strikes, instead of concentrating on getting across the Donovan Commission's message and on implementing the proposals contained in its report, which undermined an otherwise acceptable and relevant Bill and left the way wide open for the Conservatives who adopted a very different attitude.

THE INDUSTRIAL RELATIONS ACT

The Conservative approach was ill-advised. They believed that the main problem of industrial relations was the irresponsibility of trade unions and their members who refused to obey the rules of collective bargaining. This view of industrial relations, so radically different from the Donovan approach, can be traced back to the Majority Report of the Royal Commission on Trade Unions of 1869.[12] But, more recently, it had been developed in three Conservative pamphlets – *Giant's strength* (1958), *Trade unions for tomorrow* (1966) and the official party policy document *Fair deal at work* (1968). Their central argument was that the legal immunities granted to British trade unions had resulted in an excessive concentration of power without accountability. *Fair deal at work* claimed that 'Britain's industrial relations system is the least legally regulated in the world, yet no other country has granted so much legal protection to the participants. Indeed, our trade union Acts give positive encouragement to practices which society would never tolerate in any other spheres of human relationships.'[13] The Conservative answer was comprehensive legislation which, by introducing a wide range of new penalties and incentives, would ensure that trade unions and their members could not exploit their power. In this way, the Heath administration hoped not only to solve Britain's industrial relations problems but, by 'taming the unions' also to make a substantial contribution to slowing down the rate of inflation.

In introducing the Industrial Relations Act of 1971 – the first comprehensive legislative intervention in this field – the Conservative Government, for the most part, abandoned the Donovan recommendations. Instead of concentrating on reforming and extending collective bargaining, it assumed that it was possible to get rid of unofficial strikes by making trade unions the policemen of industry. It ignored the fact that trade unions were democratic organisations in which the seat of power had almost always been close to the members, and took little notice of the considered judgment of the Donovan Commission that an approach which put all the onus for policing agreements on trade unions would be 'more likely to lead to internal disruption in the unions than to a reduction in unofficial strikes'.[14]

The trade union movement, refused any consultation on the main principles of the legislation, took up a position of determined and sustained opposition to the Industrial Relations Act. Even though Robert Carr, the Conservative Secretary of State for Employment, had stated that one of the government's purposes was to strengthen collective bargaining[15], the trade unions did not believe him. In view of the lingering, if tacit, support (particularly amongst Conservatives) for the 1971 Act, it is worth recalling why trade unions felt so threatened by its provisions, and why it was so harmful to industrial relations.

To trade unions, one of the most objectionable features of the Act was that, for the first time, the right not to belong to a union was elevated to the same level of principle as the right to belong to a union. To many people, this seemed fair. (I discuss the question of individual rights in chapter 12.) But trade unions could not forget that the security of all employees depended on building an effective trade union organisation throughout the firm or industry. A man who refused to join a union in an organised factory was not only enjoying the benefits of unionism without accepting any of its obligations but could also be a potential threat to the unity of the workforce when that unity was most needed. To trade unionists, who wanted to build up their organisation and spread collective bargaining, it seemed wrong to equate the right to join a union which furthered collective bargaining with the right to non-unionism which obstructed it. They, therefore, objected most strongly to the restrictions placed on closed shops.

For the closed shop, (which in its different forms probably covers about half the total trade union membership) the Act substituted a complicated formula – the 'agency shop'. By this arrangement, a registered union could reach an agreement with management by which workers either became union members or, if they did not wish to become members, would have to pay something for its services or, in the case of genuine conscientious objectors, could make equivalent contributions to an appropriate charity. In cases where the employer refused to agree to an agency shop, there was provision for a ballot. To be successful in establishing an agency shop, however, the union had to win the support of those 'eligible to vote' – not just of those who actually voted. Where a union did not get a majority, it would be allowed another attempt only after two years. During this period, a strike called by the union to force the employer to yield would be considered an 'unfair industrial practice'. Even if the union secured a majority, it would be open for the agency shop to be challenged after two years by a dissatisfied 20 per cent requesting a new ballot. No wonder the trade unions rejected the agency shop as an unworkable compromise between the freedom not to join a trade union and the need to build up a strong trade union organisation.

The Act not only attacked the organisational basis of union power; it also threatened the position of the shop steward, who played a crucial part not only in trade union organisation but also in shopfloor bargaining.

The shop steward had emerged from the Donovan report as the lynchpin of the bargaining system.[16] According to the survey commissioned by Donovan on workshop bargaining, most managers preferred to deal with shop stewards rather than with full-time officials – presumably because of their availability and their local knowledge. Contrary to popular belief, managers found shop stewards far *less* militant than their members. To managers, shop stewards had many virtues. They acted as the workers' voice, as containers of conflict, as bargainers with management, and as management's guarantee that agreements would work. Little wonder that managers considered the shop steward's role so important.

Yet the Act contained a number of clauses, including restrictions on strike threats, which the trade union movement believed were directed specifically against the shop steward.

By omission, it also provided employers with a particularly neat way of getting rid of troublesome shop stewards. Under the section on unfair dismissals, an employer, though forced to pay compensation, was free to reject recommendations for re-instatement. Thus, even if a shop steward was proved to be unfairly dismissed, he could still be got rid of quite legally. All in all, few stewards could feel confident about their legal rights under the Act.

Trade unions also felt, with considerable justice, that their right to strike had been drastically curtailed by the Act (I discuss the issue of strikes and the community more fully in chapter 12). Indeed, there were so many legal restraints imposed on them that two leading authorities, echoing Haldane's judgement after Taff Vale, concluded that 'nobody can say precisely where the legal boundaries of strike action lie at the present time'.[17] The consequences of not being registered as a union and the long list of 'unfair industrial practices' tilted the balance of power in industry further in favour of the employers. The freedom to strike of all persons other than those acting with the authority of registered unions largely disappeared. Nearly all those organising and many of those participating in unofficial strikes (the vast majority of all strikes) were exposed to court orders to refrain from unfair industrial practices and to demands for unlimited compensation. Even the freedom of registered unions to strike was severely limited by the system of unfair industrial practices.

For a registered union found guilty of an unfair industrial practice the financial liability to pay compensation was limited in the sense that there was a maximum amount, but all the funds of a union used to finance industrial action were available for the payment of compensation awards. Moreover, any person alleging that he had suffered loss could claim such compensation. Protection against a valid claim was available only to a registered union official who could show that he acted 'within the scope of his authority' – something which was often very difficult to prove.

The trade union movement had a particular horror of the elaborate machinery set up under the Act to 'oversee' industrial relations, the cornerstone of which was the National Industrial Relations Court (NIRC). The NIRC had considerable powers. It could not only decide whether to refer the state of industrial relations in a particular industry to the Commission on Industrial Relations (CIR) but also whether to make the particular agreement on procedure recommended by the CIR legally enforceable. It could also decide whether the CIR should examine a trade union's claims for recognition or bargaining rights. It was responsible for authorising ballots on the enforcement of union recognition and on the introduction or continuation of an agency shop. And, it was the NIRC, not the government which had the ultimate political responsibility of imposing a conciliation pause or a strike ballot in cases of national emergency. Above all, it was the NIRC which had the power to fine errant unions. In view of its central role, the trade union movement decided to boycott the court, except where they had to defend their actions (though the AUEW consistently refused to appear at all despite eventual sequestration of considerable funds for 'contempt of court').

In a different context, the sections of the 1971 Act on trade union recognition, on unfair dismissals and on information for collective bargaining might have been welcomed, though they needed substantial amendment. But they could not make up for the other sections to which the trade unions objected so strongly. Conservative spokesmen have often argued that trade union opposition to the Industrial Relations Act was intemperate and biased. But, given the Act's potential effect on the ability of trade unions to organise, to negotiate, and to strike, their attitude was justified.

THE AFTERMATH

In the event, the hostility of a united trade union movement and, perhaps even more important, the indifference of major companies, substantially limited the application of the 1971 Industrial Relations Act. Trade union negotiators were successful in their instance that agreements should not be legally binding. Most employers, aware of the possible consequences for industrial relations in the future, were sensible enough not to exploit opportunities to take their employees to court. Even the Conservative Government, after an embarrassing experience over the railway unions' dispute in 1972, evidently decided that the Act's emergency powers should not be used again.

But, though the Act was not fully implemented, its harmful effect cannot be emphasised enough. It acted as a disincentive to the spread and co-ordination of trade unionism; it held up the reform and development of collective bargaining; and it soured the climate of industrial relations.

The 1971 Act's ban on the closed shop and its provisions which limited rights (including the ability to convert existing closed shops into agency shops and to secure recognition from management) only to trade unions which registered, acted, at least in some areas, as a disincentive to the spread of trade union organisation. It is true that, in many industries, the outlawing of the closed shop was ineffective; trade unionists and employers conspired together to maintain 100 per cent trade unionism on an unofficial basis. But the decision of the vast majority of trade unions not to register (the trade union movement saw the refusal to register as a key symbol of its resistance to the Act) meant that, in most cases, trade unions were not able to use the Act's recognition procedures to extend trade union membership in those industries in which the proportion of workers organised was low.

The reform and development of collective bargaining, which the Donovan Commission had recommended so strongly, was set back several years.[18] After the Donovan Report, trade union negotiators, together with the more enlightened employers, had, in a significant number of cases, begun to change the machinery of collective bar-gaining to bring it closer to the shopfloor, to reorganise dispute pro-cedures to make them more effective, and, in line with the Donovan recommendations, to redefine the status and position of the shop steward. With the passing of the 1971 Act, the situation changed. Trade union officials had now to devote much time to the legislation and its effects. They had to scrutinise agreements to ensure that they were not legally binding. They had to devise ways of protecting trade union funds from the Act. They had to warn their shop stewards of the possible consequences of disobeying the Act, par-ticularly the long list of unfair industrial practices. Reform was shelved. Shop stewards, themselves, became so uncertain of their rights that, instead of codifying their agreements with management, as the Donovan Report had recommended, many preferred to continue informal arrangements and, in some cases, to proceed without any agreement at all.

But perhaps the worst effect of the Act was its impact on the climate of industrial relations. Whilst it would be wrong to attribute a large proportion of the number of working days lost in strikes between 1971 and 1974 directly to the Act (though some strikes during this period were directly connected with the legislation), it certainly affected the general atmosphere. The Act also gave an incentive to disgruntled trade unionists and to other individual employees to take legal proceedings against trade unions, again very often to the detriment of industrial relations. And though most employers tried (as far as was possible) to ignore the legislation, a minority of employers, usually small and anti-union, used it as an authoritarian crutch. Instead of analysing why their own industrial relations were bad and doing something about it, they turned to the law (either to industrial tribunals or to the NIRC itself) and aggravated an already difficult situation. The efforts of the courts, particularly the NIRC, were usually counter-productive. Though most of the NIRC's panel members very quickly realised that what was usually needed in industrial disputes was conciliation, they had to operate the court as the law required, which, in a few celebrated cases, led to a direct confrontation between the court and the two most powerful trade unions – the Engineers (AUEW) and the Transport Workers (TGWU). This clash was harmful both to the legal system and to industrial relations. Finally, the Act undoubtedly made it more difficult for the Conservative Government to get settlements without disputes in the public sector and, when its economic policies changed in 1972, to reach a more general accommodation with the trade union movement.

The lesson to be learnt from the failure of the 1971 Act is that it is not possible, in a democratic Britain, to solve the country's economic and industrial relations problems by imposing a system of legal sanctions on an unwilling trade union movement. This does not mean that there is no room for law in industrial relations. But it must be used primarily to *strengthen* rather than as, with the 1971 Act, to *weaken* collective bargaining.

The Labour Government's Employment Protection Act (1975) which followed its two repeal Acts of 1974 and 1975 gave employees rights, including guaranteed week payments, special medical provisions, maternity pay and the right to return to work after maternity leave, rights for workers in liquidated companies, new requirements when workers were made redundant, time off for trade union and other public duties, and wider unfair dismissals arrangements. But its major objective was the strengthening of collective bargaining. Under the Act, trade unions were able to refer claims for recognition to the Advisory Conciliation and Arbitration Service (ACAS), a new independent but statutory body, which was also designed to expand the role of conciliation and arbitration in industrial disputes as an alternative to law. In cases of persistent opposition by employers, a trade union could establish a right to recognition from another body, the Central Arbitration Committee (CAC). In addition, the Act gave trade unions rights to disclosure of information for collective bargaining purposes. Once again, a trade union could use the CAC to establish the right to information. Finally, the Act contained provisions to stimulate progress towards voluntary collective bargaining in the wages council industries.[19]

The Employment Protection Act represented both a decisive break with the 1971 Act and, in its emphasis on the development of collective bargaining, a return to the line of approach recommended by the Donovan Commission. Equally significantly, the support of the trade unions for the 1975 Act marked a shift in their attitude to industrial relations law. They had now decided in its favour – provided it strengthened, rather than weakened, trade unions and collective bargaining.

The relationship between governments (of both parties) and the trade union movement in the future, as in the past, is likely to be subjected to strains. From the government's point of view, the unfettered freedom of collective bargaining presents a formidable obstacle to the success of policies to curb inflation and promote industrial recovery to the achievement of social programmes. Yet, in recent years, efforts to reach some arrangement with trade union power have foundered, in part, because (as with the 1971 Industrial Relations Act) they have been misconceived. As far as trade unions are concerned, they are entitled, in a democratic society, not only to demand basic rights of organisation, representation and dissent (including the right to strike) but also to press for a more democratic industry. However, bitter experience since the war has shown that, if trade union wage claims are pushed to the limit, the result not only makes it more difficult to maintain employees' living standards and job security but can also endanger those social priorities which the trade union movement shares with the Labour Party.

An approach to this dilemma which was based on an agreement between the government, employers and the trade union movement and which recognised trade union rights and social priorities *and* the need for a clearly defined and voluntarily accepted incomes policy should be welcomed by all parties. In practice, the pressures on both governments and trade unions for speedy results (particularly in an inflationary period) makes an effective accord difficult to sustain. But there is little alternative – unless it be the imposition of totalitarian solutions.

REFERENCES

1 K. W. Wedderburn *The worker and the law* Penguin 1971 pp. 23–25, and R. Lewis 'The historical development of labour law' *British Journal of Industrial Relations* March 1976.
2 *The worker and the law* p. 312.
3 H. A. Clegg, A. Fox and A. F. Thompson *A history of British trade unions since 1889* Oxford 1964 vol. 1 p. 305.
4 *A history of British trade unions since 1889* vol. 1 p. 310.
5 *The worker and the law* p. 17.
6 *The new inflation* p. 25.
7 For a fuller discussion of incomes policy see H. A. Clegg *How to run an incomes policy* Heinemann 1971, and *The new inflation*.
8 See John Edmonds and Giles Radice *Low pay* Fabian Society 1968.
9 *Report of the Royal Commission on Trade Unions and Employers' Associations* para. 475.
10 *Report of the Royal Commission on Trade Unions and Employers' Associations* para. 475.

11 *Hansard* 15 April 1969 cols. 1003–06.
12 *Management by agreement* p. 10.
13 *Fair deal at work* Conservative Political Centre 1968 p. 16; for a full account of the development of Conservative policy see Micheal Moran *The politics of industrial relations* Macmillan 1977 chps. 4 and 5.
14 *Report of the Royal Commission on Trade Unions and Employers' Associations* para. 482.
15 Speech to the Third Annual Forum of the Institute of Collective Bargaining and Group Relations in New York (quoted in *Management by agreement* p. 32).
16 *Report of the Royal Commission on Trade Unions and Employers' Associations* para. 110.
17 *Management by agreement* p. 38.
18 See the Department of Employment report on the impact of the Act in *Industrial Relations Report and Review* July 1975 nos. 83 and 84; also B. Weekes, M. Mellish, L. Dickens and J. Lloyd *Industrial relations and the limits of law* Blackwell 1975.
19 For a fuller discussion of the Employment Protection Act see chps. 7 and 12.

Chapter 5

The trade union response

The previous three chapters have described how the impact of
technology, the growing importance of the large firm, and the
spread of multinational corporations could reduce the effectiveness
of trade union representation; how, at the same time, employees
are increasingly demanding more fulfilling jobs, more control over
their working environment, and better opportunities for themselves
and their children in other aspects of their lives; and how governments have been driven to intervene in collective bargaining and
are likely to continue to do so in the future. This chapter examines
the effectiveness of the trade union response to these changes in
the industrial and social environment. It is argued here that this
response must be considered in the context of trade union purpose;
that there are encouraging signs of efforts to adapt functions to
environmental changes; but that this process is not yet widespread
enough, and that, more fundamentally, the trade union movement
still lacks that common strategy which is essential if it is to measure
up to what is required.

THE CRITICISMS

In assessing the trade union response, it is right to begin with
trade union achievements, which by any standards, have been considerable. Consider the record: starting with only a small minority
of mostly skilled workers as members in the 1850s and 1860s, trade
unions have grown into a very powerful movement, covering all
grades of employees and over half the labour force. Commenting
on the impact of trade union membership, Allan Flanders has
rightly said that 'there is probably no other voluntary institution
in the country which brings as many people into part-time service
on behalf of their fellows and gives them a first-hand experience of
the democratic methods of administration'.[1] And, through trade
union involvement in collective bargaining and other related instru-

ments (such as craft control and 'custom and practice'), employees have been able to obtain not only higher living standards but also a share in certain vital, if limited, areas of decision-making formerly the prerogative of management, such as recruitment, discipline, work organisation and technical change. With the creation and development of the TUC and the Labour Party, the trade unions have also been able to exercise an important influence on social and political affairs, so much so that some of the really decisive changes in this country, including the establishment of the welfare state and the introduction of the mixed economy, have been brought about, in part, through the pressure of the trade union movement. Without any doubt, trade unionism has made a massive contribution to the well-being of British society.

In the last two decades, however, trade unions have been strongly criticised, not only on the fundamental grounds discussed in chapter 1, but also in terms of their own internal arrangements. It is said that their structure, organisation and services are 'out of date', that their internal democracy has 'decayed', and that their leadership is 'weak'. But though there is some substance to these charges, they have to be considered in the right context.

As far as structure and organisation is concerned, the most common panacea put forward is that of industrial unionism.[2] As is pointed out in chapter 10, this solution not only totally ignores the historical division of the British trade union movement into mainly craft, general and occupational unions and the more recent emergence of what Professor Turner has called 'open' unionism[3] as the natural growth pattern; it also greatly underestimates, as John Hughes has noted, the benefits of a more fluid and flexible structure.[4]

This is not to deny that there *are* serious problems associated with the way the trade union movement has developed, and particularly those which arise from the overlapping membership interests of the larger unions. But, before constructing a programme of structural reform, it is essential to know *why* it is required. Is it because it is believed that industrial unions find it more difficult to resist change? Not surprisingly trade unionists find arguments on these lines unconvincing. There are stronger grounds, however, for structural reforms when these are essential for effective industrial representation.

It is also often argued that trade union services to their membership are inadequate. This is fair comment. As is pointed out in chapter 10, there are too few officials, and educational, research and other back-up facilities leave a lot to be desired particularly in view of the growth in shopfloor power and the demand for more industrial democracy. But the case for improving trade union servicing is not primarily to assist the British worker to understand what the British manager is trying to do; rather it is so that trade unionists should have at their disposal an independent and effective source of information, expertise and advice, to assist them in the achievement of their own objectives.

Turning to the question of trade union democracy, it is undeniable that practice does not always conform with theory. As Allan Flanders has pointed out, 'the emergence of a new profession, that of the trade union official, has undoubtedly influenced the democratic character of trade union organisation'.[5] However, in all unions, there are constraints from constitutional mechanisms and, more important, from shopfloor organisation on the autonomy of trade union leaders. And though (as is argued in chapter 9) experiments in membership participation already taking place need to be developed further and faster, trade unionists can be forgiven for questioning the motives of those whose own authority is in no way derived from any democratic source. Those who criticise trade union democracy should not forget that the legitimate argument for reform in this area is not the creation of a pliant, 'do nothing' unionism, but rather to ensure that, in a changing and uncertain environment, a leadership with more ambitious objectives remains in touch with and is influenced by the membership.

Indeed, when it comes to a discussion of trade union leadership, the critics often show their true colours. For trade union leaders are criticised not because they are undemocratic but because they are too 'weak'. Unlike their predecessors, they cannot, it is said 'deliver' their side of the bargain. The reason usually given for this so-called 'failure' is a curious one. It is alleged that the 1944 Education Act has creamed off the best working class brains, leaving behind only a low calibre of official from which members can choose their leaders. Hence the weakness. A mere glance at the present generation of trade union leaders is enough to disprove that theory. And from what I know of their potential successors, there is no evidence that the strain of first-class general secretaries is in danger of dying out. The real change that has occurred is in the conditions in which trade union leaders have to operate. They can no longer (if they ever could) issue commands, and expect their members automatically to obey. Rather they have to win consent by persuasion. If this is 'weakness' then trade union leaders must continue to be weak. For only this style of leadership corresponds to the facts of industrial life. There *is* a powerful case for trade union reform. But reform has to be discussed in the context of trade union purpose. Structure, organisation, services, internal democracy, leadership and so on should be considered in the light of how far they assist trade unions to fulfil their objectives in the light of modern conditions.

THE NEED FOR A STRATEGY

A more perceptive criticism of British trade unionism was made in the following terms. 'Today the unions are immensely powerful but they are not willing to run industry themselves, nor to accept terms which will make it possible for others to run it. What is needed is a new and positive ideology, positive aims for the future; without this there is no hope at all for a successful reform of trade unionism.'[6]

The lack of a positive strategy is perhaps the most glaring weakness of British trade unions today and the largest single obstacle to the development of an effective response to changes in their environment. Because of it, trade unions remain at least partially trapped within the confines of their traditional functions. As a result, they have not yet developed the representation which is required if they are to satisfy their members needs. In addition, the still almost theological commitment to old-style collective bargaining, combined with a lack of clearly defined and realistic economic and social priorities, makes it extremely hard for the movement to evolve an effective long term response to government intervention.

It is not suggested, for a moment, that trade unions should rush to adopt some high-sounding but Utopian doctrine which has no immediate relevance and no chance of being realised in the foreseeable future. What is now required is a common set of objectives or a guide to action, closely linked to existing trade union purpose and function, firmly rooted in the needs and aspirations of working people and which takes account of developments in the industrial, social and political environment.

But is a common trade union strategy attainable? W. E. J. McCarthy has warned us to be sceptical of 'references to the aims or views of trade unions in general and the "trade union movement" in particular', and has argued convincingly that 'a respect for and a delight in the differences between unions is a sure mark of the serious student of the subject'.[7] Certainly there are a number of different factors, which include the composition, attitudes and bargaining power of its members, the kind of organisational policies it pursues, the traditions and values it has acquired over the years, and the nature of its leadership, which make every union unique. Even so, it does not follow from the rich diversity of British trade unions that they cannot share common objectives. In the past, as has been pointed out above, they have united successfully behind common goals – including the development of trade union organisation, the spread of collective bargaining, the introduction of basic industrial rights and the achievement of minimum social standards. Today, all trade unions are, to a greater or lesser extent, subject to common pressures (from their members, from management, and from government) to which they must respond if they are to survive. So it is not advocating something foreign to the nature of trade unionism to argue that, while each individual union will, of necessity, extract from any general statement of aims only those parts which are applicable to its own situation, it is quite feasible – and indeed essential – for trade unions to draw up a common set of objectives, based on their shared purpose and relevant to modern conditions.

In chapter 1, the main purpose of trade unionism was defined as that of democratising and humanising industry. This implies that trade unions should seek a share in decision-making on *all* subjects which affect their members (including work design, production, investment, financial control, marketing, the direction of corporate strategy and so on) and at *all* levels from shopfloor to boardroom. It was also contended that, in an industrial democracy, trade unions have a right to be heard on the broader economic and social issues which are of importance to their members. This implies that they should seek a continuing *dialogue* with government on economic and social priorities.

A strategy which was based on these separate but interlocking objectives is likely to receive substantial support from trade union members. It should also match up to the challenges posed by changes in the industrial environment and the propensity of governments to intervene in collective bargaining. And, though the development of a common strategy will have to overcome a number of obstacles and will take time, there is more than enough evidence from changes made over the last decade to demonstrate that trade unions are quite capable, if they will it, of taking up the options outlined in the next section of the book.

COLLECTIVE BARGAINING AND BEYOND

The most important trade union function is collective bargaining. As Allan Flanders has noted, 'trade unions in Great Britain came in being, established themselves on firm foundations and extended their power and social influence mainly on account of their achievements in collective bargaining'.[8] It would indeed be wrong to minimise the successes of collective bargaining. The growth in trade union membership, particularly during two world wars, created the basis for a system by which, in many industries, unilateral regulation by management has been replaced by the joint regulation of issues both *substantive* (about the terms and conditions of employment) and *procedural* (about the way in which substantive norms are made, challenged, interpreted and applied).

The British collective bargaining system was developed primarily as an industry-level mechanism. At the end of the first world war, it was the joint industrial council (JIC), the industry-wide model recommended by the Whitley Committee, which received the support not only of government but also of the employers and trade unions. During the second world war, the next great period of trade union growth, Ernest Bevin, as Minister of Labour, gave another stimulus to the JIC concept. In 1965, there were nearly two hundred JICs; and, in the same year, in its evidence to the Donovan Commission, the Ministry of Labour reported that 'the main feature of the British system of industrial relations is the voluntary machinery, which has grown up over a wide area of employment, for *industry-wide* (my italics) collective bargaining and discussion between employers' associations and trade unions over terms and conditions of employment'.[9]

However, by the middle 1960s, the Ministry of Labour's comment was more a memorial to times past than an accurate description of present reality. Industry-wide bargaining was under severe threat, both from below and above. Below, the development of shopfloor power had led to a massive increase in the importance of bargaining at this level and also of the more informal 'custom and practice' (described by W. E. J. McCarthy as a 'protective device which workers invoke to legitimise and perpetuate those management mistakes which benefit them'[10]); so much so that the Donovan Commission estimated that domestic bargaining was almost universal among establishments with over 250 employees and which recognised trade unions, and that, in some industries in the private sector, as much as half of a worker's take home pay was usually won through plant-level negotiation.

From above, the authority of industry-wide bargaining was challenged from two directions. First, the growing importance of larger and often multinational companies had created the need for representation at a new level. Secondly, governments, concerned about the inflationary consequences of collective bargaining, had tended to intervene more directly to influence the outcome of negotiations.

The Donovan Commission's observations on the impact of shop-floor bargaining on the industry-wide system are justly well-known. It demonstrated that there were 'two systems of industrial relations', the formal one being the industry-wide collective agreement, the informal being the bargaining which takes place within the factory. It showed how the informal system generally arose out of unwritten arrangements and 'custom and practice', took place piecemeal and resulted in competitive sectional wage adjustments and chaotic pay structures, and was, in large part, outside the control of trade unions and employers' associations.[11]

Yet, though shopfloor activity creates problems for national trade unions, boards of management and governments, from the point of view of the employees it represents an important step forward in the development of individual rights at the workplace. Through plant bargaining (and through the exploitation of 'custom and practice') their representatives are able to discuss an increasingly wide range of subjects – volume of overtime, discipline, redundancy, manning, promotion and work arrangements – which are either inappropriate for discussion at national level or on which employers refuse to negotiate, unless forced to do so at plant level. No wonder that many groups of workers have learnt to put much of their trust in plant bargaining when their power can be utilised more directly.

However, shopfloor arrangements are patchy and informal; they fall far short of a full system of workers' rights. And, despite the increase in the number of subjects negotiated at plant level, issues like the control of work design and the working environment, which are of growing importance to workers, are still largely matters of management prerogative; equally important, uncertain economic conditions have made employees more aware that most *strategic* decisions are outside the scope of collective bargaining (be it at shopfloor or any other level). The predominance of the large firm, with its impact on the lives of employees, its capacity to draw on vast resources, and its ability to centralise certain types of decision-making, makes an appropriate trade union response all the more urgent. Multinationals create additional problems. What is now required is nothing less than a linked system of representation, organisation and services all the way up from shopfloor to board-room and, in the case of multinationals, the development of inter-national trade union co-operation.

The first tentative steps towards the development of a fresh trade union approach have already been taken. Trade union officials have made some attempts (for example, the ICI, Fords and Pilkingtons claims in the 1970s) to open up issues decided unilaterally by man-agement. More significantly, since 1974 the Trades Union Congress has advocated a system of employee representation at boardroom level. And there have been a number of instances of successful international trade union co-ordination. But it does not yet add up to a strategy. There needs to be a big increase in both the coverage and scope of collective bargaining: plant bargaining should be formalised and integrated with negotiations at higher levels; com-pany level bargaining needs to be developed to fill the gap between plant and industry level negotiations; in many cases, employees will also require direct representation at boardroom level; and there must be far more trade union co-operation across national frontiers. In short, there must be a radical extension of democratic control within industry.

Government attempts to influence the outcome of wage bargaining also present a serious challenge to the trade union movement. The motives which had led governments to intervene and the mistakes which they have made have been described in the last chapter, as have the difficulties that these policies have created for trade unions. Any set of counter-inflation measures with a wage restraint aspect not only threatens to undermine their traditional functions; it also runs the danger of causing a split between the leadership and membership. Yet, given that wages are a significant element in price determination, it is difficult to see any alternative.

It is just possible that, despite all the failures in the past, the long term prospects for an enduring policy are better than they have ever been. First, during the inflationary years of the 1970s (and particularly following the wages explosion of 1974–75), employees became more conscious of the impact on their living standards of unrestrained wage bargaining. Secondly, there is a growing awareness of the connection between inflation and unem-ployment. In the 1960s, when political leaders warned that inflation could lead to unemployment, they were ignored. But, when many companies went bankrupt during the recession of the 1970s, the dangers of inflation became more obvious. Thirdly, with the improvement of Britain's economic position following the exploitation of North Sea Oil, incomes policy could become less of an exercise in restraint and more of a way of planning increases in real wages.

However, if trade unionists are to agree to more than temporary limitations on wage bargaining, they will want a greater say in the management of the enterprise. In this context, more industrial democracy will not only give trade union representatives new functions to compensate for modifications in traditional ones; it will also help to ensure that the operation of the enterprise takes account of the restraint exercised by employees. And trade unionists who are deeply involved in the running of industry will be in a better position to consider the wider economic and social implications of decision-making. So a major argument for industrial democracy is that it can provide a way of reconciling the aspirations of trade unionists with the need for government intervention in the workings of the economy.

Another crucial factor in ensuring shopfloor support is a continuing commitment by the trade union leadership. Despite the lead given by the TUC over two decades, too many trade unionists still pay lip service to 'free collective bargaining' – as though it were possible in a modern industrial state to decide pay levels without regard to the consequences for the community as a whole. In the end, trade union leaders will have to accept the necessity for a continuing dialogue with government on wages; in return they should have the right to a say in the determination not only of the details of pay policy but also of overall economic and social objectives.

SOCIAL AND POLITICAL AIMS

In Britain, trade unions have never been purely collective bargaining agents. Though they have always put the main emphasis on industrial representation, they quickly understood that this had political and social implications. For, in order to create a framework in which trade unionism could function, they had to operate politically as well as industrially. They also realised that workers were consumers and parents, tenants and potential householders, sometimes unemployed and sick, and certainly, in the end, all destined to be superannuated from their employment. So (particularly after the advent of 'new unionism'[12]) they used political weapons to fight for a society which gave workers and their families adequate provision when they were unemployed, ill or old and which ensured that they had decent houses, schools, hospitals and so on.

Until the beginning of the twentieth century, trade unions were mainly interested in representation through the existing parties in parliament. But attacks on trade unionism through the courts finally convinced them of the necessity for independent political organisation. Their initial hesitancy does not detract from the success of their efforts. The Labour Party grew from what was, in the pre-1914 parliaments, little more than a pressure group without a distinctive programme of its own into, first in 1922, the official opposition and then, in 1924 and again in 1929, a government party, culminating in the general election triumph of 1945 and the notable accomplishments of the Attlee administrations of 1945–51, which implemented many of the measures for which the early trade union pioneers had fought.

By itself, the creation and the development (with trade union backing) of a major political party committed to changing society would be a big enough achievement. However, the trade union movement has also built up another organisation, the Trades Union Congress, which is, by its nature, more directly devoted to trade union objectives. And, whilst their association with the Labour party permits a direct involvement on one side of the political process, the existence of a powerful TUC gives trade unions the ability to influence both Labour and Conservative governments. The great strength of the TUC lies in its representative character; indeed, because all major unions (both manual and white collar) are affiliated to it, it is probably the most representative trade union centre in the world. It is, therefore, potentially in a position to speak for the entire trade union movement, and to expect, even when a Conservative government is in power, that it will be heard. Certainly, since the second world war, different governments have been prepared to listen and, particularly in the 1970s, to react to the TUC. At the very least, they have been made aware of trade union opinion.

But if the TUC is to be effective in getting across its views to government, it has to have the support of the affiliated unions. So far, individual unions have been uncertain about how much authority to give to the TUC. Their attitude to the TUC is similar to the Athenian view of Themistocles: 'They did not admire him, or honour him for himself, but treated him like a plane tree; when it was stormy, they ran under his branches for shelter, but as soon as it was fine, they plucked his leaves and lopped his branches.'[13] Thus the vast majority of individual unions (albeit with some difference of emphasis) gave their backing to the TUC General Council in its brilliantly successful campaigns against the Labour Government's White Paper *In place of strife* and the Conservative Government's Industrial Relations Act. In 1969, as an alternative to the use of sanctions proposed in *In place of strife*, they authorised the TUC to intervene in unauthorised and unconstitutional strikes, and when stoppages were threatened because of inter-union disputes. In 1971, to enforce its de-registration policy, which was the cornerstone of its opposition to the Industrial Relations Act, the TUC was given *carte blanche* to use full disciplinary powers over its membership. But when later in the 1970s it was a matter of developing a distinctive trade union approach to incomes policy or industrial democracy, then the TUC found it far more difficult to gain the support of its affiliates.

The motives behind the ambivalence towards the TUC by individual unions are complex. In part, it is the understandable fear of giving up some of their independence to a wider grouping. In part, it is because, for a variety of reasons, some trade unions leaders do not really want the TUC to have its own strategy. In a few cases, they believe that a more positive approach will lead inevitably to the incorporation of the movement into the apparatus of a 'capitalist' state. More commonly, however, it is an attitude of mind rather than a clearly formulated ideology. Uncertain about the industrial, economic and social policies which the movement ought to be pursuing, trade union executives are too often prepared to allow the resolutions passed at union conferences to go forward as a strategy, regardless of whether these are consistent with each other or practical in the economic climate of the time. The truth is that many trade unionists still prefer their unions to continue as reactive bodies without coherent and realistic policies of their own.

This is not to minimise what has already been achieved by the TUC. In response to the Labour Government's prices and incomes policy, it issued its first Economic Review in 1968; it also used the report of the Donovan Commission to become more actively involved in the reform of collective bargaining. Undoubtedly, however, its greatest achievement has been its sponsoring of the social contract approach in the 1970s by which, in return for the repeal of the 1971 Industrial Relations Act, the enactment of legislation to strengthen collective bargaining, the promise to further industrial democracy, and the introduction of social measures such as increases in pensions and other social benefits, the TUC undertook to restrain wage settlements.[14] After initial failure on the incomes side, the social contract achieved considerable success during the wage rounds of 1975–76 and 1976–77. More fundamentally, in the creation of structured dialogue between trade unions and government, it represented a move away from old-style trade unionism. However, as the TUC revealingly commented in 1975, 'there is as yet insufficient understanding, both within the trade union movement and outside it, of the new sense of direction which the trade union movement is taking and must take for the future'.[15] This was partly a reference to those who criticised the social contract for giving too much to the trade unions; but it was also a telling criticism of its own affiliates, not only for their failure to abide by the incomes side of the social contract during 1974–75, but also because they had not yet fully accepted the TUC's new approach. The return to 'free collective bargaining' in 1977 showed that the TUC was justified in its misgivings.

Yet the case for coherent and credible trade union policies on a number of issues is overwhelming. The need for a decisive move forward on industrial democracy and for a co-ordinated approach to pay policy has already been described. And after the failure of so many governments since the war, an independent yet realistic TUC view on economic and industrial policy is, more than ever, essential. In addition, a TUC which represents its members fully has to work out a sustained and clearly thought out attack on the economic and social inequalities which contribute to industrial divisions and continue to mar British society. More generally, if a genuine modern industrial democracy is to be developed in this country, then the trade unions must put forward their views convincingly. The trade unions have won the right to be heard; whether they are listened to with respect now depends as much on the quality of their advice as in the vigour with which they give it.

Though the TUC is in many ways the more important body, the Labour Party is still of major significance to the trade unions. It not only provides a valuable defensive weapon; it also serves as a vehicle through which trade unions can work for a society based on those democratic, humanitarian and egalitarian values to which they give the highest priority.

However, the trade unions cannot afford to take the Labour Party for granted. They have to be actively involved in its work. Obviously, there are bound to be strains from time to time between a governing party, circumscribed by power realities and seeking support beyond its traditional sources, and a powerful trade union movement jealous of its rights. What is important is that each wing of the Labour movement should know where the other stands. In the 1960s, there was some confusion, so much so that, over one major issue the *In place of strife* fiasco, the Labour Government found itself in a position of confrontation with its chief ally.[16] The understanding achieved between the trade union movement and the Labour Party in opposition after 1970 was based on a clearer recognition that what had happened then must not be allowed to occur again. Through the work of the TUC-Labour Party Liaison Committee, the Labour Party and the trade union movement united around policies to repeal the Industrial Relations Act and strengthen collective bargaining. There was also a joint agreement that, in fighting inflation, the trade unions as well as the Labour Party had a part to play. And when Labour was returned to power in 1974, the relationship between the Government and the TUC was far closer than it had been during the 1960s. However, in the uncertain conditions of the late 1970s, it is essential that this understanding is maintained.

Political involvement also implies that trade unions should take a close interest in party structure and organisation. If the return of a Labour government is in the interests of the trade union movement, then they also need a healthy and vigorous Labour Party to sustain it. Yet in parliament, at conference, and, above all, in the constituencies, the trade unions have not played as important a role as they should have done. Partly as a result of their neglect, the Labour Party is in decline. Its membership has dropped alarmingly, while its governing institutions are far more suited to a party of permanent opposition than to a party of government. The time has come for a fresh trade union initiative in Labour Party affairs.

This chapter has argued that, in many cases, the trade union response to changes in the environment has been encouraging. What has sometimes been lacking has been a co-ordinated strategy which would give their activities a new dynamism. What is now required is a set of industrial objectives, including the extension of collective bargaining and collective control over all matters which are of importance to the membership at all levels from shopfloor to the boardroom, and the formulation of coherent and credible social, economic and political aims, relevant to modern needs. A bold and determined initiative will be needed if such an approach is to be

successful. In the past, the trade union movement has proved itself
quite capable of pursuing successfully a set of common policies. It
must do so again if it is to match up to the challenge now facing it.

REFERENCES

1 Allan Flanders *Trade unions* Hutchinson 1968 p. 46.
2 See, for example, CBI written evidence to the Royal Commission on
Trade Unions and Employers' Associations 1965.
3 H. A. Turner *Trade union growth, structure and policy* Allen and
Unwin 1962 Parts III and VI.
4 John Hughes 'Trade union strategy and government' *Royal Commission on Trade Unions and Employers' Associations Research
Paper No. 5* paras. 45–48.
5 *Trade unions* p. 49.
6 A. J. M. Sykes 'Whither the trade unions?' *Engineering Employers'
Federation Industrial Relations Research Bulletin* June 1969 pp. 10–11.
7 *Trade unions* ed. W. E. J. McCarthy Penguin 1972 pp. 9–10.
8 *Trade unions* p. 75.
9 Written evidence of the Ministry of Labour to the Royal Commission
on Trade Unions and Employers' Associations 1965 p. 11, quoted in
H. A. Clegg *The system of industrial relations in Great Britain*
Blackwell 1970 p. 200.
10 See the review by W. E. J. McCarthy in the *Guardian* 27 June 1974
of William Brown's *Piecework bargaining* Heinemann Educational
Books 1974.
11 *Royal Commission on Trade Unions and Employers' Associations*
paras. 65–69.
12 See E. A. and G. H. Radice *Will Thorne* Allen and Unwin 1974,
particularly chps. 3 and 4.
13 Plutarch 'Life of Themistocles' quoted in Peter Green *The year of
Salamis* Weidenfeld and Nicolson 1970 p. 214.
14 A number of people are said to have been the architect of the social
contract, including Jack Jones and David Basnett. However, the
intellectual originator was probably Thomas Balogh in his *Labour
and inflation* Fabian Society 1970. See also Giles Radice and David
Lipsey 'A trade union view' in *A workable incomes policy* Heinemann
1972.
15 *The development of the social contract* TUC pamphlet July 1975
para. 6.
16 For an account of this episode see Peter Jenkins *The battle of 10
Downing Street* Knight 1970.

Part Two

The Drive for an Industrial Democracy

Chapter 6

Extending collective bargaining

The crucial role played by collective bargaining not only in determining pay and conditions but also in establishing a measure of control over decisions which were formerly the prerogative of management has been described in the last chapter. However, it was also pointed out that the system of collective bargaining faces challenges both from above and below. From below, a new generation of workers are demanding more from collective bargaining than ever before. They want both a reasonable standard of living *and* a more meaningful work experience and more influence over their working conditions. From above, managements of big companies take decisions which affect an increasingly large number of workers and yet remain outside the scope of collective bargaining. The growth of the multinational presents trade unions with additional problems. Equally important, governments, alarmed about its inflationary consequences, have increasingly intervened in collective bargaining – and are likely to continue to do so in the future.

This chapter examines how these difficulties can be overcome. It argues for an extension of both the coverage and scope of collective bargaining, suggests ways of integrating plant level bargaining with bargaining at higher levels, proposes more company-level bargaining, looks at developments in international trade union co-ordination and discusses a trade union approach to incomes policy.

RECRUITMENT AND RECOGNITION

As far as the spread of collective bargaining is concerned, about 13 million out of 16 million manual workers and 6 million out of 10 million non-manual workers are covered by negotiating machinery (including statutory wage fixing bodies).[1] But this overestimates the influence of collective bargaining. Over $3\frac{1}{2}$ million workers are within the scope of wages councils and the two agricultural boards for England and Wales and for Scotland, and only half of these are covered by collective bargaining.[2] About 8½ million workers (or over a third of the workforce) are not covered by genuine collective bargaining. In addition, plant level or domestic bargaining, which, as we have seen, is essential to the establishment of workers' rights, probably affects only a minority of employees, possibly even a minority of manual workers.[3] So trade unions must ensure that there is an effective system of bargaining at all levels throughout industry.

The prerequisite for extending collective bargaining is an increase in trade union membership, which still only covers just over half the working population. In a previous chapter, it was argued that, though traditional methods of organisation were less applicable to the non-unionised sectors, there were other factors which could work in the favour of trade unions. In particular, the growth in white collar membership in the last few years suggest that a combination of growing bureaucratisation, persistent inflation, the insecurity produced by higher levels of unemployment, and changing employer attitudes to union recognition has led to a situation in which we can expect at least the majority of white collar workers becoming union members.[4] The large and growing numbers of married women who are returning to work full-time after completing their families are also providing an increasingly solid basis for union recruiting drives.[5] However a really dramatic increase in union membership during the late 1970s and 1980s will depend on two things: a far greater allocation and direction of trade union energies and resources to recruitment, and an effective method of forcing reluctant employers to concede trade union recognition and negotiating rights.

What is required from the trade union movement is a commitment to extending membership as a matter of priority. No one should underestimate what is involved. The high turnover in some of the organised industries makes it difficult enough even to maintain membership. For example, the General and Municipal Workers' Union (GMWU) has to recruit well over 100,000 new members annually merely to make up for those members who have lapsed. And, whereas at least part of the overall increase in trade union membership in the 1960s and early 1970s was the result of more effective retention and the 'closing up' of sectors in which trade unions were already strong, membership expansion in the future will require new initiatives. If the percentage of the labour force organised is to be expanded past the 60 per cent mark, then a greater effort will have to be made in the unorganised areas. The successes in the white collar sector by trade unions like the National Association of Local Government Officers (NALGO) and the Association of Scientific, Technical and Managerial Staffs (ASTMS), the Association of Professional, Executive, Clerical and Computer Staff (APEX), the National Union of Bank Employees (NUBE) and the Association of Clerical and Technical Staffs (ACTS), the white collar section of the Transport and General Workers' Union (TGWU) and amongst women workers by the General and Municipal Workers Union (GMWU), the National Union of Public Employees (NUPE) and the Confederated Organisation of Health Services Employees (COHSE), shows what can be done. It is essential that initiatives like these are sustained. Here the TUC has a great responsibility. It cannot, of course, physically recruit members itself; that is a job for the individual unions. But it can, through its industrial committees, remind individual unions of their responsibilities and co-ordinate their efforts. For their part, individual unions must not resent the intervention of the TUC, provided, of course, that it is done with tact and with a knowledge of the difficulties involved. Unions must be reminded that, though competition can often be a spur to recruitment, it must not be allowed to become a thinly disguised form of inter-union warfare.

The key to the organisation of the under-organised occupations, groups and industries is specialisation – specialisation in recruitment and servicing. The spectacular increases in white collar membership in the late 1960s and early 1970s occurred partly because the unions involved were prepared to take account of the particular attitudes and needs of these workers.

Though the similarities between white collar and manual workers in work experience are growing, many white collar workers remain suspicious of the traditional trade union techniques, particularly the strike weapon. So, in order to recruit and maintain white collar workers in membership, trade unions have to put on a sophisticated face. There is also evidence that separate organisations for white collar members pays off. The unions catering specifically for white collar workers, like NALGO, ASTMS, APEX and NUBE, have grown the fastest, while other unions, like the TGWU, the Engineers (AUEW) and the GMWU, which organise other groups as well, all have white collar sections which are distinct from the rest of the union.

The successful organisation of female workers also partly depends on a specialised approach. The truth is that, though women are a vital part of the labour force, their rewards and job opportunities

are still far inferior to those of men. The Equal Pay and Sex Discrimination Acts are helping to change the climate of opinion. But,
if there is to be real equality, then there will have to be a revolution in training facilities and job opportunities open to women.
Only about 11 per cent of women are serving apprenticeships compared with 42 per cent of the men – and most of these are apprenticeships in hairdressing and manicure.[6] As the White Paper *Equality
for Women* pointed out, 'the restricted nature of the opportunities
open to young women to train for skilled work reinforces the
tendency for women to fill the lower paid, least satisfying job. They
are less likely to be promoted than men and are generally treated
as unsuitable to be in authority over men.'[7] The central role now
played by married women in the labour force also underlines the
need for their particular requirements, including part-time work,
flexible working hours and paid maternity leave, to be fully
recognised.

Trade unions must, therefore, give top priority to the fight for
equality for women. They must also face up to the fact that one
of the main barriers to an expansion of female membership is the
attitude of male trade unionists. It is sadly the case that, though
the proportion of women workers in trade unions increased from one
quarter to one third between 1961 and 1971, there has *not* been a
corresponding increase in the numbers of women officials or of
women on trade union governing bodies. Yet, in the end, the best
recruiting sergeants will be those trade unionists (both men and
women) who show that they understand the problems of working
women.

Another major unorganised area is the service sector. In that part
of this sector which is in the hands of the community there is
already a high level of unionisation (though, as COHSE, NUPE
and, to a lesser extent, the GMWU have shown, there are still gains
to be made by closing up relatively strongly organised areas). But in
industries such as distribution, motor repair, hotel and catering, the
proportion of workers unionised is very low. The problems of
organisation are formidable. Small units predominate, turnover is
high, and there is an above average proportion of women. However,
there is some evidence that a recruiting strategy which recognised
the special characteristics of workers in these industries could
succeed.

The hotel and catering industry presents an interesting case study.
Because of the seasonal nature of much of the trade, there is a
high labour turnover. Many of the workers come from abroad, in

some cases from countries with no strong tradition of trade union-ism. So, if trade union organisation is to take root, it has to be based on the hard core of permanent employees and, in par-ticular, on the kitchen staff, who tend to have a more developed sense of solidarity. Trade union recruiting drives have also to take account of the peculiarities of the industry, particularly the special relationship between customer and worker. The efforts of the GMWU and the TGWU (who have divided up hotel and catering between them on a company basis) have shown how it is possible to establish a solid foothold in a problem industry. What is now required is a major allocation of resources by the trade union move-ment to recruitment in those parts of the service sector which remain unorganised.

Organisation however cannot be considered in isolation from collective bargaining. For a union's appeal to workers is largely based on its ability to achieve results at the negotiating table. Hostile employers are well aware that a union which cannot service its mem-bers adequately finds that they drop out of membership. So, in an industry which is, in any case, difficult to organise, all the employer has to do is to wait for the first flush of enthusiasm for the union to evaporate in the face of his refusal to negotiate; the underlying factors which work against trade union organisation (such as high turnover, small establishments and an apathetic workforce) will do the rest. The crucial role of employers in the initial establish-ment of trade union organisation has been confirmed by a number of studies.[8]

The Donovan Commission, therefore, proposed a system of com-pulsory recognition. A trade union which, though it had a fair amount of support in a particular plant or company, yet found management continuing to resist its demands for recognition and negotiation, would be able to get the case referred to the Commis-sion on Industrial Relations (CIR), which, after finding out whether or not the union had achieved a reasonable membership, would issue a report. If the employer continued to refuse to recognise and negotiate with trade unions in those cases in which the CIR had found in the union's favour, the CIR would be empowered to recommend that the union should have the right of unilateral arbitration. The 1971 Industrial Relations Act also provided for trade union recognition, though of a much weaker kind than that proposed by Donovan. For a CIR recommendation to be enforce-able against an unwilling employer the union had to apply to the National Industrial Relations Court for a ballot to be held, in which it had to show that it had the majority of the membership. But, as the Donovan Commission pointed out, to insist on majority support (or even a particular percentage) before granting recognition was to stack the cards against the union. 'The fixing of a figure in this way might set up an impossible barrier to a union which could, if only it were granted recognition, organise a majority and represent them successfully.'[9]

The recognition provisions contained in the 1975 Employment Protection Act were potentially more favourable to the unions. A trade union could refer not only recognition issues but also extensions to the scope of collective bargaining to the Advisory Conciliation and Arbitration Service (ACAS) for its assistance. If attempts at conciliation failed, ACAS was empowered to report its findings. Provided it considered that the union had the support of the employees, it was able to recommend recognition. In the event of the employer refusing to comply with the recommendation, the trade union could refer the case back to ACAS for an award which would become part of the employees' contract of employment. This system will probably need to be strengthened; provided this happens and if it is fully exploited by the unions and backed up by the necessary recruiting efforts, there could be a major increase in trade union organisation.[10] It could also give unions in the more difficult industries an independence from management which they have sometimes lacked in the past.

The wages councils could also play a more important role in encouraging collective bargaining. One of their original functions, as conceived under the 1918 Trade Board Act, was the promotion of collective bargaining. In some cases, wages councils have been dissolved because of the development of effective collective bargaining in the industries concerned: and about half the workers in the wages council industries are covered by collective agreements. But the wages councils have not been sufficiently effective in promoting collective bargaining. It is true that the industries covered by wages councils (there are two main groups – clothing manufacturing and the distribution and service industries) have a number of characteristics including a large proportion of part-timers and small units, which make them exceptionally difficult to organise. Trade unions, however, complain with some justice, that so far from being a spur to recruitment, the low rates provided by wages councils and their slowness in paying increases discourage workers from joining trade unions. So, what is required is a far more interventionist wages council system.

The greater scope to fix terms and conditions given to the wages councils, along with the new right for a trade union to force employers to pay the 'going' negotiated rate and the establishment of a half-way house (the statutory joint industrial council) between a wages council and collective bargaining in the Employment Protection Act, is a step in the right direction. But more is needed. Part of the agenda for each wages council meeting ought to be devoted to examining the progress of unionisation and the development of collective agreements. There ought also to be a powerful full-time secretariat whose main responsibility should be to prod reluctant employers into granting recognition rights to unions and to remind unions of their recruiting responsibilities. In short the main aim of the wages councils ought to be to work themselves out of a job.

THE EXTENSION OF PLANT BARGAINING

The effectiveness of collective bargaining cannot, however, be judged only in terms of its spread. It needs also to be considered in the light of its relevance to modern conditions. If trade unions are to ensure that collective bargaining fulfills the aspirations and needs of their members and also matches up to the challenge of the large corporation, then its scope must also be widened.

The key principle that needs to be accepted not only by management but also by trade unions is that there must be no limit to the agenda of collective bargaining. In the words of McCarthy and Ellis, 'there would no longer be any room for a doctrine of employer "reserve rights" or "managerial prerogatives",'[11] and trade unions would have the right to influence managerial decision-making in any area which they considered affected their members' interests. Thus every issue relevant to the enterprise could potentially be the subject of joint decision-making.

In the following chapter, it is argued that, in order that trade unions should participate in strategic decision-making, there must, in most cases, be an extension of collective bargaining to boardroom level, although in a somewhat different form from traditional collective bargaining. But, for the achievement of results in the boardroom, there must also be an effective system of joint regulation, at every level – all the way up from shopfloor to boardroom. Indeed a strategy for democratic advance has to be primarily based on a vigorous shopfloor democracy. For, unless there is employee influence over those managerial decisions which affect them directly, 'industrial democracy' will remain a slogan. Employees who do not even have a say in these kind of decisions are unlikely to show much interest in decisions which are seemingly more remote. In such a situation, representatives at a higher level would not get the support they need to press home their point of view, and there would be a danger that apparently democratic arrangements would, in reality, be a cloak for the unilateral exercise of managerial prerogative. There must, therefore, be a radical extension of plant bargaining, backed up by strong shopfloor organisation.

The wide coverage of plant bargaining was discussed in the last chapter. Shop stewards bargain over many wage issues, including piecework and other bonus payments, plus payments for dirty work, job evaluation, merit money and up-grading. They bargain over many aspects of work, including its distribution, its pace, the manning of machines, the transfer from one job to another, the introduction of new machinery, the taking on of new labour, the number of apprentices and the acceptance of up-grading. In some companies they have even begun to bargain over change itself. Even in plants where there is no piecework, no job evaluation and no overtime, shop stewards negotiate over crucial safety and health questions (a development which is being accentuated by the establishment of joint health and safety committees under the 1974 Health and Safety Act) and over working conditions in the plant; they represent their members and negotiate with management on questions of discipline (over reprimands by foremen, over suspensions and dismissals) and over short time and redundancy issues.

But, although shop stewards negotiate over a wide variety of topics, the advances made at shopfloor level are patchy and informal. As William Brown has shown 'in much of British industry "custom and practice" is king'.[12] Though it is right that the shape of bargaining in a particular plant or firm should suit the circumstances and needs of the workers concerned, there are severe disadvantages in a largely informal system. 'Custom and practice' can be revoked if, for whatever reason, the balance of power changes inside a plant. It is much more difficult for management to go back on a written agreement which, in essence, establishes a system of plant level rights. A formal system is also likely to be more equitable between one group of workers and another than 'custom and practice'. And reference to written agreements stimulates a *spread* of rights from one plant to another which, by its nature, is much less likely in the case of 'custom and practice'. It is, perhaps, an indication of the benefits of codification that the main obstacle to the writing down of agreements should come from management rather than from the unions. Lower management is unwilling to commit its 'custom and practice' transgressions to paper in case they are disowned by senior management, while senior management remains reluctant to give shop stewards the recognition implied by codification of 'custom and practice'.[13] Thus, if there is to be a meaningful extension of plant bargaining the most advanced practice must be universalised by a trade union campaign for written agreements.

There are a number of areas, however, where even the most energetic and ambitious shopfloor representatives have had little influence but which are of great importance to workers, in particular manpower and training policy and the design of work.

The recession of the 1970s has led to far more agreements at plant level to mitigate the consequences of cutbacks in production, including 'no compulsory redundancies' clauses, the adoption of natural wastage policies, guaranteed-week and early retirement arrangements, additional redundancy payments and transfer and retraining within the company or plant.[14] There is, however, a need for a shopfloor say at an earlier, more strategic stage. Hence the case for shopfloor involvement in manpower planning and in the related question of training.

It is true, of course, that many firms not only have no manpower planning policy but very little planning of any sort. And the most technically perfect planning cannot secure the future or even forecast, with any accuracy, shifts in consumer demand. But, from the workers' point of view, it is essential that, if sudden interruptions are not to occur in their employment, companies should be forced by shop stewards to plan their manpower requirements ahead, and to carry out these policies in such a way that the interests of the workers are taken into consideration. Shop stewards should be equipped by their unions to negotiate in this field and should also, if they wish, be able to call on the services of trained experts, competent to evaluate manpower plans.

The related problem of training is also crucial to employees. Even in times of relatively high unemployment, there is an unsatisfied demand for some types of skill. Academic research has also confirmed the obvious point that access to the better paid and more interesting manual jobs is dependent on skill – and conversely that low pay is a function of lack of skill. The inequality of women at work is also partly caused by inadequate opportunities to acquire skills. With the stimulus given by the Industrial Training Act of

1964, and the 1973 Employment Training Act, training is becoming less a matter of 'time-serving' and more a genuine exercise in acquiring a range of skills which a worker will be able to use throughout his working life; so the expansion of and access to training is all the more vital to workers. Yet, though there are trade union representatives on the Industrial Training Boards and on the Training Service Agency, at shopfloor level there has been little worker representation. Shopfloor representatives need, as a matter of right, to participate in the formulation and administration of policy on training. This is not only of importance in job training, but also in ensuring that some of the funds for training are spent, under trade union auspices, for the training of shop stewards.

The alienation felt by many workers and their growing demand for more satisfying work has already been described in chapter 3. There is now a great deal of evidence that the monotony, anonymity and lack of autonomy associated with much industrial work leads to boredom and stress as well as absenteeism, high labour turnover and industrial disputes.[15] It would be wrong to imply that *all* jobs can be made more satisfying, or that making work more satisfying can supply a complete answer to the problem of alienation, which is also related to wider issues of inequality, including those of rewards and power (though a 'satisfied' worker is also likely to support extensions of industrial democracy at higher level). But there are now enough successful cases of improvements in the quality of working life for trade union representatives to take the redesign of work very seriously indeed.[16] Such potentially creative concepts as *job rotation, job enlargement, job enrichment* and *autonomous work groups* are far too important to be left to management. It is essential that techniques, which have demonstrably provided at least some alleviation in the boredom and monotony of work, should be fully exploited by shop stewards. Trade union education departments have a responsibility to see that trade union representatives understand the implications of this new approach.

On the advice of the tripartite steering group on job satisfaction, (which includes both the Confederation of British Industry and the TUC) the Department of Employment set up, in 1975, a Work Research Unit to provide a free advisory service on job design projects and to carry out and commission research in job satisfaction. This initiative provides a useful start. But there may also be a case for following the West German example and giving government help to companies, which, with the agreement of trade union representatives, are prepared to carry out experiments in redesigning work processes.[17] When management and trade union represent-atives (who would normally be shop stewards with direct knowledge of the work experience involved) agree on the outlines of an experiment which might otherwise be initially uneconomic, they would be able to submit their plans to the Work Research Unit for vetting. If successful the project would qualify for government grants. Support might include assistance with training, start-up allowances, tax allowances and possibly machinery and equipment grants. It might also be necessary to obtain a government commit-ment to the project for a limited period in order to give firms the initial confidence to undertake the experiments.

In Norway and Sweden, there are even more ambitious 'self determination' schemes, which, mainly as a result of trade union pressure, seek to combine experiments in job design with the setting up of autonomous employee groups which control the shopfloor (that is to say, planning work, establishing production goals and having responsibility for running operations). In Britain some of the functions of these groups (though there are already examples in this country of successful formal experiments in autonomous groups) are already exercised by work groups and their representatives; it may well be that a shopfloor which also had control over manpower planning, training, safety and work design would be coming very near a situation of almost complete employee control at this level which could later be formalised by the setting up of statutory joint shop and plant committees throughout industry.

Finally plant bargaining, like other levels of bargaining, needs to be backed by a regular provision of information. Both the 1975 Employment Protection Act and the 1975 Industry Act ensure that trade union representatives have access to relevant information. Under the Employment Protection Act, a reluctant employer is eventually forced by an award of the Central Arbitration Committee (CAC) to supply information for collective bargaining purposes, while, under the Industry Act, an employer must supply certain types of information to a union which demands it. But, though the Industry Act defines the kind of information (including numbers employed, capital expenditure, output, productivity and sales) which must be provided, with certain safeguards, to trade unions, the Employment Protection Act leaves it to the decision of the CAC, in conjuction with the code of practice issued by the Advisory Concili-ation and Arbitration Service.[18] The TUC has suggested that accredited representatives should be entitled to information on man-power, earning and financial information (including sources of revenue costs, directors' remuneration, profits, performance indications and worth of company). Representatives should also have the right to information which might help them form a view on the prospects of the company, including details of new enterprises and locations, prospective closedowns, mergers and takeovers, trading and sales plans, production and investment plans, manpower and recruitment plans, etc. In addition, there should be the following information for individual employees: all information circulated to shareholders, terms and conditions of employment, a job specification (including responsibilities, management structure, and health and other possible hazards), employment prospects (including promotion opportunities and plans to expand or contract the workforce) and access to their personal files.[19]

HIGHER LEVELS OF BARGAINING

Though priority should be given to the development of plant bargaining, this does not mean that there is no longer a role for bargaining at higher levels. It is certainly important that each level of bargaining should be confined to those matters which they are capable of regulating. Thus, as the Donovan Commission pointed out, it is useless to attempt to regulate at a higher level those matters which are more appropriate to the plant. But, equally, a system of bargaining confined to the plant would be powerless to set up minimum standards across industry and would also leave most strategic decisions in the hands of management. What is required is a multi-dimensional approach which brings together joint regulation at all levels.

At industry level, there is already, as has been described earlier, a developed bargaining structure. This will continue to determine minimum pay and conditions. Union negotiators should use joint industrial councils (JICs) as one of the means of tackling the low pay problem. JICs are well placed to examine the implications of squeezing differentials, including the reaction of the higher paid and the employment consequences of helping the low paid. In addition joint industrial councils should build up a role in regulating shop-floor bargaining. The job of national negotiators will be partly to bargain over the framework in which this takes place and to monitor its progress. National trade unions will also need to assist the spread of local bargaining. The support of union educational, technical and research services are obviously of importance in this context.

There is, however, still a major gap between bargaining at shop-floor level and industry-wide negotiations. In most industries, there is very little bargaining at the company or group level, where, as we have seen, most of the important decisions are taken. Yet, without company bargaining, there is a danger that shopfloor bargaining, even if reformed and extended, will remain sectional and localised, while industry-level negotiations will become even more remote from the shopfloor. Company bargaining will become even more essential if the developments in collective control outlined in the next chapter come about. Unless there is an effective negotiating structure at this level, the employee representative on the board is likely to find himself isolated and ineffective. The trade union movement must, therefore, create a comprehensive bargaining structure (perhaps based on the joint representation committees proposed by the Bullock majority)[20] at company and group level as a matter of urgency. The objectives would be to assist in the monitoring of plant bargaining, to negotiate wages and conditions, to open up corporate policy to discussion (assisted by the information provisions in the Industry Act), and to provide employee directors with the support they will require to make their presence felt in the boardroom.

In chapter 2, the challenge of the multinational company to national trade unionism was underlined. There is a clear need for a response by trade unions, co-operating, like the multinational, across national frontiers. Yet, as the TUC has admitted, international trade union co-ordination cannot be said as yet to amount to a major countervailing force.[21] There are formidable difficulties in the way of successful international co-ordination between unions, including political and religious divisions, differences between collective bargaining systems, and the underlying organisational problems.

In France and Italy, the major unions, which are affiliates to the Communist controlled CGT and CGIL, are not affiliated to the international trade secretariats or to the ICFTU. Even the Dutch trade union movement, which is otherwise relatively powerful, is split on religious lines. Then there are differences in bargaining structures. In some countries, national or industrial level bargaining is more authoritative than in others. There is a particularly striking contrast between the British pattern of negotiations with its developed plant bargaining and the more centralised systems of Scandinavia and Western Germany. There are also differences in legal systems which will obviously make for a varied trade union response. In the United States, Germany and Sweden, for example, there are legal restraints on the right to strike in sympathy. Perhaps most important of all are the sheer organisational difficulties in the way of international action. This is partly a matter of resources; the international trade secretariats (ITS) of the International Metal Workers' Federation (IMF), the International Chemical and General Workers' Federation (ICF), the International Federation of Commercial, Clerical and Technical Employees (FIET) and so on just do not have the money, staff, or information at their disposal to counterbalance the international companies. But, as the TUC shrewdly pointed out, perhaps the most fundamental problem is the natural desire of national trade union leaders to preserve their own independence and the reluctance of trade unionists to become involved in other countries' problems. A survey of Canadian Chrysler workers revealed their willingness to help American workers but few were ready to help British or Mexican workers.[22]

The ultimate trade union aim may be a fully fledged international bargaining system but this is not likely to be achieved in the foreseeable future. Indeed the only genuine examples (the United Automobile Workers' claims on behalf of both American and Canadian car workers with Chrysler, General Motors and Fiat) come from the North American continent. The circumstances which make international negotiations possible here are obvious – cultural unity, a similar standard of living, a virtual common market, an identical trade union and bargaining system. But these are combinations of factors which trade unions in other parts of the world cannot hope to enjoy at least in the next few years.

Given the difficulties, the most productive approach for British trade unions to adopt is one that builds on existing trade union strengths and practices. In the immediate future, the main priority should be to develop information gathering both by national unions and by the international trade secretariats to strengthen the international councils for particular companies set up by the various secretariats, and to extend the already considerable ad hoc bilateral assistance to trade unions in dispute with a multinational. There may be occasions when it will be possible to launch more ambitious exercises. The co-ordinated effort by the ICF affiliates against the French-based multinational chemical firm, St. Gobain, in 1969 is an example of what can be achieved in favourable conditions. Though the unions concerned presented separate claims, the fact that they bargained simultaneously and co-ordinated as far as possible their date of settlement enabled the power of the stronger unions to be used on behalf of the weaker.[23] But, for a number of years to come, this type of international action is likely to be the exception rather than the rule. More commonly, as with the European Metal Workers and Philips, international trade union committees will hold joint meetings with multinationals to discuss issues outside wages, such as investment, technological change, training, transfers and redundancies. These consultations may provide the basis for more ambitious initiatives at a later stage.

However, international trade union activity will not, by itself provide enough countervailing power. Trade unions will also have to demand the assistance of governments, acting both nationally and internationally. Nationally, governments can do something to set the framework for multinational investment. But it is quite clear that the only really effective governmental response to multinational power is an agreement between governments either on a regional or international basis.[24] So, in addition to building up bargaining at multinational level, trade unions will also have to act as pressure groups on national governments and also on regional and international agencies.

WHAT KIND OF INCOMES POLICY?

In a previous chapter both the reasons for government intervention in collective bargaining and the problems that this has created for trade unions have been described. But, whatever the difficulties, trade unions have to accept that it is not possible to isolate collective bargaining and its results from the rest of the economy. There *is* a relationship between increases in wages on the one hand and price increases and the level of employment on the other. So a trade union movement that puts a high priority on rises in real living standards and full employment cannot, in all honesty, deny that it is entirely legitimate for the government to have a view on what happens and what should happen at the negotiating table.

But, if governments are entitled to have a policy on incomes, it is only right that trade unions should be able to participate in determining that policy. The key question is, of course, within what sort of framework the policy should work. The whole history of incomes policy has so far been shaped not only by the mechanics of a particular policy but more significantly by the background against which it has operated. Thus the 1964–70 Labour Government's policies were undermined by the slow growth of the economy while the 1970–74 Conservative Government's policy was fatally flawed by the anti-union posture and reactionary social policies which that government had previously adopted. In chapter 8, there is a detailed discussion of trade union social and political objectives. What needs to be said here is that the movement must decide for itself the conditions which it wishes to attach to its collaboration in an incomes policy. Part of the value of the social contract approach (whatever the shortcomings of its first stage) was that the trade unions were prepared to accept this wider definition of their role.

Though the creation of the right social and economic framework is the critical factor in the success or otherwise of an incomes policy, the technical details (the criterion, the exceptions, the monitoring body, the powers it possesses and so on) are also important. The failure of both the last stage of the Conservative incomes policy and the first stage of Labour's social contract are evidence of that. The Conservative incomes policy was too rigid to allow for any exceptions, while the first stage of the social contract was so imprecise that different people were able to make their own interpretations of what the policy actually meant. So it is essential that the trade union movement has a clear idea of what kind of policy it prefers.

From the trade union viewpoint there are three vital ingredients in an incomes policy – clarity, some flexibility (but not too much), and fairness. Clarity is essential. Most of the stages of the incomes policy of the 1964–70 Labour Government were so complex that they had little hope of being understood at the shopfloor level. The merit of the stage 3 (4 per cent + £1) of the Heath policy and stage 2 of the social contract (£6 flat rate) was that at least their objectives were easily intelligible. And, though it is not always possible to express targets solely in terms of a flat rate because of the impact on wage structures, there is always a strong case for simplicity.

There must also be arrangements for genuine special cases, whether it be those groups like local authority workers, (who are amongst the lowest paid) or those like the miners (who have powerful economic and social grounds for exceptional treatment). On the other hand, too many exceptions destroy the policy. A balance must be struck.

Perhaps the most important factor; however, is fairness. This does not only mean consideration for the low paid and a just reward for skill and exceptional work. It also implies that those trade unionists who settle within the limits of the policy ought to have some guarantee that others are doing the same. This is the force behind the argument for a *statutory* policy. My own experience, however, is that legal enforcement is, in most circumstances, counter-productive. If an incomes policy is to work, it will, in any case, need a consensus of opinion behind it, whilst a policy which has legal sanctions provides its opponents with an argument they would otherwise lack. However, to have any chance of lasting success, a policy must have the full backing of the TUC, more co-ordination of pay claims, and possibly also the support of a monitoring body, preferably set up on a tripartite basis. Only then are trade unionists likely to accept it on a long-term basis.

This chapter has suggested ways in which collective bargaining can be extended both in spread and scope. It has also outlined a rational trade union response to government intervention. However, there is also a need, as is argued in the next two chapters, for trade unions to devise new forms of collective control and to decide on their social and political objectives.

REFERENCES

1 These figures are based on the *New Earnings Survey 1973* HMSO 1974.
2 See written answer from the Department of Employment in *Hansard* 31 October 1975 cols. 627 and 628.
3 *Hansard* 31 October 1975 cols. 627 and 628, and estimate in *The system of industrial relations in Great Britain* p. 247.
4 G. S. Bain and R. Price *Union growth and employment trends in the United Kingdom 1964–70* Industrial Relations Research Unit 1972, and the same authors' 'Union growth revisited' *British Journal of Industrial Relations* November 1976.
5 *Women and work* Department of Employment Manpower Paper no. 11 1975 chp. 1.
6 *Women and work* p. 37.
7 *Equality for women* Cmnd 5724 HMSO September 1974 p. 2.
8 *Royal Commission on Trade Unions and Employers' Associations Research Paper no. 6*, and *The growth of white-collar unionism* Oxford University Press 1970 chp. 8; and *Union growth and employment trends in the United Kingdom 1964–70.*
9 *Royal Commission on Trade Unions and Employers' Associations* para. 254.
10 The long drawn out Grunwick dispute indicates that there may have to be some changes in the Employment Protection Act.
11 *Management by agreement* p. 96.
12 William Brown *A consideration of custom and practice* SSRC Reprint Series no. 13 p. 61.
13 *A consideration of custom and practice* p. 59.
14 For examples, see *Industrial Relations Review and Report* nos. 134 August 1976, 141 December 1976, and 153 and 154 June 1977.

114   *The Industrial Democrats*

See *On the quality of working life* Department of Employment Manpower Paper no. 7 1973 for a concise survey.
16 *On the quality of working life* chp. 5; *Making work more satisfying* Department of Employment 1975; and Lisl Klein *New forms of work organisation* CUP 1976 pp. 43–70.
17 See *Working power* p. 18, and Lisl Klein's article in *The Times* 20 June 1977.
18 Disclosure of information to trade unions for collective bargaining purposes *ACAS Code of Practice* No. 2 HMSO 1977.
19 *Industrial democracy* TUC 1974 p. 13.
20 *Report of the Committee of Inquiry on Industrial Democracy* HMSO 1977 chp. 19 paras. 29–32.
21 *International companies* TUC 1970 p. 17.
22 *International companies* p. 21.
23 *International trade unionism* pp. 12–21.
24 For example, the O.E.C.D. guidelines published as a Government White Paper *International investment: guidelines for multinationals* Cmnd. 6525 June 1976, and the work of the United Nations Commission on Multinationals.

Chapter 7

Towards industrial democracy

The creation of a humanised industry will require trade union participation in all decisions which affect members' interests – at whatever the level at which these decisions are taken. The main argument of this chapter is that, if this objective is to be fully achieved, a new form of joint regulation will be required. For, though a reformed and extended system of collective bargaining must be the basis of a democratic strategy for industry, there should also be, where appropriate, an employee voice at boardroom level, closely linked to collective bargaining but expressed in a different institutional form. Whereas the traditional subjects (like pay and conditions) or the obvious omissions (like the design of work, training and manpower planning) arise naturally out of the immediate preoccupations of the workers, more remote but equally vital issues (such as investment, reorganisation and the nature of corporate strategy) are more difficult to introduce into conventional collective bargaining. There is, therefore, a strong case for a right to employee representation on boards of enterprises, as well as the development of a new type of bargaining to cover strategic issues.[1]

This chapter defines industrial democracy, explores the problems involved, and suggests ways of bringing about democratic reform.

THE 'GREAT' DEBATE

Industrial democracy is on the British political agenda for the first time since the 1930s. The EEC Commission has put forward proposals concerning employee participation, including one for a 'European company' statute and, more significantly, for the draft fifth directive to apply to all public limited liability companies in member states, which could well affect the United Kingdom.[2] At the two general elections of 1974, the three major political parties set out policies for increasing employee participation. In January 1975, 250 MP's voted in favour of a private member's bill (introduced under the house of commons' ten minute rule) to establish 50 per cent employee representation at boardroom level – a record for this kind of bill.[3] Partly as a result of this pressure, the Labour administration set up an inquiry, under the chairmanship of Lord Bullock, into boardroom representation in the private sector which reported in 1977; then, after a year's consultation, the government published its own white paper (see Appendix). In 1974, the TUC Congress, in a decisive break with its previous line, accepted a report which called for 50 per cent employee representation in the boardroom[4], whilst the CBI has also agreed that changes are needed. Meanwhile, there are frequent and often fierce debates about industrial democracy in trade union branches, in management circles, on the media, and amongst academics. Yet, despite the growing interest, there is little agreement about what this means or what is the most effective way of bringing it about. Indeed, when the ideas behind the slogans are explored, it becomes clear that the various bodies and interests have very different approaches.

The Conservative Party, which (as was described in chapter 4) when in government, devoted a good deal of time and energy to trying to tame the trade unions and, in some respects, to weaken collective bargaining, has nevertheless accepted that large and medium sized firms should be required to develop consultative procedures. But, though the Conservatives are not, in principle, against some employee representation at board level, they tend to be sceptical about its widespread application. The Liberal Party has had a rather more coherent and consistent view. For a number of years it has advocated the setting up of statutory works councils on the German model, and the extension of profit sharing; more recently, it has argued for a system of employee representation on boards, again mainly based on the German model.[5]

The CBI is in favour of a compulsory system of consultative arrangements, arrived at through 'participation agreements' between management and employees. It is, however, firmly against statutory employee representation at board level, parity of representation between shareholders and employee representatives, and a trade union monopoly to choose directors.[6] The British Institute of Management (BIM) also supports participation agreements.[7] The views of the CBI and BIM reflect a growing interest among progressive managements in developing more democratic styles of supervision, devising better systems of consultation and communication, and experimenting with ways to increase job satisfaction.

A major criticism of the Conservative and management proposals, and also (though to a lesser extent) of those of the Liberal Party, is that they run the risk of giving employees 'the illusion of involvement without the reality of power'.[8] Industrial democracy should be defined primarily in terms of power-sharing and *not* in terms of consultation, job involvement, profit sharing, valuable though these are. Thus an effective democratic strategy must genuinely change the balance of power within an enterprise in favour of employees and not merely give a democratic facade to an otherwise authoritarian structure. Trade unions are, therefore, entitled to be suspicious of any management-orientated approach which does not shift power and influence towards employees. By the same token, they are also right to reject any new structure or machinery which, however democratic it appears on paper, subtracts from the existing source of employee power, i.e. trade union organisation.

This does not mean that good job design which increases an employee's scope for autonomy and self-expression is not important or that the development of more democratic styles of management should not be encouraged. On the contrary, we have already seen (in chapter 3) that employees are becoming increasingly dissatisfied with jobs which are unrewarding in human terms. And there is also a clear link between job satisfaction and industrial democracy, in that the greater the involvement in work the more meaningful the involvement in the running of the enterprise.[9] But, even so, increasing job satisfaction by itself does not redistribute industrial power. Similarly, though it is obviously an important step forward that management should adopt a style which accepts that workers are human beings, a belief in consultation does not add up to industrial democracy.

The fear that new democratic machinery will undermine existing sources of employee power is not motivated by any exaggerated concern for trade unions as trade unions. No institution has a divine right to exist. But the truth is that trade unions are the only available source of employee power. Through collective organisation, employees, though powerless individually, have been able to establish joint regulation (particularly at shopfloor level) over a number of vital subjects. It is certainly the case that the strategic corporate decisions remain largely outside the control of collective bargaining. But whilst accepting the limitations of collective bargaining, it is necessary to emphasise that the continuing existence of trade union organisation is the only real guarantee against manipulation of democratic machinery by management or shareholders.

So to be meaningful any democratic strategy must be underwritten by trade union organisation and built on existing trade union achievements in negotiation and representation.

SHIFT IN TRADE UNION OPINION

It is because trade unions have so clearly understood the power realities that they have previously concentrated their resources on collective bargaining as the most fruitful means of democratising industry. However, a growing number of trade unionists are now convinced that some additional method of control is also required. This shift in opinion is worth examining in some detail, because it was shaped not so much by ideological considerations but by what happened in British industry during the 1960s and in the early 1970s. As industrial conditions deteriorated, so some trade unions changed.

Traditionally, British trade unions fought shy of participation in management. It is true that the Guild Socialists, who advocated a trade union partnership with the state to run industry, were influential in some trade unions between 1910 and 1926. Then, during the second world war, joint production committees of managers and shop stewards discussed such a wide range of subjects, above all in the engineering industry, that many saw joint consultative arrangements as an important step towards industrial democracy. In practice, however, management's insistence that joint consultation should be kept separate from collective bargaining meant that, after the war, the effectiveness of joint consultative committees was extremely limited (except in the nationalised coal industry). And with the growth in plant bargaining, shop stewards did not see why there should continue to be different arrangements for dealing with issues which, though they were wider than wages and conditions, could still be matters on which opinions might differ. As a result, consultative committees were either brought under the influence of collective bargaining or became very anodyne indeed.

In the debate at the end of the war on how to run nationalised industries, the TUC had already set its face against workers' control or employee participation in management. Indeed, it gave its backing to the Morrisonian concept of a public corporation without direct trade union representation. The 1944 TUC document on post-war reconstruction argued that 'it does not seem by any means certain that it would be in the best interests of the work people of a nationalised industry to have, as directly representative of them, members of the controlling board who would be committed to its joint decisions . . . trade unions should maintain their complete independence'.[10] Trade unionists were appointed to the boards of the nationalised industries but always from outside the industry concerned. Thus, while many other European countries negotiated for works councils and, in the case of West Germany, for employee representation on supervisory boards, the British trade union movement was content to rely on collective bargaining (and, to some extent, political power) to influence management.

However, during the 1960s, trade union attitudes began to change. In 1966, the TUC told the Donovan Commission that 'there is now a growing recognition that at least in industries under public ownership provision should be made at each level in the management structure for trade union representatives of the work people employed in these industries to participate in the formulation of policy and in the day-to-day operation of their industries'.[11] A year later, an influential Labour Party working party, under the chairmanship of the Transport and General Workers' Secretary Jack Jones, also called for experiments in 'new forms of worker's participation' within the public sector. While its report emphasised the crucial role of collective bargaining in the development of industrial democracy, it concluded that workers' representatives (not necessarily full-time officers of the union) should be appointed to the boards of nationalised industries.[12]

This shift in the official TUC view partly reflected what was happening in industry. Worsening economic conditions highlighted the weaknesses of traditional collective bargaining. Unilateral managerial decisions about redundancies and closures revealed, in a dramatic and painful way, its limited scope. The recession also underlined the subsidiary role of joint regulation. It became increasingly clear that it was not enough to have control over wages and conditions; these were, in a large part, dependent on earlier decisions on investment, production and marketing and so on, over which trade unions had no influence at all. The initial shopfloor response was usually a defensive reaction to managerial threats of closures; examples include the famous work-in during 1971–72 at the Upper Clyde Shipbuilders which saved four yards and the sit-ins at Plessey (Alexandria), Fisher-Bendix, Allis Chalmers and the former British Leyland factory at Basingstoke. But increasingly shopfloor representatives began to explore more positive and ambitious strategies. These ranged from the participation scheme at British Leyland, the union proposals for more effective management at Lucas, the shopfloor involvement in the Harland and Woolf experiment, and the workers' co-operative at the former Norton Villiers Triumph factory at Meriden. In addition, in the nationalised industries, some trade unions wished to expand their role. In particular, the post office unions won support both from the government and from their members for a system of employee representation at boardroom level, which was introduced in 1977. These initiatives and the extensions of collective bargaining (described in the previous chapter) created a new climate in which a planned and concerted strategy for furthering industrial democracy became both more necessary and more likely to succeed.

Thus the TUC was in part responding to pressures from below when in 1974 (after an interim document in 1973) it produced its own policies on industrial democracy which were accepted by the 1974 congress – though it was significant that major trade unions, including the GMWU, the AUEW and the Electricians (EETU-PTU) expressed considerable reservations. Like the 1967 Labour Party report, it concluded that the major way to extend collective control of workpeople over their work situation would continue to be through the strengthening of trade union organisation and the widening of the scope of collective bargaining. However, because the extension of collective bargaining would leave 'a wide range of fundamental managerial decisions affecting workpeople . . . beyond the control of workpeople'[13] the TUC report proposed that elected trade union representatives should form one half of a new supervisory board, which would constitute the supreme authority and also appoint the management board in all companies employing more than 2,000 people. So the TUC had officially opted for full employee participation in management.

The controversial majority report of the Bullock Committee on industrial democracy, which was published in January 1977, was, in the main, a triumph for the official TUC view.[4] This was hardly surprising as the majority included such prominent trade union leaders as Jack Jones of the transport workers, Clive Jenkins of ASTMS and David Lea of the TUC. It proposed a right to boardroom representation, through trade union machinery, on all companies employing 2,000 workers and over. This right would be 'triggered off' when a trade union or several unions represented 20 per cent or more of the employees, who would then be balloted to find out if they were in favour; to be successful, the majority would have to equal at least one-third of those eligible to vote. The unions involved would then be entitled to set up a joint union committee or joint representation committee (JRC) at company level which would be responsible for appointing employee representatives at boardroom level.

The Bullock majority, however, decided against a two-tier board system (as the TUC had originally suggested in its 1974 report) and instead came down in favour of direct employee representation on existing company boards. According to the so-called '2x + y' formula, they proposed an equal number of employee and shareholder representatives who would jointly agree on a third and smaller number of independent members. On all questions concerning management and the use of resources, the reconstituted board would have final responsibility as well as acquiring exclusive powers of initiative from the shareholders on a number of other issues (including the winding up of the company and disposal of parts of the undertaking). In addition, directors would be obliged to take account of employees' as well as shareholders' interests.

The majority report was widely criticised. Not surprisingly, given its initial position, the CBI rejected its proposals. More disturbingly for the TUC, the three major unions which had been sceptical about its 1974 report came out in opposition. Most serious of all, by-election losses forced the Labour government to rely on a parliamentary arrangement with the Liberals, who were also hostile, so there was no parliamentary majority for Bullock. The following section examines some of the objections to the Bullock report.

CONCEPTUAL PROBLEMS

There are a number of difficult issues raised by the idea of employee directors. Is it desirable or, if desirable, possible to achieve meaningful board level representation? And is there not a danger that involvement in the running of the enterprise would undermine trade union independence? How far is it possible to reconcile the economic objectives of private sector companies with genuine employee representation? Can industrial democracy be combined with efficiency? These are all questions which the exponents of employee directors have to answer.

As to the desirability of employee participation in managerial decision-making at boardroom level, it is quite clear that, despite collective bargaining, most of the strategic decision-making remains exclusively in managerial hands. Yet, as was argued in an earlier chapter, decisions at this level can profoundly affect workers' lives. It is certainly the case that any democratic structure has to be firmly based on a reformed and extended plant level bargaining, so that those issues which are of immediate importance to employees are the subject of joint regulation. But, while acknowledging the importance of what happens at shopfloor level, one must also recognise the effect that higher level decisions, particularly about investment and redundancies, can have on the working environment. Indeed, most top level decisions, even if about such apparently remote matters as financial control or marketing, can have profound shopfloor consequences. So employees have a direct interest in what happens at boardroom level.

But even though the worker director concept may be desirable can it ever become more than an empty institutional charade? In the past, employee power has been most successfully exercised at shopfloor level and usually about a limited range of subjects, associated with pay and conditions; the more remote the issue, the less effective the pressure. Is it really conceivable that there can be sustained shopfloor backing for boardroom participation?

Paradoxically, the best way to make employee representation meaningful at boardroom level is by the development of a strong shopfloor democracy. For, while employees who have no say in those decisions which are most immediate to them will normally be little interested in matters which seem more distant, those employees who have a real measure of control over their working environment are more likely to be aware of the connection between what happens at shopfloor level and decisions in the boardroom and, therefore, are likely to be more concerned about the activities of their representatives in the boardroom. In their turn, employee directors, who are backed by strong representative institutions at lower levels, will not only be more effective at boardroom level; they will also provide an increased and regular flow of information about the company to employees at the 'grass roots'. The EEC Green Paper commented that an attractive feature of employee participation at boardroom level was that such participation appears to have a generally positive effect on the other forms of employee participation existing in relation to the companies in question.[15]

Industrial democracy should, therefore, be a comprehensive process, capable of influencing *all* levels of decision making. To be fully effective, it must involve both participation by employees at lower levels *and* participation at boardroom levels. The distinction which the CBI draws between lower level participation and representation in the boardroom is not a real one. Both involve participation – though at different levels. The truth is that what the CBI is really concerned about is the 'power-sharing' aspect of the employee director system. Yet participation without a sharing of power (as with so many consultation schemes set up after the war) is not worthy of the name at whatever level it takes place. What is required, above all, is a *multi-dimensional* approach which links together joint regulation at all levels. If employees are to influence strategic decisions, they should have a right to direct representation in the boardroom. However, participation at this level alone without strong representation at lower levels would be almost totally ineffective. Worker directors must have the support of an extended system of collective bargaining. What is needed is a *continuous* system of representation from shopfloor to boardroom.

Some trade unions argue that, in order to influence boardroom decisions, it is not essential to have direct employee representation. Collective bargaining, if suitably reformed and extended, can, by itself, provide an effective way forward. The GMWU have proposed a general legal requirement for all employers to negotiate with trade unions on strategic issues – a view which was accepted in principle by the 1977 TUC conference.

Though agreeing that boardroom representation is one possible option, the union considered that its approach 'will mean a form of industrial democracy more clearly related to the historic and organic development of collective bargaining and trade union machinery in this country'.[16] A reformed system of collective bargaining is the indispensable basis of a successful democratic strategy; there is also, as is argued later, a good deal to be said for an extension of collective bargaining to cover strategic issues. However, there will also be a need for an additional type of joint regulation, clearly linked to collective bargaining but expressed in a new institutional form. So far, collective bargaining has been a largely reactive process, a response to more fundamental decisions taken elsewhere. And, in many cases, even a reformed system of collective bargaining is likely to leave strategic decisions outside the scope of joint regulation. Whereas subjects like the design of work and manpower planning arise naturally out of the immediate preoccupations of the workers, more remote but vitally important questions could only be introduced artificially and certainly rather slowly into collective bargaining. As the EEC Green Paper pointed out, 'employee representation on company boards, alone among existing forms of employee participation, provides an opportunity for the employees of an enterprise to be involved on a relatively *continuous* (my italics) basis in the process of strategic decision-making at the highest level of the enterprise by which they are employed'.[17] So if employees are to influence the major decisions, there is a strong case for at least a right to boardroom representation.

The Electricians Union (EETU-PTU) was a more vehement critic of the Bullock proposals. That union believes that a system of employee representation at boardroom level could undermine trade union independence. 'Management's job is to manage, while trade unions exist to consider, contest and oppose, if necessary, the exercise of managerial prerogatives.'[18] Direct involvement in managerial decision-making would lead to split loyalties, to the detriment of employee interests.

One difficulty in allaying the understandable fears about boardroom representation expressed by trade unionists is that there is little direct British experience from which to judge. The worker director experiment in the national British Steel Corporation, which was introduced in 1967, is of some interest but it should be remembered that these directors were appointed (not elected) to advisory divisional boards – and not to the main board on which the strategic decisions were made. In addition, the directors were initially not allowed to retain their links with the trade unions and there was no mechanism for reporting back to the shopfloor. In 1972, the TUC Steel Committee negotiated with the British Steel Corporation improvement in the system of representation, including the right of employee directors to hold union office and to represent specific areas. However, the boards on which these directors sit have continued to be advisory. One study of the experiment concluded that the scheme has not led 'to the representation of shopfloor interests at board level or a feeling of involvement in the organisation on the part of the workforce',[19] though the worker directors in British Steel believe that their contribution has been a significant and pioneering one.[20]

Given the dearth of native examples, and with our membership of the European Community, it is not surprising that the Bullock Committee should have commissioned a study on the European experiences which focused, in particular, on the German 'co-determination' system.[21] This was established directly after the war, when the German trade union movement had only just been set up again after its destruction by Hitler. The German trade unions believed that they needed at least some form of employee representation in management if they were to prevent the emergence of anti-democratic forces, including big business, which had helped Hitler to power. However, given their weakness, particularly at shopfloor level, they accepted that the system should be based on works councils; and, with the exception of the Co-determination Act of 1951 covering the coal and steel industries, they also failed to get the principle of parity between employee and shareholders' representatives accepted. Elsewhere, only a third of the members of supervisory boards were employee representatives. However, in 1976, the German government, with a Social Democrat Chancellor, legislated to strengthen employee representation in the rest of industry (though, at the insistence of the Free Democrats one of the employee seats is reserved for senior management and the shareholders are able ultimately to insist on their nominee as chairman). Significantly, pressure for the change came from the German trade unions which had concluded from the experiences of the coal and steel industries that, provided there was a parity system, a considerable measure of power-sharing could be achieved *without* undermining trade union independence.

Other developments of interest to the British trade unions took place in Norway and Sweden during the 1970s. In both these countries a powerful trade union movement supported a Labour government in introducing worker participation in management. Collective bargaining, though more centralised than in this country, was already strong and, as was pointed out in the previous chapter, some ambitious experiments in increasing employee control over the working environment had been undertaken with full union support. During 1976, the Swedish Government, at the insistence of the trade unions, also introduced legislation to extend collective bargaining. However, the trade unions felt that additional employee participation was needed at boardroom level. As the Swedish Confederation of Trade Unions (LO) argued in its report on industrial democracy, representation at this level, though debatable in isolation, was of very great political value in obtaining information and influence as well as being in itself 'something that is no more than just' when it was part of a wider democratic programme.[22] By a law in force since 1973 (and continued in 1976) Swedish trade unions had the right to elect two representatives to the board of all limited companies employing over 100 workers.

In Norway, there is a slightly different system. In 1972, company legislation was amended, so that representative assemblies were set up in all joint stock companies with over 200 employees. These assemblies, one third of which were elected by and from among the company's employees, were given powers over company policy, including all major decisions on investment, reorganisation and nationalisation, and were also made responsible for the appointment of the board of directors, one third of whom could be employees' representatives. In contrast with German co-determination laws, the powers of shareholders were specifically limited, while those of employees were increased. As far as trade unions were concerned, the government stressed the need for links between the representative system and trade union organisation. Trade unions were able to nominate candidates for the assemblies, including their own officials, while employee representatives were encouraged to keep in close touch with their trade union organisation. So, both in Norway and Sweden, the trade unions have backed measures to promote employee participation in management, in the belief that this would increase industrial democracy without at the same time, weakening their position.

But whatever the lessons of foreign experience, it is as well to recognise that those trade unionists in this country who are concerned about the independence issue represent an important strand in trade union thinking. They must, in their turn, accept that the problem is in essence no more than another facet of the traditional trade union dilemma mentioned in chapter 7. Trade unions derive their power and motive force for change from the conflict of interests inherent in industry. Yet, in order to protect their members' interests and secure improvements for them, they have to reach agreement with management. Thus collective bargaining is itself a form of 'participation in management', 'a collaboration' over important, if limited, issues. So what is at issue in the debate over industrial democracy, is not the *principle* of participation (trade unions already participate) but the *way* in which that participation is exercised.

The Bullock report concluded that the only effective way that trade union independence can be combined effectively with participation in management at boardroom level is if employee directors are on the supreme body of the company in *equal* numbers to shareholder representatives and, at least, in part as *representatives* of the employees. Bullock also argued that representatives should be chosen through trade union machinery.

The argument for parity was put by the Bullock majority as follows: 'In our view, it is unreasonable to expect employee representatives to accept equal responsibility unless, through equal representation on the board, they are able to have equal influence in the decision-making process.'[23] Parity not only strengthens the position of employee representatives within the board but also builds up their authority with their constituents. It thus opens up the possibility of effective joint regulation of strategic decisions. The insistence on the representative nature of employee directors is also important. This is not to imply that employee directors should not share responsibility for decision-making (particularly if their obligations specifically include the interests of employees). But they are also there to enable the voice of those who are mainly affected by decisions to be heard within the board.

The case for representation through trade union machinery is a strong one. It is difficult to see how boardroom level participation could work without trade union involvement. Obviously, if the trade unions decided to boycott the new system, as they ignored the consultative arrangements after the war, it would not get off the ground. It is also a matter of practical mechanics. Trade unions provide the obvious link with the shopfloor. Without them employee representatives would quickly lose touch with those they represent. It is revealing that, in Germany, those employee representatives who were originally non-union usually join after a few months. And how are boardroom representatives going to be trained and serviced unless by trade unions? As Eric Batstone has written 'trade union support is generally an important condition for any democratic institution since it provides strength, a means of integration into a wider system of representation, and constitutes an organisation with a considerable degree of independence from management'.[24]

The most difficult criticism to refute is the libertarian one. In one sense, the libertarian argument is only partly relevant within industry. Without organisation, the individual employee would be powerless; hence the case for trade unions. However, it is difficult to answer those who ask why democratic rights should be confined to trade unionists. The Bullock majority implicitly acknowledged the force of this point of view when they proposed that there should be an initial ballot of all employees, irrespective of whether they were trade unionists. The question is whether it is possible to go further to satisfy the libertarians without losing the backing of trade ought to be elected by a ballot of all employees and that any scheme of boardroom representation. The Manifesto Group of backbench Labour MPs proposed that boardroom representatives outght to be elected by a ballot of all employees and that any employee should be able to stand.[25] It pointed out, however, that their exclusive operation of the trigger mechanism when combined with an agreed slate of trade union candidates would give trade unions a *de facto* monopoly of employee representation in firms employing 2,000 workers and over (where as Bullock showed, average trade union membership is at least 70 per cent[26]).

The practical effect of these proposals – parity representation, employee directors as representatives, and strong trade union involvement – would be to extend joint regulation to the boardroom. As the West German Biedenkopf Commission noted, parity representation gives 'something akin to negotiation'.[27] The employee representatives will tend to act as a group, with a specific viewpoint on some issues, of which account has to be taken. However, there is no reason why this influence at a new level should compromise trade union participation in collective bargaining. While employee representatives on the board will have a valuable contribution to make on manpower issues, they would obviously not want to get involved in the details of bargaining strategy, particularly if there is a dispute. Usually negotiators and boardroom representatives will be different people; most boardroom representatives, though remaining closely linked to the trade unions, will no longer have the time to be bargainers as well. In any case, trade union representatives are already faced with conflicts, particularly those between the contradictory demands of particular groups. The kind of clashes that are likely to occur in the new situation – between the employee director and the negotiator, or, more seldom, between the varying roles of the same trade unionist – are different only in degree from those that already occur. The best guarantee that employee directors will make a good job of representation is, as with trade union negotiators now, a powerful independent and lively shopfloor, linked to an effective system of bargaining at company level.

There is a further trade union point of view that has to be considered. The AUEW argues that, though it might be possible to establish employee representation on the boards of *nationalised* industries, the conflicts of interest inherent in capitalism would mean that employee boardroom representation in *private* industry would either be ineffective or work at the expense of trade union independence.[28] A lucid statement of this (basically Marxist) point of view was put to the Fabian working party on industrial democracy in the following terms: 'In private industry, the dominating motive is to maximise the return on capital with little or no regard to social costs. This disregard for social costs, together with the possibility of increasing private profit by exploiting labour, provides the real conflict of interest inherent in capitalism . . . Workers' representatives sitting on the board of a private firm would never be able to surmount this conflict, even though on some issues they would find common interest with the employer.'[29]

As the 1967 Labour Party working party report rightly pointed out, it would probably be easier, because of the wider public sector objectives, to introduce employee directors into nationalised industries. It is also true that, throughout much of private industry, there is a developed collective bargaining system which already gives employees rights in certain areas. But the point has been made earlier that most strategic decisions are outside the scope of collective bargaining – and that traditional collective bargaining is a second order activity, a process of reaction to decisions taken elsewhere. Something more is needed in the private as well as in the public sector. It was this argument, above all, which persuaded the TUC to argue for a representative system at board level covering both the private and public sectors. Otherwise, employees in private industry would have to be content with less representative rights than their colleagues in the public sector.

Employee representation on boards of private companies need not freeze the pattern of industrial ownership and prerogative (as some argue happened in West Germany as a result of the co-determination laws). Indeed, the proposals of the Bullock majority to redefine directors' responsibilities to take account of employee interests and to ensure that, on the key issues, the board (on which there is parity between employee and shareholders' representatives) either has the final say or exclusive powers of initiative, represent a significant curtailment of the rights of capital.

However, it may well be that some trade unions, particularly those which have ideological objections, will not wish to exercise their right to boardroom representation. It is, therefore, important that there should be a non-mandatory system which is only triggered off if the trade union, or unions, representing a substantial number of employees *and* a majority of employees equivalent to at least a third of those entitled to vote, are in favour.

If some trade unionists are concerned about the implications of employee participation in management, many managers are even more apprehensive about its effect on decision-making. Will it be possible to combine democracy with efficiency? The multi-dimensional approach which has been outlined above – a strong shopfloor democracy, a major extension of collective bargaining and parity employee representation on boards – does offer a good prospect of introducing for the first time a real measure of democracy into the running of the enterprise. It is not surprising that managers, naturally uncertain about their role in a new structure, should be fearful lest the speed and secrecy which is sometimes necessary in industrial decision-making be sacrificed in a slow and potentially conflict-ridden democratic process.

It is important for all involved in the argument to realise that, whatever the system, there has to be a management function. Earlier syndicalist schemes were usually marred by the assumption that there was no role for management. But, given the size and complexity of industrial enterprises, the modern solution (as is recognised even in the Yugoslav workers' council structure) is not to abolish management but to democratise it. In the new democratic structure, management will still have the key part to play; it will, however, owe its position, not to rights of property and prerogative, but to its specialist skills and its ability to convince employees that it is right.

The effect on management of industrial democracy is more fully considered later. What needs to be said here is that the old basis of its authority has been largely eroded. So whatever the other requirements of its decision-making, management is unlikely to be able to run industry unless it is able to secure the consent of the employees. In a democratic enterprise, management's authority will be clearly derived from decisions taken after the impact on employees has already been fully discussed rather than from a dubiously based and frequently resented prerogative. In the new context, it should become far easier to innovate. Democratic management will also be able to tap a fresh pool of ideas and skills. So the close involvement of employees and their representatives should enable the enterprise to operate more and not less effectively than in the past.

As far as boardroom conflict is concerned, there is already a potential clash between the different interests and viewpoints at present represented there. One argument for the introduction of employee representation is that it will provide, for the first time, a means of resolving the different attitudes and interests of management and employees on the major corporate issues at the crucial policy formulation stage. Indeed, the evidence from foreign experience is that employee representatives play a constructive role,[30] and, despite the apprehensions about 'wreckers in the boardroom', there is no objective reason why this should not be the case in this country. As the AUEW position illustrates, those who have an ideological objection to private enterprise are far more likely to reject the employee director system from without than attempt to destroy it from within. Those managers who are still concerned should read the constructive manifesto of the worker directors in British Steel.[31] The vast majority of employee directors are certain to adopt their approach. However, an additional managerial worry is that confidential information will be leaked to competitors. Given the employee representative's interest in the future of the enterprise, such misbehaviour would be highly improbable. Certainly breaches of confidentiality in Sweden and West Germany by boardroom representatives are extremely rare.[32] However, there is a case for adopting a two-tier board structure, with a powerful supervisory board appointing and overseeing the work of a much smaller executive board. This would establish overall democratic control, while leaving management broadly responsible for the day-to-day running of the enterprise. Even if it were decided to retain unitary boards, in practice these mostly act very much in a supervisory capacity. There is also much to be said for having either a chairman elected by both sides or perhaps a number of additional directors, also elected jointly. This would enable decisions to be reached in the case of deadlock, and so prevent the enterprise grinding to a halt.

PRACTICAL DIFFICULTIES AND PRACTICAL ANSWERS

Besides the conceptual problems discussed above, there are also some very real practical difficulties to be overcome. There is the task of devising a fair system of representation. In any large firm there are many different groups including the unskilled, semi-skilled and skilled, as well as the clerical, technical and supervisory staff, with differing and sometimes conflicting interests. In addition, it should not be forgotten that managers are also employees. There is also another point of view besides that of the producers – the consumer or community interest. Yet how can consumers be adequately represented at enterprise level? We also have to face up to the diversities and complexities of the mixed economy. In the private sector, there is the varying size of companies which range from those employing 50,000 or over, to those with only a handful of workers. In the public sector, there is the difficulty involved in applying the same democratic solution in the public services, particularly those run by elected representatives, as in the nationalised industries. Finally there is the problem of multinationals.

The need for a strong trade union involvement has already been stressed, because it provides the only worthwhile guarantee that any new form of democratic representation is not used against the interest of employees. A special position for trade unions does not mean monolithic representation. On the contrary, one of the strengths of the trade union movement is its diversity. British trade unionism, catering for many different types of employee up to and including management, is well suited for the kind of democratic advance proposed by the TUC. But in those enterprises in which there are a number of unions special attention will need to be given to inter-union agreement on representation – as is the normal practice in collective bargaining. Joint representation committees will help; but in difficult cases it will probably be necessary to make provision for intervention by the Advisory Conciliation and Arbitration Service.

Managers as well as employees have a right to representation. For managers are themselves employees with rights of their own – as a number of unions have recognised. It would be wrong, however, if management *qua* management had a special place reserved for them on supervisory boards. For it is not from their role as management but from their position as employees that their claim to representation derives. Managers, who are now joining trade unions in increasingly large numbers, must be able to play their part in electing representatives on to supervisory boards. In addition, they are, of course, likely to be elected on to the board as representatives of the shareholders – and also there, in an ex-officio capacity, as part of the management board. So they should not expect a further 'bite of the cherry'.

The crucial role of trade unions in the extension of industrial democracy throws a heavy responsibility on them. Their internal democracy is of critical importance. For, if employee representatives are considered merely as part of management without accountability, they could spark off a shopfloor revolt against the whole idea of industrial democracy. So, if the employee director system is to succeed, trade union democracy must be fully effective. The TUC should, therefore, ask individual unions, as a matter of urgency, to look at their electoral and report-back machinery with great care, in order to ensure that employee directors represent the views of and remain in close contact with their constituents. There will also be a need to examine existing organisational structures. The successful introduction of an effective system of employee representation is bound to strengthen workplace trade unionism. Trade unions will have to consider the relationship of national and regional officials and their governing bodies to the shopfloor in the light of this development. They will also have to discuss inter-union links, particularly in view of the necessity for multi-union representation on the joint representation committees.

There will also have to be an extensive development of trade union education, training and research facilities. It will partly be a question of equipping employee directors for their new functions and seeing they get the back-up services they require. Equally important, however, is the general educational effort that will be required if employees and their shopfloor representatives are to understand the implications and advantages of the new democratic system, and be in a position to question and influence their board-room representatives.

Lastly the onus will be on the trade unions to expand the system. If the case for an exclusive trade union trigger is to be sustained, there must be a major drive to spread trade union organisation beyond its base in the large companies. This is an additional argument for a TUC initiative in stimulating recruitment in the unorganised enterprises and industries.

Obviously employees, management and shareholders are not the only parties with a legitimate concern about the behaviour of the enterprise. The consumer and the community as a whole have an interest in seeing that the enterprise does not enrich itself at their expense. In classical economic theory, the producer served the good of the community by looking after his own. The 'free market' system ensured that the consumer was able to exercise his choice. In practice, a combination of oligopoly and private and state monopoly has meant that consumers have far less choice than the traditional economists supposed.

It is, however, difficult to see how the consumers' interest can be directly represented within the enterprise. There is no identifiable constituency. The complexities of appointing consumer representatives to the board of every company would be great. How would they be elected and how would they carry out such a general responsibility? In view of these problems, it would be unreasonable, except in the nationalised industries, to expect direct consumer representation. It is certainly the case that, with the extension of public enterprise and public shareholding under the National Enterprise Board, there will be more government appointments to company boards. But elsewhere the government itself will remain the real representative of the consumer and the community – and it will be through government policies on pricing and taxation that these interests will be best protected.

Any democratic strategy has to take account of industrial realities.

In the private sector, top management and many trade unionists have misgivings. As far as the public sector is concerned, there is a crucial distinction between the nationalised industries and the public and local authority services. The form of industrial democracy in the public services, particularly those which are already democratically controlled by the community, is likely to be rather different (though even here there may be a case for some worker representation at the appropriate level); here further discussion and examination is certainly needed. In the nationalised industries, however, parity representation for elected employee representatives on the main board is entirely applicable, though the relevant minister must retain the power to appoint the non-employee directors and the chairman of the board as representatives of the community interest. Above all, we have to recognise that attitudes and practices will have to undergo some modification if the new system is to be successful. The management attitude to the Bullock report was somewhat hysterical, while as the 1977 TUC Congress debate showed, the trade union movement is still divided in its approach.

There is, therefore, a strong case for a phased introduction of industrial democracy.[33] In the scheme proposed by the Manifesto Group, the first phase would come into operation with the assistance of enabling legislation which would permit the appointment of employee representatives at boardroom level and extend company directors' obligations to take account of the interests of employees. The first phase would be a period of experimentation which would allow time for management and unions to agree on participation arrangements covering strategic issues.[34] These arrangements are likely to cover extensions of collective bargaining as well as boardroom representation (though following the Post Office example there could be a more rapid move forward on parity representation in the nationalised industries if the trade unions wished). These agreements should be registered with an Industrial Democracy Commission which would also be available to give advice to both sides of industry on the introduction of lower level arrangements where appropriate and the development of adequate training and communication systems (see Appendix).

The second phase, which would establish a right to boardroom representation, would come into operation some years later. The main arguments for introducing the legal option of a formalised system of boardroom representation are that it provides an incentive for management and unions to agree on their own arrangements in the first phase, and offers a way forward in those cases in which managements have resisted union requests for boardroom representation.

There remains the problem of multinationals. It is only fair that there should be a right to boardroom representation in any foreign controlled enterprise employing 2,000 or more people in the United Kingdom. However, that right does not necessarily give employee representatives the ability to influence decisions made at head offices outside this country. Obviously, solutions to this difficulty can only be reached in the context of an international or regional approach (mentioned in the previous chapter).

Thus it is probable that there will be a number of different approaches to industrial democracy. In most nationalised industries, parity employee representation at boardroom level is likely to be introduced during the next decade. In the private sector, we can expect a more varied pattern. Some trade unionists may wish to rely on the extension of collective bargaining alone, while in other companies they will opt for the worker director system. There must also be a place for producer and other forms of co-operative enterprise. In all cases, it will be necessary for the trade union movement to monitor the introduction of new systems, if they are to get the maximum benefit from diversity.[35]

The underlying contention of the last two chapters has been that there is now a strong case for more industrial democracy, extending all the way up from the shopfloor to the boardroom. Evidence of substantial support amongst employees and their representatives for such a development suggests that new democratic structures are likely to have firm foundation, provided they are supported by trade union machinery and built on existing collective bargaining systems. What is now required is a continuous system of power-sharing (employees' representatives and management) throughout industry which will link together all levels of decision-making. This will involve trade unions in new responsibilities, particularly as regards recruitment and training. It will also make it even more essential that the reforms in internal union democracy, as outlined in a following chapter, are carried through. But the rewards for decisive policies on industrial democracy will be high. For, if even some of the proposals suggested in chapters 7 and 8 are implemented, they will lead to a more democratic and humane industry.

REFERENCES

1 Part of this chapter draws on the arguments of the Fabian pamphlet *Working power*, and on the Fabian Society's evidence to the Bullock Committee published as *Workers in the boardroom* Fabian Tract 1976.
2 'Employee participation and company structure' EEC green paper *Bulletin of the European Communities* Supplement no. 8 1975.
3 *Hansard* 15 January 1976 cols. 464–74.
4 *Industrial democracy* TUC pamphlet 1974.
5 M. Fogarty *Company responsibility and participation* PEP 1975 pp. 64–69.
6 See the CBI evidence to the Bullock Committee.
7 *Employee participation* British Institute of Management 1975.
8 W. W. Daniel and Neil McIntosh *The right to manage* PEP 1972 p. 125.
9 F. E. Emery and Einar Thorsrud *Form and content in industrial democracy* Tavistock Publications 1969 pp. 26–30.
10 *Post-war reconstruction* TUC pamphlet 1944 para. 99.
11 *Trade unionism* TUC 1966 para. 262.
12 *Report of the Labour Party working party on industrial democracy* Labour Party pamphlet 1967.
13 *Industrial democracy* para. 84.
14 *Report of the Committee of Inquiry on Industrial Democracy.*
15 *Bulletin of the European Communities* Supplement no. 8 1975 p. 38.
16 *Industrial democracy* GMWU policy statement 1976.
17 *Bulletin of the European Communities* Supplement no. 8 1975 p. 38.
18 EETU-PTU evidence to the Bullock Committee.
19 P. Brannen, E. Batstone, D. Fatchett and P. White *The worker directors* Hutchinson 1976 p. 236.
20 *Worker directors speak* ed. J. Bank and K. Jones Gower Press 1977.
21 *Industrial democracy: European experience* HMSO 1977.
22 *Industrial democracy* Swedish Confederation of Trade Unions 1972 p. 105.
23 *Report of the Committee of Inquiry on Industrial Democracy* p. 95.
24 *Industrial democracy: European experience* p. 34.
25 See my article in the *Guardian* 14 June 1977 for a comment on the Manifesto Group document.
26 *Report of the Committee of Inquiry on Industrial Democracy* p. 15.
27 *Industrial democracy: European experience* p. 65.
28 *Investigation into the scope of industrial democracy* AUEW 1976.
29 *Working power* p. 13.
30 *Industrial democracy: European experience* pp. 26–28, 65–66.
31 *Worker directors speak* pp. 3–5.
32 *Report of the Committee of Inquiry on Industrial Democracy* p. 90.
33 This was proposed by the 1972 Industry Group, the Fabian working party on industrial democracy, and the Manifesto Group of Labour MPs in submissions to the Government following the publication of the Bullock Report.

34 See the article by John Lloyd in the *Financial Times* 6 January 1978.
35 David Watkins *Industrial common ownership* Fabian Society 1978; also Peter Jay *Employment, inflation and politics* Institute of Economic Affairs 1976, and Samuel Brittan's essay 'Property rights for workers' in his book *The economic consequences of democracy* Temple Smith 1977.

Chapter 8

The wider objectives

In an industrial democracy, trade unions have the right to be heard and to have their views taken into account by government. In previous chapters, it was argued that a coherent and realistic definition of trade union social and economic objectives was required if the trade unions were to make this right effective. The enduring challenge to collective bargaining requires a considered trade union response. And, given the industrial and economic weakness of Britain, an independent and credible trade union view is more than ever essential. Finally, trade unionists are pressing for a more just society; so the trade unions have to have a social policy.

This chapter discusses the reasons for trade union involvement in the political processes, describes how it has evolved and attempts to outline the main principles on which a positive trade union strategy for industrial relations, for industrial and economic policy, and for social policy should be based.

TRADE UNIONS AND POLITICS

At the outset it must be recognised that there is a strongly held view, not confined to the right of the political spectrum, that trade unions should not be involved in politics at all. Their role, it is argued, should be solely industrial; they should operate strictly as 'business' unions without any wider objectives. Such arguments, however, are based on a misunderstanding of trade union purpose and of the nature of the economic, social and political obstacles which prevent them from fulfilling that purpose.

From their beginnings trade unions had to act politically in order to create an environment which was favourable to trade unionism; even in the twentieth century, there have been a number of occasions, as far apart as the 1901 Taff Vale judgement and the 1971 Industrial Relations Act, when the trade union movement has been provoked by attacks on what it considered to be its legitimate activities into intense political activity. The truth is that, despite their long history, trade unions are still only grudgingly accepted. And whenever they raise their sights and try to move away from being management's junior partner toward the more substantial role of democratising and humanising industry, then attempts are made to stop them, not only from within but from outside industry as well. The Industrial Relations Act of 1971 was, at least in part, an attempt to tame the growing power of the shopfloor; it was only natural that such a political intervention should trigger off a political reaction by the trade union movement. After a fierce battle against the Act, it turned to the Labour Party not only to repeal it but also to introduce new legislation which would help to produce an environment which was more favourable to trade unions and to the aspirations of its members. Thus it is inevitable that the battle to create a better industrial society should have political implications. Trade unions will be forced into the political arena, whether they like it or not, either to protect themselves from their opponents or to secure changes in the industrial framework which will make it easier for them to fulfil their role.

It is also natural that trade unions should want to be involved in the determination of national economic and industrial objectives. It is not intended to discuss the place of trade unions in economic theory.[1] Since Keynes, however, it has been widely recognised that governments have a crucial role to play in influencing the level of consumption, investment and employment. It is no exaggeration to say that, in a modern economy, the jobs and living standards of workers will depend, to a considerable extent, on the effectiveness or otherwise of government measures. Given the obvious implications for trade unionists of government policy, it was not surprising that trade unions should have wished to have a say in policy-making. And the sluggish post-war performance of the British economy (at a time when other rival economies were expanding more successfully), the persistence of industrial and regional weaknesses, and, in the 1970s, the twin menaces of a fast rate of inflation and a high level of unemployment made it inevitable that the trade union movement should develop views of their own about economic and industrial policy.

The opponents of a wider role for trade unions ignore a further point. As was pointed out in chapter 5, trade unions have to represent the needs and interests of their members in the broadest sense. Though their prime function is industrial representation, they have to take into account that workers are also consumers and

parents, tenants and potential or actual householders, sometimes
sick, disabled or unemployed, and eventually old-age pensioners.
So trade unions have not only to fight against deprivation and
inequality at work; they have also to act as a pressure group for
social justice in the widest sense. Inequality is, in any case, indivisible. Many studies have shown how inequality at the workplace
is, at least in part, shaped by other inequalities – in family conditions, in housing, in schooling and so on.[2] So a trade union movement which confined its concern to industrial conditions alone would
be falling down on the job.

There is a yet more fundamental reason why trade unions should
be involved in the political process. Democratic governments,
above all, have to secure the consent of the governed. In an industrial democracy, this means that they have to pay particular attention to the producer groups, which include the trade unions. So, in
modern Britain, the trade union movement has the right not only
to be heard but also to insist that its views be taken into account.

But to argue that trade unions should be involved in politics is
quite different from saying that they should run the country. Since
the general strike of 1926, the trade union movement has fully
accepted the supremacy of a democratically elected government.
Thus both over the 1971 Industrial Relations Act and the miners'
dispute of 1973–74, the TUC made it quite clear that it was not
directly challenging the Conservative Government's authority, however wrong it believed its policies to be. In February 1974 it was the
Cabinet of Mr. Heath, not the trade unions, which precipitated a
general election over the issue of the miners' dispute. Most trade
union leaders, though they rejoiced at the opportunity they now
had to get rid of the Conservatives, were also deeply dismayed that
trade unions should be accused of trying to take over the country.
Earlier, in their fight against the Industrial Relations Act, they had
firmly rejected the idea of direct action. The correct procedure,
which the trade union movement adopted, was to campaign vigorously against the Act, to refuse, as far as was legally possible, to
co-operate in its implementation, and to work for the return of a
government pledged to repeal that legislation. Though there may
sometimes be a case for 'propaganda' strikes, there are overwhelming arguments against general strikes undertaken with the express
purpose of forcing a democratically elected government either to
drop legislation or (even more dangerous) to leave office altogether.
Apart from its probable ineffectiveness (there are few examples of
successful political strikes), such conduct is fundamentally undemo-

cratic. It also encourages unscrupulous opponents to take similar action when a government more favourable to the trade unions is in power. The ways of democracy may sometimes be slow and uncertain but it ill behoves the preponents of a more democratic society to argue for unconstitutional short cuts. The proper democratic behaviour is not direct action but political pressure, legitimately applied.

The concept of direct action is, in any case, based on the incorrect assumption that the main function of trade unionism should be political. One cannot emphasise enough the primacy of the trade unions' industrial role. Their social and political involvement derives from and must remain subsidiary to their major task of democraticising and humanising industry. If they concentrated on social and political objectives to the detriment of their industrial objectives, they would be failing their members. Workers join and remain in unions so that they can be protected and their interests furthered within industry. Trade unionists are right to continue to reject the blandishments of Marxists who seek to politicise them to overturn the system undemocratically. Of course, within industry, trade unions are, in the deepest sense, political, in that they seek to change the balance of power in favour of the workers. And, as has been previously argued, they have an important social and political role to play in the world outside. But, whilst the trade union movement must be involved in politics, it cannot afford to neglect its primary purpose of industrial representation. If trade unions become indistinguishable from other political parties and movements, then it is almost certain that, even if they succeed in capturing power, the workers' views, without the continual pressure of trade unions acting as trade unions, would be ignored by a new political élite. For, only if trade unions behave like trade unions, can workers be sure that their views will be heard both within industry and in society as a whole.

DIALOGUE WITH GOVERNMENT

If the trade unions are to be effective politically they must maintain a continuous dialogue with government upon the basis of an independent yet credible set of industrial, economic and social policies.

Trade unions are now involved in a whole range of official institutions. They play a major role in the National Economic Development Council (set up in 1962 to assist economic planning and to help stimulate economic growth) and in the subsidiary Economic Development Councils and sector working parties. They are also represented on the National Enterprise Board (established in 1975 to act as a state holding company and a spur to economic regeneration). They participate, together with management representatives, in such organisations as the Health and Safety Commission, the Manpower Service Commission and the Industrial Training Boards. And the trade union movement is also prominent in the work of the Advisory Conciliation and Arbitration Service (created in 1974 to provide independent arbitration and conciliation). Above all, the social contract approach pioneered in the 1970s led to the development of a regular and wide-ranging process of consultation between the Labour government and the trade union movement.

In the eyes of some critics, trade union participation in outside institutions – especially those set up or inspired by government – amounts to little more than 'corporatism' – that is to say, a state of affairs in which trade union independence is fatally compromised by their involvement with the apparatus of the state. Ralph Miliband, for example, has written that '. . . their incorporation into the official life of their countries has mainly served to saddle them with responsibilities which have further weakened their bargaining position, and which has helped to reduce their effectiveness'.[3] However, as is described in chapter 12, others say that governments have given away too much to trade unions. Certainly, there are costs as well as benefits for both trade unions and government. The relationship is in the nature of a bargaining one, in which in order to reach conclusions which are beneficial to both parties, there has to be some compromise.

In considering the Miliband argument it should be remembered that trade union involvement in these official and semi-official institutions and relationships is not only comparatively recent but is also something they have had to fight for. *The Times* correspondent who, in his reply to the vote of thanks to the press at the end of the 1945 Trades Union Congress, told delegates that 'You have no longer any need to thunder; you have only to whisper and Ministers tremble and Field-Marshals bend their knees' was referring (with appropriate journalistic licence) to something that had only just happened.[4] Though beginning with the 'Treasury' agreement of 1915, Lloyd George took trouble to involve the young trade unions in the running of the 1914–18 war, it took another war and the appointment (by the Coalition Prime Minister, Winston

Churchill) of Ernest Bevin, then General Secretary of the Transport and General Workers, as Minister of Labour, before the trade unions established their right to be heard and to participate in appropriate institutions. And it was many years later, after the successful resistance of the TUC to the Industrial Relations Act, before Whitehall finally recognised them as a power in the land.

Trade unions have also been persistently discriminating in their attitude towards organisations. Thus, while agreeing to join the National Economic Development Council, the TUC refused to have anything to do with the National Incomes Commission established in the same year (1962) to oversee incomes policy. Similarly, it was totally hostile to the Conservative Government's desire to secure trade union representatives as members of the National Industrial Relations Court, and, when industrial tribunals were given new functions under the Industrial Relations Act, it instructed all affiliated unions to request those members who served on those courts to resign. If the trade union movement has traditionally been more co-operative with Labour governments, it is because it believed that its needs were more likely to be satisfied under a Labour than under a Conservative administration. But it has, in the past, agreed to participate in institutions set up by both Labour and Conservative governments because it considered that it would be in the interests of its members. Trade unions rightly believe that such subjects as economic planning, industrial policy, training and manpower questions and social issues are too important to be left to governments and employers; and that the viewpoint of employees can only be fully taken into account if trade unions are also involved in the determination of policy.

It was this consideration, above all, which led the trade union movement to adopt the social contract approach described in chapter 5. From the viewpoint of the Labour leadership, the social contract was a frank recognition of trade union power. A Labour Party, which in government had been involved in a clash with the trade unions over *In place of strife*, had to show anew that it could get on with the unions. Equally important, it needed a credible policy on incomes. As the experience of the Heath administration had shown, no counter-inflation policy was likely to work for long unless it had the support of the unions. From the point of view of the trade unions, it certainly involved acceptance that wage bargaining could not be considered in isolation from the wider interests of trade unionists or from its impact on the community as a whole. On the other hand, for the first time, they were able to trade their support on this issue for an agreement to introduce a number of measures of importance to trade unions, including the repeal of the Industrial Relations Act, legislation to extend collective bargaining, and substantial increases in social benefits. Thus, the trade unions used the social contract as a lever to raise their bargaining power with government. In a very real sense, closer involvement increased their political effectiveness.

However, if the trade unions are to continue to rebut the charge of corporatism, they have to show results from their participation in the political process. In part this depends on the TUC having the support of its affiliates for its views (see chapter 11); it is also a question of effective trade union back-up services (see chapter 10); equally important (and this is the subject of this chapter) is the need for putting forward policies which carry conviction. Here, internal consistency, ordering of priorities, and an appreciation of realities are all essential. This is not to argue that trade unions should behave like governments. Their primary job is to articulate the aspirations of their members. Thus they cannot support for any length of time policies which their members reject – a point which government should note. But a close attention to the needs of the membership should not imply that the task of trade union leaders is merely to put forward a series of unco-ordinated and unrealistic demands. No industrial society possesses such a super-abundance of resources that choices about their allocation do not have to be made. Even in a fast growing economy, it is just not possible to achieve dramatic increases in spending on houses, schools, hospitals, social benefits and increases in real wages all at the same time. In Britain, which has suffered from persistent economic and industrial weakness for many years and which has been one of the last to recover from the recession of the 1970s, there is unlikely to be room for substantial increases in overall living standards for the next few years – whatever the impact of North Sea oil. Of course, in an inegalitarian society there is always room for redistribution of wealth. But even a large-scale redistribution cannot begin to satisfy all society's needs. Sometimes, there may be scope for the reallocation of resources away from one type of expenditure towards another (say, from defence to social benefits). But here again there is a limit to the amount of reallocation that can be undertaken in a given period of time. As far as defence expenditure is concerned, in a world of power politics even a neutral nation (as Sweden has found) has to spend money to defend itself. So short of Utopia, defence cuts cannot possibly finance all the increases desired in other kinds of social expenditure. However, it is certainly a trade union interest to examine the redistributional effectiveness and value for money of all public expenditure programmes. Trade unionists should also avoid the mistake of believing that industrial profits provide a bottomless pool of wealth from which extra resources can be readily raised for social needs. Quite apart from the decline in the profitability of British industry[5], it is not always realised that profits have an important function in any economy (be it privately owned, publicly owned or a mix of the two) because it is the major source of investment. Even a nationalised industry has to provide a large part of its investment from its own resources – in other words, from the profits of the organisation.

So, while it is natural that trade union *members* should continue to put forward demands on all fronts, trade union *leaders* have the responsibility of pointing out that they cannot be satisfied all at once. Trade unionists may 'cry for the moon' but, if they are not to become entirely cynical, their leaders must point out the difficulties. In the long run, nothing undermines authority so completely as the failure to deliver. Trade union leaders who are prepared to point out realities often discover that their honesty and courage is rewarded. The 'dutch auction' approach is, in the end, self-defeating and should be abandoned once and for all in favour of a more far-sighted and clearly thought out strategy. On the other hand, trade union leaders have to avoid the other mistake of refusing to take up any position at all. If they do so they weaken themselves. There is an analogy here with collective bargaining. The initial demand is crucial. If it is pitched too high, it is laughed out of court; if too low, the subsequent agreement may be overturned. A realistic posture backed by rational argument has far more chance of success. In a wider discussion with government, a trade union movement which has already defined its objectives coherently and realistically has a clear advantage. Definition, by helping to delineate the grounds of debate, escapes the weakness of a purely practical approach. The remaining sections of this chapter attempt to outline the principles on which a trade union strategy should be based. Industrial relations, economic and industrial policy, and social affairs are examined in turn.

INDUSTRIAL RELATIONS

British industrial relations are and are likely to continue to be mainly shaped by voluntary agreements between trade unions and

employers. The difficulties created by comprehensive labour legislation have been described in chapter 4 (though the case for some
form of statutory protection against arbitrary trade union behaviour
is reviewed in a later chapter). However, trade unionists should
not allow their traditional hostility to legal enactment to blind them
to the constructive part that the law can play in redressing the
industrial balance.

In a series of statutes, the 1974 Labour Government created a new
framework in which the rights of employees and their trade union
representatives were extended. The two Acts which repealed the
Industrial Relations Act of 1971 also re-enacted its provisions against
unfair dismissal, except that they removed statutory protection for
workers dismissed as a result of closed shop and other union
security arrangements (though these continued to be protected by
common law rights and by appeal to the TUC's review committee).
More important was the 1975 Employment Protection Act which,
as has already been described, gave employees rights in a number
of areas, including unfair dismissal, redundancy, guarantee payments, maternity, insolvency of the firm and time off work, and also
strengthened collective bargaining by its provisions on trade union
recognition, on disclosure of information and on wages councils.
Other Acts which reinforced the position of employees and trade
unions included the 1975 Sex Discrimination Act, the 1974 Health
and Safety at Work Act and the 1975 Industry Act. In some areas,
the law may need amending. The long-drawn-out dispute at
Grunwick and subsequent judgements in the courts cast doubt on
the effectiveness of the Employment Protection Act in cases in
which employers are really determined to resist trade union recognition even though it is supported by a large section of the workforce; disturbances outside Grunwick also raised anew the issue
of picketing. The law on picketing which was re-enacted by the
1974 Repeal Act established the right to picket. There is, however,
still obscurity over whether pickets are allowed to stop vehicles
going into factories and how many are allowed to picket. There is
a strong argument for modernising the law to allow a right to stop
vehicles; there is also a case for a limitation on numbers. Even
though strengthening amendments may be required, it is certainly
true that a significant shift in power should result from these
developments in industrial law, provided trade unions are prepared
to educate their members to know their rights and exploit the
opportunities which the new legislation affords them.

However, further legislation will be needed. There is a case for an extension of individual and trade union rights in the area of manpower and training. Under the Employment Protection Act, an employer is obliged to consult with a recognised trade union if he is proposing to make 100 or more employees redundant within a period of ninety days, at least ninety days before these employees are made redundant. In cases of ten or more employees being made redundant within a period of thirty days, the employer must consult at least sixty days before. The employer also has to notify the Department of Employment at the same time. However, as both the employment and training functions of the Department of Employment were hived off by the 1973 Employment and Training Act, the employment and training agencies ought also to be informed. More fundamentally, there ought to be a right to training; all citizens over the age of sixteen should either be in a job or in education *or*, if they wish it, in training. And employers should not only tell trade unions about future redundancies. They should also be obliged to discuss their manpower and training requirements with trade union representatives.

If there is to be a major step forward in the joint regulation of work design, help from government will probably be needed. The first priority should be for an expansion of trade union education in this field. But, as was suggested in chapter 6 there is also an argument for government backing for worthwhile work design schemes which have secured trade union agreement. In which case, amendments will be required to the 1972 Industry Act to enable the Departments of Industry and Employment to provide the relevant financial support.

Perhaps most important of all there should be an Industrial Democracy Act to assist the spread of industrial democracy. In the previous chapter it was argued that there should be a phased introduction. In the first phase, company directors' obligations would be extended so as to include employee interests, the appointment of employee representatives would be permitted, and an Industrial Democracy Commission would be set up. Only in the second phase would a right to boardroom representation be established – though only in firms employing 2,000 workers and over and where the trade union or unions representing a substantial number of employees are in favour and a majority of employees (equivalent to at least a third of those eligible) vote in the affirmative. Employee representation would be on the top board of a two-tier structure; this top board would be the supreme corporate authority in a number of strategic areas; and there would be parity between employee and shareholder representatives in the private sector and between employee and government-nominated representatives in the nationalised industries (though it may be possible to secure an agreed build up towards parity). With respect to the appointment of employee representatives, there ought to be a right of appeal for *all* employees. However, the provision of a trade union trigger and the special position of the joint representation committee should ensure that trade unions dominate the elections (see Appendix).

In the past, trade unions have been justified in their hostility to industrial relations law. But the legal enactments of the 1974 Labour Government have been of great benefit; and trade unionists ought to support legislation which assists the spread of collective bargaining, helps the extension of industrial democracy and guarantees employee rights.

ECONOMIC AND INDUSTRIAL POLICY

It has been asserted above that a credible and consistent trade union view on economic policy is essential, given the key role that a successful economic strategy can play in sustaining employment and in raising the living standards of employees.

For some time our economic performance has been worse than most of our main competitors. Over the last three decades, our economy has grown more slowly than that of any other member of the twenty-one nation OECD group (a group that includes Turkey, Greece, Portugal, Italy and the Republic of Ireland, as well as Japan, West Germany and the United States). Over the last decade, our rate of growth has been only half that of the group as a whole.[6] Admittedly, with the advent of North Sea oil, British prospects have been substantially improved. However, our situation cannot be considered in isolation. The events of 1970s (particularly the quadrupling of oil prices in the autumn of 1973) have dealt the industrialised and developing countries a blow from which they have been slow to recover.[7] There have also been disturbing reports of the possibility of a world energy gap opening up by the end of the 1980s.[8]

It is against this background of world uncertainty that the trade union movement has to put forward its views. The TUC has consistently argued the case for economic growth; it has rightly pointed out that only through sustained growth can the living standards of its members be increased and their employment be secured. Growth also provides the essential financing motor for increasing the key social expenditure programmes, including the improvement of the environment. But the performance of the British economy, despite the commitment to growth by successive governments, has not only failed to match the record of other rival economies but also to live up to its own productive potential.[9] Both monetarist and Marxist critics claim that the relative British economic failure illustrates the ineffectiveness of Keynesian techniques of demand management.[10] A more balanced judgement would be that, in this country, demand management has been misapplied. Growth has either been almost wholly sacrificed to some other objective or been allowed to degenerate into an unsustainable boom. Thus the Labour administrations of 1960s put sterling first, while, in 1972–73, the Conservative Government (after a period of deflation) emulated the unwise example of the 1964 Maudling strategy and engineered an unbalanced and short-lived expansion. Growth remains the priority; but it cannot be sustained either where demand is deficient or by resort to printing money. The first leads to decline in output, unemployment, and poor use of investment, while the second results in inflation, balance of payments difficulties and further unemployment. What trade unions require is neither deflation nor a mad dash for growth but steady demand and monetary management, related to a realistic growth strategy.

The trade union movement has an important contribution to make to economic growth. For if inflation is to be contained and industry to remain competitive, there has to be a continuing prices and incomes policy. In chapter 6, the conditions for a successful policy were examined. It was argued that, while certain ingredients such as clarity, fairness and some flexibility were essential, the economic and social framework was even more important. In the next section, the movement's social priorities are analysed. As far as economic objectives are concerned, the priority of growth of output has already been stressed. But, here the argument is partly circular. The trade unions understandably demand expansion as one of their conditions for the prices and incomes bargain. Yet, without a prices and incomes policy, a sustainable rate of expansion of output and real incomes is unlikely to be achieved. Trade unions also ask for price control. However, given the fact that prices of raw materials and food are largely outside national control, there is a limit to what can be done. But there is a case for a powerful Prices Commission and for a sympathetic approach by government itself, particularly in those areas where it is able to influence prices without undermining other parts of its strategy.

The trade unions also have a responsibility in the area of productivity. As was pointed out in chapter 1, there is little doubt that our productivity record compares unfavourably with many of our competitors. In the longer run, persistent over-manning is a major factor in our economic weakness and, therefore, contributes to the slow growth in living standards and unemployment. There is a strong case for a more vigorous and constructive trade union approach on this issue, particularly if it is considered against the background of an active manpower and employment – creating policy (see below).

However, as the TUC has pointed out, there are other requirements for economic growth. The trade union movement, during the long recession of 1974–77, called for selective import controls. Although there is a case for import controls on a temporary basis, both to protect individual industries and to help the balance of payments, they are no substitute for improvements in industrial performance. They risk retaliation by competitors, which not only harm export industries but slows down world trade. They should, therefore, be used only sparingly or if there is no alternative. Another instrument is a change in the external exchange rate, either by devaluation or by allowing the currency to find its own level on international markets. The advantage for a country in a weak position like Britain is that such action gives its exports a competitive edge; unfortunately it also usually increases the value of imports more quickly than that of exports. In any case, as the TUC has accepted, exchange rate variations and import controls, though useful weapons in a government's economic armoury, do little more than buy time for more fundamental industrial changes.

The most essential condition for improving industrial efficiency is a sustained period of economic growth. For obvious reasons, enterprises (whether private or public ownership) are most likely to invest when markets expand. Thus our poor growth record goes far to explain our inadequate investment level. But, if a cautious but firm commitment to growth must be the first trade union requirement from government, trade unions are right to insist that there is also an important role for government in assisting industry to identify its market opportunities, in stimulating investment in key industries and companies, in promoting structural change and in overcoming those bottlenecks, whether of labour or materials, which have so often held up economic growth in the past.

Classical economists and, curiously enough, many businessmen still believe that government intervention in the economy is, at best, ineffective and, at worst, actually harmful. Prosperity is best achieved by leaving individual enterprises alone to manage their own affairs. On the other hand, some trade unionists, as well as some socialists, are equally adamant that total public ownership alone will produce a British 'economic miracle'. Both models are too simple.

The classical model assumes that, provided the individual entrepreneur maximises his profit, competition will ensure that there is no conflict between his private interest and the public good. In reality, in a number of areas such as housing, education, health, social benefits, and other essential utilities (like electricity, coal, gas, water and so on) the market system works so imperfectly and inefficiently that, in the interests of the community, the state has to intervene.

In any case, industry expects the support of government to correct a deficiency of demand and, sometimes, to bail it out when the going gets rough. In addition, in order to achieve community objectives, governments have had to introduce measures to control inflation, to improve the balance of payments, to stimulate investment and technological innovation, to assist regional development, to secure and create employment, to ensure an adequate supply of skilled manpower and to preserve the environment. So, whatever the theoretical beauties of the classical model, it hardly corresponds to the needs of a complex industrial society.[11]

However, the Marxist belief that taking private industry into public ownership provides the only solution to British problems is almost equally misplaced. Certainly, there are arguments for an extension of public ownership beyond the public utilities and steel. Already the weakness of large parts of the manufacturing sector has compelled the Labour Government, like the preceding Conservative administration, to take a number of important companies (including British Leyland, Alfred Herbert, and ICL) into total or partial public ownership. During 1976, the shipbuilding and aircraft industries, both already dependent upon public funds, were nationalised. In the future, it is likely that the National Enterprise Board, the state holding company set up in 1975, will establish further companies in key sectors of the economy in order to act 'as highly competitive price-leaders and pace-setters, provide a yardstick for efficiency, support the government's investment plans, and above all produce a better product or service'.[12] In addition, nationalisation is the weapon of last resort to be used against the 'unruly' multinational. There are also grounds for extending public ownership for social reasons, as with community ownership of development land under the 1975 Community Land Act. But, if there is a case for further public ownership as a selective weapon, the idea that the creation of more and more industry-wide state monopolies will transform the British economy is largely beside the point. There is some evidence that during the 1960s the nationalised industries had a marginally better efficiency record than many industries in the private sector.[13] But the reasons for this country's poor economic performance since the war are related less to the question of ownership than to the ineffective economic management and planning mechanisms of successive governments and the inadequate level of investment and use of resources by individual public and private enterprises. There is also the cost in terms of individual liberty to be considered; it is no accident that the 'command' economies of Eastern Europe in which the private sector has been virtually eliminated are also one-party states – without free speech, free elections, or free trade unions. So, if selective and strategically directed public ownership remains an essential instrument, it is only one of a range of economic weapons which an interventionist government must employ to improve our economic and industrial efficiency.

But to be effective, government intervention must be coherent. What is needed is an economic and industrial plan, closely linked to industry's needs, related to a clear set of priorities, and backed by an effective political will. Strangely, after the collapse of George Brown's National Plan in July 1966, 'planning' became an almost unmentionable word. Instead of trying to improve the system of planning, both Labour and Conservative governments abandoned the idea altogether. It was not until the November 1975 Chequers meeting of Government, TUC and CBI that the first tentative steps of trying to develop a more sensible approach were taken. Yet other countries, even those which, like Japan, have traditionally adopted less overtly interventionist policies, have evolved far more effective economic and industrial plans. It is not so much a question of intricate and complicated economic projections (though forecasts, particularly of government growth plans, have a part to play): it is far more a matter of determining priorities in the light of needs, finding out the implications of these priorities for other policies, drawing conclusions and sticking to them. Politicians – and trade unionists – should remember that nothing is so harmful to industry as continual shifts and turns in policy. A coherent government strategy provides a framework in which enterprises can, themselves, plan more effectively.

There has been a largely sterile debate which has included some
trade union leaders between the advocates of company planning
agreements and those who favour sectoral planning. The truth is
that both kinds of planning are necessary. There is a strong case
for developing planning agreements with the largest corporations
(including nationalised companies and multinationals) because they
play such an important part in the economy. However, for the
purposes both of analysis and implementation, it is also essential
that planning covers not only the leading but also the less effective
companies in a sector. An illustration of the need for this is the
finding of the National Economic Development Office study which
shows that the significant difference in efficiency between British
and foreign companies lies not so much in the gap between the
best companies, but in the wider disparity between the best and the
average companies in Britain compared with abroad.[14] In addition
to company and sectoral arrangements, there are, however, two
further basic requirements for a successful planned system. The
first is an effective planning unit *within* government. Where precisely
this should be located (whether in the Department of Industry, or
under the joint sponsorship of the Departments of Industry and
Treasury or attached to the Prime Minister's office) is not so
important as the necessity of having such a unit. Without a planning
office of its own, government will find it more difficult to decide
on its own priorities or take initiatives in company and sectoral
planning. The second essential is the *consent* of industry. We are
fortunate enough to have in this country an organisation, the
National Economic Development Council (NEDC), on which both
sides of industry are represented. The NEDC, which has survived
different governments and their changing attitudes to planning,
acts both as a forum for industry and as overseer of the work of
the Economic Development Councils for individual industries and
is, therefore, in a good position to influence sectoral behaviour. So
the TUC is right to have pressed for an increased role for NEDC
in the planning process.

Successful planning is not only a matter of the right coverage
and organisation; it is also a question of backing up the plan with
the right kind of instruments. The instruments are required for
three main purposes – for stimulating investment, for industrial
restructuring and for ensuring that the most effective use is made
of manpower. As far as investment is concerned, it has been argued
above that the main stimulant to investment is economic growth;
but trade unionists should not forget that a reasonable return on

capital is also essential, in order to allow resources to be ploughed back into the company in the form of investment. The government has, in addition, a wide battery of weapons, ranging from loans on easy terms, tax allowances, and investment grants to location controls, buying an equity stake, and outright nationalisation. These can be crucial in promoting investment in key companies or sectors, in bringing forward projects which would have otherwise been delayed, or in ensuring that a company expands in a development area. It is, however, essential that these weapons are used both *selectively* and *strategically*. General handouts of public money are usually a waste of resources, as are subsidies to companies which are either not viable in the medium term nor of vital importance to the economy. Though, in this area, government already has adequate instruments to hand, there is one outstanding gap. There is clearly a need for a state *investment* bank, able to tap the resources of pensions and insurance funds, and which would provide medium and long term finance for industry, particularly for small and medium sized firms.[15]

As far as industrial restructuring is concerned, the state holding company, the National Enterprise Board has a major role to play in improving efficiency in key sectors (it is already heavily involved in motor manufacturing, machine tools and computers). Perhaps in co-ordination with the state investment bank, the resources available to it should be increased. In some industries, there is a strong case for linking the provision of public investment money with rationalisation (as with the ferreous and non-ferreous foundries, machine tools, and clothing industries). And in any discussion of restructuring, the regional dimension should not be ignored. For the regional problem is mainly one of industrial imbalance – an over-concentration of the less dynamic industries.[16] Once again, regional incentives should be linked (perhaps through regional development agencies) with the creation of a better industrial balance. The benefits of such a policy could be substantial. If all regional economies could be brought up to the standards of the most efficient, the national economy would gain considerably in strength.

However, the growing unemployment of the 1970s underlines the need for the development of employment policy, complementary but no longer subsidiary to economic and industrial policy. Since the beginning of the 1960s, the trend of unemployment has been moving consistently upwards through successive cycles; and, according to a study by the Department of Employment, an extra 680,000 jobs will have to be found between 1977 and 1981 – and a further million in the years to 1985.[17] Though much unemployment has been caused by economic recession, there are disturbing signs that an increasing proportion of unemployment is caused, not so much by insufficient demand but more by structural factors. As the higher level of unemployment in some areas suggests, this is partly a regional problem. The disproportionate numbers of unskilled and young workers unemployed provide further evidence of flaws in the labour market. In addition, a fundamental shift in the demand for labour may also be taking place. The decline in manufacturing jobs is partly a function of the poor relative performance of British industry. But, even if the competitiveness of this sector was considerably improved, it is unlikely to lead to substantial increases in manufacturing jobs. Quite apart from the spare capacity which will have to be absorbed before employment increases, investment in the next few years is likely to be directed towards rationalisation and increases in productivity and will therefore destroy jobs as much as it creates them. So additional measures are required to ensure that economic growth brings enough extra employment to bring down the numbers of unemployed by a really significant amount.

Under the 1974 Labour Government, manpower policy has received much more attention than before; but it has primarily been concerned with issues such as job placement, mobility and training, and only temporarily and experimentally (though very successfully) with job creation. This is not to say that conventional labour market policies are not extremely useful, as well as cost effective. School leavers who are equipped with the skills required by employers and who are aware of where the demand for their skills is located, are more likely to get jobs. And if it were possible to upgrade the skills of more unemployed manual workers, this would not only be good for the economy but also reduce the level of unemployment.[18] However, employment creation must now become a central rather than subsidiary part of economic and industrial strategy.

What is needed is a manpower plan, which monitors the job potential of different sectors of the economy and suggests policies to improve that potential. In the manufacturing sector, the case for increasing shiftwork should be seriously encouraged, as it combines gains in productivity with increased employment. With respect to public services, priority should be given to projects that provide the most jobs, while possibilities in the market-orientated private service sector (banking, insurance, tourism, etc.) must not be ignored. In addition, the government should introduce direct labour subsidies where they can help create permanent jobs. A reduction in the number of hours worked during the week, as well as a lowering of the retirement age, may also have to be considered. If underemployment, with all that could mean socially and politically, is not to become a permanent feature, then a whole range of unorthodox measures will have to be taken by government, employers and trade unions alike.

Finally, both government and employers must realise that an increase in industrial democracy is an essential part of economic and industrial policy. If, as has been argued above, the use that is made of investment and manpower at the level of the individual enterprise is a key factor in economic growth, then it follows that the attitude of employees is of vital importance. For, in many firms, they have the power to delay or prevent the introduction of new plant and techniques. So the involvement of workers and their representatives in the running of the enterprise is not a marginal luxury but critical to economic recovery.

TAXATION AND PUBLIC EXPENDITURE

The inequalities in British society were noted in chapter 7. In terms of personal wealth, 1 per cent of the adult population owns 28·1 per cent of the total, 5 per cent owns 53·9 per cent, while the bottom 80 per cent owns 17·6 per cent.[19] As far as the distribution of income is concerned, the top half of income recipients received just over three-quarters of the total of pre-tax personal incomes, whilst the lower half had to share between them less than one-quarter of the total. There are also wide disparities of opportunity in terms of housing, medical care, pensions, education and job prospects. In addition, over 4 million have incomes below the supplementary benefit level.

The traditional response of the Labour movement has been the linking of progressive taxation with redistribution in the form of public expenditure on social programmes. The 1976 TUC Economic Review commented that 'the combination of a progressive system of taxation together with redistributive public expenditure is the main mechanism in the drive for social equality'.[20] Undoubtedly, this approach has had an impact. Over the last forty years, the share of personal wealth and income held by the very wealthy has declined, though some of the benefits of this have gone to those in the upper middle ranges. With respect to the distribution of income, the measures of the Labour governments of the 1940s and 1960s have had a significant egalitarian effect. The Royal Commission on the Distribution of Income and Wealth concluded that 'the combined effect of the tax system, the receipt of transfer payments and direct and indirect benefits in kind is a major redistributive one'.[21] The development of a whole range of social programmes has also substantially improved the quality of people's lives. As Howard Glennester has pointed out, they 'enable individuals to survive the burdens of sickness and the heavy cost of schooling, child bearing and setting up home as well as the interruptions of earnings, through illness, unemployment, widowhood and old age'.[22]

But whilst progress has been made, the differences in wealth and income are still far more than can be justified by any rational criteria, while what Anthony Crosland called 'the stubborn residue of grinding poverty'[23] persists. And, in a slow growing economy, it is difficult to finance growth in public expenditure – particularly at the explosive rate of the early 1970s. The time has come for the trade unions, whose members' tax burden has increased considerably in recent years, not only to back the TUC's call for a fairer distribution of wealth and income but also to demand a review of the effectiveness of social expenditure programmes both in terms of redistribution and of value for money.

The capital transfer tax, which was introduced by the Labour Government in 1975, and which is levied at rates rising to 75 per cent on estates worth more than £2 million, is the first effective tax on inherited wealth. There is also a case for an annual wealth tax on those with large fortunes, provided it is co-ordinated with other taxes on capital.

As regards the distribution of employment income, the Royal Commission on the Distribution of Income and Wealth agreed that 'a broad consensus over pay relationships would be a desirable goal',[24] while the TUC has called for the adoption of a ratio of about seven to one (the kind of ratio obtaining in the Scandinavian countries) between top salaries and the medium wage.[25] One argument often used against such a limit on higher salaries is that it would lead to a damaging 'brain drain' to other countries. There is little hard evidence, however, that this is likely to happen. On the other hand, agreement on a top salary level might make it easier to achieve an overall consensus on relativities between different groups of wage earners and, thus, to preserve a balance between maintaining differentials and improving the position of the low paid. It is certainly worth attempting, as part of a prices and incomes policy, to reach an agreed solution on the gap between higher incomes and the mass of wage-earners.

There must also be reforms in the income tax system. The decline of the tax threshold in relation to average earnings has meant that tax has become a heavy burden on low income earners, even including those entitled to supplementary benefit. There is certainly an overwhelming case for raising tax thresholds and for making a more radical effort to solve the 'poverty trap' problem by linking policies for wages, taxation, and benefits more closely together. Here, the introduction of the child benefit scheme to replace the family allowances and tax reliefs for dependent children is a step in the right direction. In the longer term, the introduction of a negative income tax needs to be seriously considered.

There is, however, also a tax problem for the average wage earner. Whereas in 1960–61 a married man on average earnings paid a tenth of earnings in income tax, in 1975–76 he was paying nearly a quarter of his income in income tax. And though, as was argued in the previous paragraph, there may be scope for increasing the tax burden on the better off in some respects, it has been estimated that, even if no taxpayer was left with more than £8,000 per annum after tax, this would increase the yield by only about 6 per cent.[26] In a fast expanding economy, it might be possible to finance increases in public expenditure by growth. But in the three years up to 1976, output rose by less than 2 per cent, while public expenditure increased by nearly 20 per cent in volume. At a time of recession, it made sense to run a large public sector deficit. However, when the economy began to recover again there were dangers that the financing of such a deficit would lead to increased inflation. So the Labour Government was faced with the alternatives of either increasing taxation very substantially, or of cutting back public expenditure programmes and thus avoiding taxation increases which might have provoked a widespread revolt amongst trade unionists against public expenditure as a whole.

In any debate on public expenditure, it is right that the trade unions should reaffirm their commitment to a high level of public spending, which is essential for a prosperous and civilised society. It is also understandable that individual unions should want to fight for particular spending programmes (the Railwaymen's Union (NUR) has naturally argued against cuts in railway subsidies, while the local authority unions have protested against cuts in their spending programmes). However, it is also important that the trade union movement as a whole should be concerned about the value for money and the redistributive effect of public spending. This is not to say that our public expenditure is particularly extravagant or notably more generous than other countries. The percentage of our GNP spent publicly is no higher than most of our competitors; and Britain is devoting less of her total wealth to social security, health and welfare provision than any of the continental EEC countries.[27] Indeed, if our economy grew faster, there would be a strong case for increasing many programmes. But, in time of slow growth, increases in public expenditure can only come from more taxation on trade unionists (many of whom already feel over-taxed) or from deficit financing which can lead to price increases (at a time of already high inflation). The conclusion is unavoidable; until we achieve faster growth, the gains in welfare are likely to come more from cost effectiveness and better redistribution than from big increases in public spending. In any case if the TUC is to defend the concept of public spending and head off the discontent of its members, it must put itself at the head of the campaign for more effective public expenditure. For this, it will need far more information than the government currently provides. Public expenditure White Papers should link expenditure with taxation plans, while the policy options and assumptions behind different programmes as well as their distributional impact should be made public.[28] In these ways it should become possible to compare different programmes both for cost and redistributional effectiveness, thus making it easier to ensure value for money and to concentrate resources where they are most needed.

THE INTERNATIONAL DIMENSION

It is impossible to discuss trade union economic and social objectives without some reference to the international context. As British trade unions have found to their cost, the position of this country as a major trading nation and its relatively weak industrial performance make its economy peculiarly vulnerable to shifts in world demand and movements in the international money markets. In addition, post-war developments on the European continent, particularly since the creation of the EEC, have forced this country to make difficult choices about its future. Finally, the more uncertain world economic conditions following the traumatic events of the early 1970s and the possibility of a world energy gap at the end of the 1980s cannot be ignored by trade unionists.

It would be unfair to condemn the trade union movement for its insularity. Indeed, it has played a major role in the development of international trade unionism, including the creation of the European TUC. However, the TUC decided against British entry into the EEC in 1972 and later rejected the Labour Government's renegotiated terms. It took the view that the common agricultural policy was against British interests, and that the EEC budget was weighted in favour of the original members, especially France. It also feared the domestic impact of German competition. Given the weakness of the British economy, these were all legitimate doubts. But most trade unions (though, as the 1975 referendum showed, not a majority of their members) failed to attach sufficient weight to the longer term advantages – the benefits of a larger market, the support of the stronger European economies, and the potential social and political gains of belonging to a wider community.

Now that the question of British membership has been settled by the 1975 referendum, the British trade unions must try to influence the future direction of the European Community. This is not just a matter of playing their part in Community institutions. Equally important is the development of specifically trade union aims. Three areas are of special significance: the establishment of guide lines for multinationals; the expansion of Community social and regional programmes; and the strengthening of both industrial and political democracy within the EEC. It is now essential not only for British but also for European trade unionists that the TUC assumes a creative role within the Community.

British trade unions must also continue to lend their authority to the view that world problems – the recession in world trade, the possible energy gap, and the disparities of wealth between the industrial and developing world – can be solved more by international co-ordination and co-operation than by purely national solutions. If each country turned its back on the other, the living standards of all would suffer. Thus internationalism is no luxury; it is essential for the interests of those whom the trade unions represent.

Trade union involvement in politics is inevitable and desirable. And if trade unions are to represent their members adequately, they have to develop a series of coherent and credible objectives in the industrial relations, industrial and economic, and social policy fields. In doing so, they increase their political effectiveness and make Britain more of an industrial democracy.

REFERENCES

1 For a review of this question see Giles Radice 'A trade union view of economics' in *Uses of economics* ed. G. D. N. Worswick Blackwell 1972.
2 For example, *The disadvantages of inequality* ed. Roger Berthoud PEP 1976, and *Labour and inequality* ed. P. Townsend and N. Bosanquet Fabian Society 1972.
3 Ralph Miliband *The state in capitalist society* Weidenfeld and Nicolson 1969 p. 161; for a discussion of trade unions and corporatism, see Colin Crouch *Class conflict and the industrial relations crisis* Heinemann 1977 pp. 255–72.
4 Quoted in *Trade unions* p. 157.
5 See *Financial performance and inflation* National Economic Development Council report February 1976.
6 Calculated from OECD and other sources.
7 See *Towards full employment and price stability* OECD June 1977, the report of a group of independent experts.
8 *World energy outlook* OECD report 1977; for the British situation see the *Third Report from the Select Committee on Science and Technology* vol. 1 HMSO 1977.
9 See R. Bacon and T. Eltis *Britain's economic problem* Macmillan 1976 chp. 2.
10 For a monetarist view see Milton Friedman *Unemployment versus inflation?* Institute for Economic Affairs 1975; for a partly Marxist view see Stuart Holland *The socialist challenge* Quartet Books 1976.
11 There is a useful chart in *Britain's economic problem* p. 2.
12 Anthony Crosland *Socialism now* Jonathan Cape 1974 p. 38.
13 Richard Pryke *Public enterprise in practice* Macgibbon and Kee 1971.
14 *The UK and West German manufacturing industry 1952–72.*
15 See John Hughes *Funds for investment* Fabian Research Series March 1976.
16 For example, the Northern Region Strategy Team's *Main report* vol. 1 1977.
17 *Department of Employment Gazette* June 1977; and for a discussion of manpower and employment policy see my article 'Where have all the jobs gone?' *Socialist Commentary* September 1977.
18 See *A five year plan* Training Services Agency (TSA) HMSO 1974, *Vocational preparation for young people* (TSA) HMSO 1975, and *Young people and work* Manpower Services Commission May 1977.
19 For summaries of their findings see *Royal Commission on the Distribution of Income and Wealth* report no. 1 HMSO 1975 pp. 156–59.
20 *Economic review* TUC 1976 p. 63.
21 *Royal Commission on the Distribution of Income and Wealth* report no. 1 para. 172.
22 Howard Glennester 'In praise of public expenditure' *New Statesman* 27 February 1976.
23 Anthony Crosland *Social democracy in Europe* Fabian Tract 1975 p. 7.

24 *Royal Commission on the Distribution of Income and Wealth* report no. 3 para. 144.
25 *Economic review* TUC 1976 p. 68.
26 *Public expenditure up to 1979–80* Cmnd 6393 HMSO 1976.
27 *Social security in the European Community* PEP 1975.
28 See *Constraints and choices: social policy and public expenditure* Centre for Studies in Social Policy 1976, and the *Fourth Report from the Expenditure Committee* HMSO 1977.

Part Three

The Implications

Chapter 9

Trade union democracy

The following section examines the implications of the trade union objectives outlined in previous chapters. It considers in turn trade union democracy, trade union structure and services, the role of the TUC and the Labour Party, and the impact on the community as a whole.

This chapter discusses trade union democracy – a subject which is important enough in its own right but which will assume an even greater significance if industry becomes more democratic. Trade unions derive their *raison d'être* and their strength from representing their members. Whenever they depart from their democratic function, they are fatally weakened. If a trade union leadership gets too far ahead of its membership, it will quickly discover that it represents nothing but itself. And a do-nothing leadership will eventually find that either its members will join another union or, where this is not possible because of closed shop arrangements or membership agreements with other unions, that they will act independently. Trade union participation in a democratic structure which extends to *all* kinds of industrial decision-making will make it all the more essential that trade union members and their shopfloor representatives are fully involved. If membership endorsement is lacking, the experiment in industrial democracy will either become an empty charade or provoke a damaging shopfloor revolt. There is also the question of individual rights; in this respect, the behaviour of a more powerful trade union movement must be of the highest standard. Lastly, a permanent trade union dialogue with government requires the continuing support of trade unionists if it is not to degenerate into a kind of corporatism. So trade union democracy is crucial to the main themes of this book.

THE IRON LAW OF OLIGARCHY?

In a previous chapter, it was pointed out that one of the current criticisms of trade unions is for their 'lack of democracy'. There is nothing particularly novel in this; indeed the most formidable critique of trade union democracy ever made was put forward by the German academic, Robert Michels, at the beginning of the twentieth century. Michels' famous work was mainly concerned with political parties; but he also concluded that 'in the trade union movement, the authoritarian character of the leaders and their tendency to rule democratic organisations on oligarchic lines, are even more pronounced than in the political organisations'.[1] He gave a number of reasons why the 'iron law of oligarchy' was applicable to trade unions: it was impossible, because of the need for a permanent organisation and for organisers to conduct negotiations and arrange strikes for trade unions, to operate on the basis of direct democracy; officials stuck like limpets to their jobs for mainly economic and social reasons; and, because of their expertise and prestige, the membership acquiesced in their virtual permanence in office. Oligarchic control was also reinforced by mass apathy: 'The majority of members are as indifferent to the organisation as the majority of the electors are to parliament.'[2] Michels pointed out that institutional needs could supplement and even displace the original goals of an organisation: 'The . . . doctrines are, whenever requisite, attenuated and deformed in accordance with the external needs of the organisation. Organisation becomes the vital essence . . . More and more invincible becomes its aversion to all aggressive action . . . Thus, from a means, organisation becomes an end.'[3]

On the surface, there seems to be much in British experience to support Michels' argument. Officials *have* gathered much of the decision-making power into their own hands. General secretaries usually remain in office, once elected, until they retire. The development of collective bargaining, particularly at national level, has resulted in a great deal of power being given to full-time officials. In a number of unions, officials are appointed, not elected. And even when they are subject to re-election (as in the predominantly craft unions), the man in possession has an inbuilt advantage. In some circumstances, trade union officials can become divorced from their members; even when this has not happened, the emergence of the professional trade unionist has undoubtedly modified the democratic character of trade unionism.

Of course, in almost all trade union rule books, there remain formidable constitutional checks on the arbitrary abuse of power – all the way up from the union branches, through district and regional committees, to union executives, conferences and final appeal courts. In theory, the membership, through its elected representatives at union conferences and on governing committees at various levels, is supreme. In practice, the situation is somewhat different. Participation in elections, as membership involvement in union affairs generally above shopfloor level, is usually low. The power of conferences, in the rule book usually the dominant body, is in reality limited. In some cases, conferences are only bi-annual. Even when they take place annually, they usually only determine broad lines of policy; in normal circumstances it is just not possible for a conference to control the twists and turns of a fast moving negotiating situation. The powers of union executives vary. But, in many unions, executives are composed of those who (even when directly elected from the shopfloor) are professionals in all but name.

However, despite these developments, it is not the case that power in trade unions is concentrated solely in the hands of the officials. On the contrary, in a very real sense, power comes from below. Professor Clegg, in his survey of trade union government, concluded that 'it is clear that British trade unions are not autocracies, and that trade union members have available a number of channels, varying from union to union, through which they can exert influence over their leaders'.[5] He pointed to the existence of factions within trade unions, to the effect of the separation and decentralisation of power, and to the influence of full-time officials, in close contact with the members, as checks on the leaders. He also argued that low polls in union elections do not necessarily prove that the votes are unrepresentative of the views of the membership as a whole.

As far as union elections are concerned, the dominant influence tends to be that of the shop stewards. In a few unions, polling, because of exceptional circumstances, is high. Mineworkers, who vote at the pit head, usually achieve a 60 per cent level.[6] But, in the majority of unions, balloting takes place at branch level and the level of involvement, even for major posts, is far lower (though this is disguised, as in the cases of the GMWU and USDAW, by the system of allowing the majority decision of those attending branch meetings – probably little more than 5 per cent – to cast the vote of the whole branch membership as a block). There is some evidence that voting by postal ballot leads to rather higher levels of participation. In the engineering section of the AUEW it is said that the change to election by postal ballot (made in 1973) has trebled the level of participation – from about 10 per cent to about 33 per cent.[7] But, in most circumstances and in most trade unions, the shop stewards, who are the most frequent attenders at branch meetings and to whom the members are likely, in any case, to turn for advice as to the merits of the different candidates, decide the outcome of the elections. Thus 'trade union elections can be represented as a form of indirect election'.[8]

In nearly all unions, channels exist through which opposition can be voiced. The engineering section of the AUEW and the mine-workers have an unofficial party system which is expressed in left-right terms, while in most unions, there are industrial and geographical alliances which coalesce from time to time. Even in those unions in which the leadership is generally considered to be in a powerful position, there are ways in which those who wish to challenge the platform can exert an effective influence. The GMWU has had, for many years, a 'mainstream' Labour leadership. But this does not mean that there is no opposition. On the contrary, a dissident viewpoint has only to capture one of the regional delegations to be guaranteed a hearing at conference. And, in the 1972 election for general secretary, there were a number of different factions (including not only those representing regional interests but also radical opinion as well); as it turned out, conditions were favourable for the election of a national official, David Basnett, whose backing by the younger modernising element made up for his lack of initial support in the biggest regions.

There are also other powerful checks on the central authority in most unions. The best known example is the separation of power in the engineering section of the AUEW (which is said to be based on the constitution of the United States). The main features of this system are strong district committees which join together to elect delegates to the union national committee, a seven member executive elected by separate constituencies, and a president and general secretary elected by the whole union. The power of the two chief executive officers is circumscribed not only by the executive but also by the virtual autonomy of the district committees, on which shop stewards are heavily represented. Other unions also have a decentralised structure. In the NUM, the areas are very powerful, so much so that, in some respects, the national union amounts to little more than the old Miners' Federation. Though in 1975 there were some changes in the government of the GMWU, which are described later in this chapter, the regions have retained their traditional autonomy and are represented on the union's governing body. Even in the TGWU, whose constitution is in theory far more centralised than either that of the NUM or the GMWU, the role played by the trade group committees and secretary in industrial affairs gives them considerable influence, and, though the TGWU regional secretaries cannot be members of the executive, the career of Jack Jones shows that it is possible for a regional official who is in close touch with his shop stewards to build up a position of power within the union.

In democratic theory, trade union officials, as full-time professionals, are part of the union oligarchy. In practice, they often act as channels for the views of the membership and, therefore, as a check on the leadership. It is not surprising that this should be so. As part of their duties, officials are in constant contact with union activities. They are thus in a position to gauge the feelings of the members and transmit them to the union leaders.

But the most important check on trade union leaders is the increase in shopfloor power. Though the spread of closed shop arrangements and of inter-union membership agreements prevents most discontented trade union members from 'voting with their feet' by joining another union, the rank and file in many companies and industries are now in a position either to act independently of the leadership or to exert considerable influence over it. This development has had a salutary effect on trade union leaders who, because they operate within a culture which is expressly democratic, are, in any case, more likely to pay attention to their members' views.

This suggests that pessimistic accounts of trade union democracy have been over-concerned with formal mechanisms and have ignored the realities of trade union power. The priority today is not so much to design new constraints on the arbitrary use of power (though, as is argued later, these can be of use) but to devise ways of increasing shopfloor involvement and influence in trade union decision-making, so that trade union leaders, while providing effective leadership, remain responsive to their members.

THE ROLE OF LEADERSHIP

Trade unions need leaders. Their role may have changed in emphasis and style. In the conditions of the 1930s when there was little shopfloor bargaining or overt pressures from the shopfloor, a more authoritarian form of leadership may have been viable. Today any trade union official who attempts to act in an authoritarian way is in immediate danger of having his decisions rejected.

He has to win the consent of his members through persuasion; he cannot expect their automatic obedience. As Jack Jones has pointed out, 'the power of the leader is not that of controlling the members . . . it must be the authority that comes from persuasion, experience and judgement . . . he has to involve himself in making policy, discussing strategy, and deciding tactics *with* the officials and stewards, and not *for* them'.[9] But to accept that their role has changed is not to say that there is no longer any place for trade union leaders. On the contrary, a creative and determined national leadership is as necessary today as it ever was.

It is possible to conceive of a trade union movement fragmented into a collection of purely factory-based unions without national leadership, but this would certainly reduce the effectiveness of trade unionism.

Consider, first, the power position. A trade union which was based solely on a single factory or even on a single company would be quickly picked off by an employer in a dispute. The strength of a group of workers is derived not only from its own bargaining position, but also from the power of other groups and also of workers in other factories. It is true that, in some industries, certain occupations and factories have more bargaining power than others; but, in order to buttress the position even of powerful groups of workers, a trade union official needs to have the ability to call on other workers in other factories. And when it comes to supporting those workers who are in a weak bargaining position, then a wider backing is absolutely essential. The watchword of the GMWU – through unity strength – is no outworn cliché; rather it is a simple acknowledgement of the power reality. Any claim which has more than local implications has to have the backing of all the workers involved.

The need for a wider dimension is not merely to maximise trade union power. It is also to ensure that employees have a better chance of influencing their working environment. A trade unionism which was confined purely to plant level would be unable to influence decisions which are made at a higher level and yet, as we have seen, affect the lives of workers very considerably. It is little use a union being perfectly equipped to establish employee rights at plant level if the framework within which plant level decisions are taken is still decided unilaterally at boardroom level. Workers need their representatives to participate in managerial decision-making at all levels. Trade unions also need to be able to argue at national level with governments, particularly about their attitude towards unions and collective bargaining, their management of the economy and their handling of social affairs. Even shopfloor activity is more effective if it is part of a wider programme. Of course, in any shopfloor bargain many items will be particular to that plant or factory – and, in any strategy for shopfloor advance, some elements will be emphasized more in one factory than in another. But, as has already been pointed out, the spread of plant bargaining is uneven; in some factories and companies workers' representatives have won the right to bargain about a whole host of subjects, while, in other factories, even those shop stewards who represent work groups in a potentially powerful position have been left far behind. What is needed above all is strategy and co-ordination. In short, if trade unions are to represent their members effectively, there must be a coherent response at all levels at which decisions are made.

If there is to be a coherent trade union response, then national leaders are needed. No trade union programme can be effective unless it is based on the needs and aspirations of the membership; but if the members' demands are to be organised in a consistent and realistic set of policies, there must be leadership. A trade union congress carries a series of resolutions which may or may not be consistent with each other and which may or may not be realistic. Union branches may want rapidly rising money wages and strict price control at one and the same time; they may want a substantial improvement in the position of the low paid while, at the same time, maintaining differentials; they will almost certainly want higher pensions and other benefits, better housing, more schools and more hospitals, and so on, irrespective of economic conditions. So, while conference resolutions fix the parameters for trade union policies, someone has to try to set the priorities – and that someone can only be the leadership. Even in the more limited sphere of collective bargaining, some freedom must be entrusted to the trade union negotiator. Of course, the industrial conferences and negotiating committees (which are considered later in this chapter) will provide the framework within which he operates. And he will be constantly aware of the need to reach a settlement which is acceptable to his members. But, in most negotiations, there will have to be an ordering of priorities; to achieve some objectives, others will have to be postponed or modified. At every stage, the official will have to use his own judgement – an essential ingredient in successful leadership. And, even though the system of boardroom representation will be based on the company, it will require the training, servicing and monitoring which only the national trade unions can provide.

There is, in truth, no substitute for leadership. A purely localised trade unionism would not only be far less effective in power terms; it would also fail to protect and advance workers' interests in the way that is now required. An imaginative and courageous high command is needed to translate the aspirations of the shopfloor into a consistent and realistic strategy. Trade union leaders, like politicians, must, at all times, listen to and articulate their members' views. But again, like politicians (and managers), they have to set priorities and formulate policies. And although they cannot order, only persuade, this persuasion is and should be a vital element in trade union democracy.

TRADITIONAL METHODS

But, if modern trade unionism requires leadership, it also needs a vigorous lay democracy. As has been argued previously, if industrial democracy is to become a reality, the shopfloor must be fully involved. And if trade union leaders are to take part in a permanent dialogue with government on industrial relations and economic and social issues, they will need to ensure they have the backing of their members. Over the last decade, some important initiatives to improve trade union democracy have already been taken. This suggests that the right approach is for the best union practice to become more widespread.[10]

It is, however, important to realise that there can never be an entirely uniform response. Trade unions will differ according to their membership and industrial situation. Thus a solution which seems suitable to a union like the engineering section of the AUEW, whose members are in a strong bargaining position, may be less appropriate to other unions, like the TGWU and the GMWU, whose membership is both less skilled and more general. But, if there can be no hard and fast blueprint, it is quite proper to put forward a set of guidelines for internal democratic advance.

It has already been argued that the main emphasis in any reform programme should be on devising ways of increasing shopfloor involvement in trade union decision-making, rather than on designing new constraints on the use of trade union power. However, if trade union membership is to be expanded and to become the main basis of participation in industrial democracy, then there must be effective safeguards for individuals, particularly against arbitrary refusal to admit workers to membership and against unreasonable exclusions from membership. The Donovan Report recommended the adoption by unions of standard rules on admission, exclusion, discipline, disputes between a union and members, and elections. It also advocated the setting up of an independent review body to which, in the last resort, trade union members would have the right of appeal.[11] Following the Donovan Report, the TUC circulated to trade unions recommended rules, including the points mentioned by Donovan, and also suggested that unions should have an effective appeals system as part of their rules to which aggrieved individuals could apply. Though there was an encouraging initial response from a number of unions to the TUC initiative, trade union hostility to the wide powers over trade union rule books, given to the registrar and to the courts under the 1971 Industrial Relations Act, set back the impetus of reform. When the Labour Government repealed this Act in 1974, it did not take up the Donovan proposal and instead the TUC agreed to establish a body whose members were appointed after consultation with the Secretary of State for Employment, to which aggrieved individuals could, in the last resort, appeal. It is too early to say whether this new machinery will prove adequate. What is clear, however, is that the TUC must ensure that *all* trade union rule books contain adequate safeguards and that, in addition to common law rights, there is an effective appeals procedure. For, if trade union power is to be increased, trade unionists will need to be even more on their guard than in the past against the misuse of that power (see chapter 12 for a fuller discussion of this vital point).

Turning to the question of shopfloor involvement in decision-making, it is well to consider, first, whether it is possible to improve the traditional methods of participation, through the election of officials and the strengthening of executives and conferences.

Those unions with a strong craft basis, like the engineering section of the AUEW and the EETU-PTU, have laid the greatest stress on regular direct elections as the best means of ensuring that officials remain responsive to the membership. Many other unions, including the TGWU and the GMWU, believe that, though elections have a role to play in furthering participation, it is equally important to give officials, once they have proved their ability, some prospect of continuous service. Elections have obvious advantages, in that officials with the widest appeal are chosen, while those who have lost the confidence of the membership can be replaced.

Certainly, in choosing the chief executive of a union, there are overwhelming arguments for elections. Whether there ought also to be regular re-election (say once every five years) is more debatable. While the fact of having to face re-election is at least a partial guarantee that a general secretary will not lose touch with his members, regular election can sometimes encourage persistent factionalism. However, those unions without a re-election process ought at least to insist on a relatively young retiring age for their leaders. The pressures on general secretaries are immense and, in most cases, they will already have done their best work by the time they have reached sixty.

As far as less senior trade union officials are concerned, it is difficult to lay down any hard and fast rule. The strict adherence by the engineering section of the AUEW to the craft tradition of direct and regular election of all classes of full-time officials has much to recommend it. But against the craft approach, one has also to take into account the need for well trained and efficient officials who are sometimes prepared, in the long term interest of their members, to put their own authority on the line. However, when trade unions do elect their officials, it is essential to ensure that elections are fairly conducted and as many members vote as possible. The pithead balloting which has such a beneficial effect on turnout in the National Union of Mineworkers (NUM) elections is a special case (though there may be lessons here for other mainly industrial unions); but there is no reason why balloting by post, which is already the rule for elections in the EETU-PTU and in the engineering section of the AUEW, should not be more widely adopted. It would be wrong to impose this by law. But there is a stronger case for government assistance in meeting the increasingly heavy cost of postal ballots.

The role of the executive becomes crucial when trade union officials are appointed and not elected. Allan Flanders argued persuasively that 'in this case it is the more important to ensure that policy decisions are made by "lay" representatives of the members if an uncontrolled bureaucracy is to be avoided'.[12] It has been pointed out earlier that, in many cases, the so-called lay representatives are full-time union representatives and very often become professionals. However, the all lay executives of the NUR are allowed only a three-year period in office, after which they are not allowed to stand for re-election. In a number of white collar unions, which almost always appoint their officials, there are strong lay executives; two examples are NALGO and the National Union of Teachers (NUT). During the 1970s, other unions have increased the proportion of lay members on their executives. In 1975, the GMWU executive, on which there had been four regional secretaries and five lay members, was expanded so that, in addition to the chairman and the general secretary, each of the ten regions was represented by two lay representatives, in addition to the regional secretary. During 1975, NUPE also increased lay representation on its executive.

The limitations on trade union conferences in relation to industrial negotiations have already been stressed. However, they have a vital part to play in voicing members' general demands and in settling the framework of trade union policy. It is, therefore, essential that those who attend conferences should fully reflect the views of the shopfloor and not just those of a minority. It is particularly import-ant that younger members and female trade unionists should be present. Too often trade union conferences seem to be attended by delegates who are overwhelmingly male and middle-aged. This is perhaps the reason why some of the vital shopfloor issues, such as job satisfaction, control over the working environment and equal opportunity have not yet been reflected adequately in conference resolutions. If the membership is to participate in union govern-ment, then union conferences must represent more accurately (perhaps through a system of quotas) the views of trade union members.

NEW FORMS

But, increasingly, trade unions have realised that they need to create *other* ways of involving their members and their representa-tives in their work. Like management and government, they have had to come to terms with the growth in shopfloor power. If they were to represent their members adequately, they had to build new machinery to bring the shopfloor and its representatives into closer contact with their officials, and make negotiating bodies more responsive to their demands. A number of useful devices, which are examined below, have been developed to encourage shopfloor involvement. But perhaps more crucial than any of them is the change in the trade union attitude to the representatives of the shopfloor – the shop stewards (who are likely to play an even more important role in the new system proposed in this book).

In 1968, the Donovan Commission had criticised trade unions in the following terms: 'We believe that the processes of union government should be modified to accommodate shop stewards and work groups more adequately than they now do.'[13] Since then, there has been a marked change in official trade union attitudes. Whereas, at the beginning of the 1960s, many trade union officials tended to look on shop stewards as a challenge to their authority, now these are seen increasingly as vital to trade union organisation. One of the key figures in this shift of opinion was the general secretary of the TGWU, Jack Jones, who was elected in 1968. The TGWU has a lay executive, but traditionally this has been dominated by the general secretary, while, as a general union with a predominantly semi-skilled membership, full-time negotiators had a great deal of autonomy. Jones, with direct experience of the car industry and engineering in the Midlands, realised that the growth of shop-floor power made it essential to give shop stewards more influence and prestige within the union. Using his powerful position as general secretary, he emphasised the key role of shop stewards and the necessity of involving them in the work of the union. In 1969 he outlined his aims as follows: 'I am working for a system where not a few trade union officials control the situation but a dedicated, well-trained and intelligent body of trades union members is represented by hundreds of thousands of lay representatives every one of whom is capable of helping to resolve industrial problems and assist in collective bargaining and the conclusion of agreements.'[14]

The other large general union, the GMWU, was slower to respond to the growth in shopfloor power, in part because of its base in the public sector. But, following increased militancy amongst its public sector employees at the end of the 1960s and the traumatic effect of the 1970 Pilkington strike which appeared to be as much a strike against the union as against the employers, and with the advent in 1972 of David Basnett, (the national official involved in the Pilkington strike of 1970[15]), as general secretary, the executive put its authority behind a policy to increase the influence of the union's shop stewards and to promote their participation in decision-making. In other unions, like the EETU-PTU, USDAW and NUPE, there were similar developments. However, in the engineering section of the AUEW, shop stewards had always played an important role. Indeed, there is provision for direct representation of shop stewards on the union's district committees, while many of the remaining committee members are shop stewards. Thus, the union's leaders saw little need for any new initiative, even though the union's back-up services for their shop stewards were inadequate.

However, it is indeed becoming increasingly clear that a strategy for increasing shopfloor participation in trade union affairs has to ensure that shop stewards have not only the opportunity to participate but also that full use is made of that opportunity. It is not just a question of devising the right institutional arrangements, important though these are; it is also necessary to provide shop stewards with support so that, in terms of information, training and facilities, they are in a position to argue their case within the union from a position of some strength. The next chapter looks at the gaps in union servicing in more detail, particularly in relation to bargaining and industrial democracy. However, what is true in this context applies equally to that of internal democracy. Without more effective trade union education, shop stewards will not be in a position to take advantage of internal democratic reforms; they will also be less well equipped to discuss corporate policy with their boardroom representatives at report-back meetings.

A number of methods have been developed to encourage shop-floor participation in the main work of trade unions, collective bargaining. These include reference back and lay representation on negotiating bodies. The idea that, after negotiations, officials should refer back settlements to the membership for their approval was initiated by the TGWU and has been adopted by a number of unions. Though it may not always be appropriate, it has obvious advantages. Some unions have also put shopfloor representatives onto negotiating bodies. Again, it is obviously useful to have shop-floor opinion represented at negotiations though, in a situation in which a union has only a limited number of seats and represent-atives, and representatives are responsible to members in a large number of small sites and plants, representation by an official may sometimes be more effective. However, in the new democratic structure at enterprise level (proposed in chapter 6 and 7) the joint representation committee (JRC) will play a crucial part, and it is essential that this should be predominantly a committee of shop-floor representatives.

One of the most interesting developments has been that of the industrial conference. The idea was pioneered by the EETU–PTU in the aftermath of the Communist ballot-rigging scandal. The new leadership abolished the old area committees and set up in their place industrial conferences for shipbuilding, electricity supply, engineering and electricity contracting. Every year, shop stewards in the industry concerned come together for an area conference, and every other year they elect delegates and forward motions to a national conference.

Other unions have created similar structures, including the GMWU and USDAW. The GMWU (though it is, as mentioned earlier, more regionally decentralised than the TGWU) lacked the trade group structure which made it easier for that union to involve its shop stewards in the shaping of bargaining strategy. So, in 1969, the GMWU set up a system of conferences for all its major industries, at which shopfloor representatives could partici- pate in the determination of negotiating policy. After a few years' experimentation, the system was reviewed.[16]

Though the union's congress remained the supreme authority, the industrial conferences had developed considerable power in their particular section of industry. Originally, half a dozen industrial groupings had been envisaged as forming the basis of the industrial conference system; in practice, however, industrial conferences had been convened for narrower groupings and directly related to specific negotiating machinery. A much wider and more detailed list of industries for which a conference should be held was, there- fore, drawn up in 1975. In order to make these conferences fully representative of shopfloor opinion, a number of other specific recommendations were also made; these included regular convening of annual regional conferences prior to a national conference, a uniform system of elections for both regional and national con- ferences, and a more effective system of reporting back to branches. So the industrial conference is potentially an extremely useful way of influencing negotiating policy; it could also become the forum at which experiments in boardroom level representation were reviewed.

So far we have considered ways in which trade unions can be made more responsive to shop stewards. We need also to consider how the union contacts its members. It has already been shown in chapter 3 how trade union branches are inadequate as channels of communication with the membership, because the vast majority of union members simply do not bother to attend meetings. For most members, their shop steward is the contact with the union; so giving shop stewards a greater say in trade union affairs in itself improves democracy within trade unions. But it is also important, particularly with the advances in industrial democracy proposed in this book, that union members themselves have some opportunity of being involved.

Outside critics often argue that trade union democracy would be improved by frequent balloting of members. Their assumption is that, if trade union leaders were forced to consider their members over disputes, there would be fewer strikes. The Donovan Commis- sion, however, pointed out that there was little justification for the view that workers were less likely to vote for strike action than their leaders.[17] Experience during the 1970s on the railways and in the mining industry certainly confirms the commission's opposition to compulsory ballots.

There is, however, a case for the use of ballots in the right circumstances. They can sometimes prevent a trade union leadership from going out on a limb over an issue where membership backing is not wholehearted, or alternatively give it the confidence which comes from solid support. But ballot of the membership needs to be part of an overall democratic system, one of an armoury of weapons which a trade union leader needs to stimulate membership participation. By itself, it is no panacea.

It is of more importance to reform and supplement the trade union branch. The branch remains essential both as an administrative unit and a meeting place for shop stewards. But, unless it is based on the workplace (something which is sometimes not possible where there is a wide scatter of membership) and meets there too, it is of little use as a vehicle for membership participation. If branches cannot be thus reformed, they will need to be supplemented by membership meetings at factory or on site. Such changes will become even more necessary if the report-back arrangements, so central to the representative system at boardroom level, are to be effective.

Finally, trade unions need to ensure that their internal communication is more effective. They must examine the role of union journals and see that at least the majority of their members get a copy. There is also a strong case for a lively correspondence column, which acts as a forum for debate within the union and a vehicle for membership feedback.

Extensions of trade union democracy will be essential if the new democratic system, proposed in earlier chapters is to become a reality. What is now required is an increase in shopfloor participation in decision-making, in order to ensure that trade union leaders, whose role continues to be of great importance, remain responsive to their members. This chapter has suggested that the most practical way forward is for the best union practice to become the rule rather than the exception and has proposed a younger retiring age for general secretaries, and particularly where they are not re-elected, government assistance to defray the cost of postal ballots, predominantly lay governing bodies where officials are not elected, shopfloor participation in negotiating and other bodies (including joint representation committees), more industrial conferences, more workplace branches and shopfloor meetings (which will become even more important if employee representatives at boardroom level are to keep in touch with their constituents).

REFERENCES

1 R. W. E. Michels *Political parties* (1911) English edition 1915 p. 143 (quoted in Richard Hyman *Marxism and the sociology of trade unionism* Pluto Press 1971 p. 14).
2 *Political parties* pp. 50–51.
3 *Political parties* pp. 369–73.
4 See *Marxism and the sociology of trade unionism* p. 11.
5 *The system of industrial relations* p. 112.
6 *Royal Commission Research Paper no. 5* Part 2 p. 47.
7 See Robert Taylor 'Towards more union democracy' *Socialist Commentary* December 1974.
8 *The system of industrial relations* p. 82.
9 Jack Jones in *The Sunday Times* 1 March 1970.
10 The rest of the chapter is based on my article 'Democracy within the unions' *Socialist Commentary* September 1974.
11 *Royal Commission on Trade Unions and Employers' Associations* paras. 648–69.
12 *Trade unions* p. 50.
13 *Royal Commission on Trade Unions and Employers' Associations* paras. 196–99.
14 Jack Jones *Trade unionism in the seventies* TGWU pamphlet 1970.
15 The Pilkington dispute of 1970 was as much a strike against the union as against the company.
16 *Industrial conferences* GMWU report 1975, and the earlier GMWU policy document *Union reorganisation* 1969.
17 *Royal Commission on Trade Unions and Employers' Associations* paras. 426–30.

Chapter 10

Trade union structure and services

This chapter looks at trade union structure and services. The case for reforms in trade union structure and for expansion of trade union services is already compelling; it becomes overwhelming if the implications of the democratic objectives outlined in the previous section are taken into account. As it is, the existing trade union structure is, in some respects, already a barrier to effective representation. If a new level of representation at boardroom level is added, then it becomes all the more essential that trade unions change themselves. Similarly, trade union services are even now inadequate. How much worse will they appear, when trade unions adopt new functions?

INDUSTRIAL UNIONISM: THE WRONG SOLUTION

As far as trade union structure is concerned, the criterion by which it should be judged should not be how far it matches up to some ideal form but to what extent it assists in the achievement of trade union objectives. If, in some respects, particularly in relation to the high standard of representation and co-ordination which is now required, existing trade union structure is a hindrance, then there is a strong case, not for the espousal of a particular organisational panacea but for the adoption of detailed measures which will remedy the shortcomings.

As was mentioned in chapter 5, some advocate a trade unionism organised on a partly industrial basis. But arguments for industrial unionism ignore both the historical and more recent development of British trade unions and the advantages which are derived from the present structure.

The fact is that industrial unionism arrived too late on the scene in this country. By the time it appeared 'substantial parts of the territory which industrial unions might be expected to occupy had already been possessed either by stubborn, craft-conscious unions or by the new amorphous general labour unions'.[1] The first stable trade union organisation, which emerged during the third quarter of the nineteenth century, was craft-based. The growth of the Amalgamated Society of Engineers (the forerunner of the AUEW) and the Amalgamated Society of Carpenters and Joiners (the forerunner of UCAIT) depended largely on the ability of skilled craftsmen to control entry to the labour market. The second type of organisation – general unionism – traces its existence back to the 'new unionism' of 1889. The unions which sprang up were literally new, not simply because they grew up then but also because they recruited among groups of mostly unskilled workers previously almost untouched by trade unionism.[2] In addition (though this often came about by accident) many of these unions were general. Setting out to cater for particular groups of workers like gas workers, and dockers, they found others clamouring to join. This general form of organisation, though it might at first be built on only a few industries, formed the base for future development, and led, through the great amalgamations of the 1920s, to the two giant general unions of today – the Transport and General Workers' Union and the General and Municipal Workers' Union.

Thus, when industrial unionism was first advocated in the years after 1909 by syndicalists and by those who believed in a more 'rational' trade union structure, the organisation of skill across industrial boundaries proved an unsurmountable barrier to its spread. In addition, in many industries, the more adaptable general unions were in a better position to organise and service their membership than purely industrial unions, so much so that, despite the growth of some mainly industrial unions, such as the miners, the railwaymen, the steel workers, and the post office workers, it was the general unions who benefited most from the first great period (1911–21) of trade union expansion.

The predominant position of general and craft-dominated unions was confirmed in the second period of trade union growth, during and immediately after the second world war. Significantly, by then the craft unions had modified their orginal recruiting techniques. In 1926, the Engineers opened their ranks to unskilled male engineering workers, and, when female employment expanded during the second world war, women also became eligible for membership. Other craft unions (including the electricians, the vehicle builders, the foundry workers and the building trade workers) followed their example. By adapting their methods in this way, some of the craft-dominated unions began to match the pace of general workers union growth to the extent that, out of the six major unions today, two, the Engineers and the Electricians, were formerly craft unions which had become less exclusive.

The emergence of white collar unionism added to rather than simplified the variety of trade union structure. Though the majority of white collar workers belong to exclusively white collar unions, manual unions (including the Transport and General Workers, the General and Municipal Workers, the Engineers and the Electricians) are extending their organisation into this field. Of the white collar unions, some are organised on occupational lines, others are multi-occupational, while a few, including the biggest of all, the National Association of Local Government Officers, might be said to resemble a general union recruiting in the public sector white collar catchment area.

Thus the tendency of British trade unionism has not been towards industrial unionism. On the contrary, as John Hughes pointed out in his research paper for the Donovan Commission,[3] the main trend is one of continued growth, partly by amalgamation, of large open unions, which are not necessarily entirely general in their approach to organisation and recruitment, but take a broad defini-tion of their sector of operation and of the occupational grades they organise. The dominance of this trend is illustrated by the fact that all of the six largest unions – the TGWU, the AUEW, the GMWU, NALGO, the EETU-PTU, and NUPE – can be described as open.

The strength of open unionism means that, short of a major cataclysm, the construction of British trade unions on industrial lines is not a practical possibility. As the Donovan Commission pointed out, it would mean the dismemberment of almost every major and expanding union in the country and it is, therefore, highly improbable that the British trade union movement will ever agree voluntarily to industrial unionism.[4]

In any case, there is a positive case to be made for open unionism. New technologies are continually breaking down conventional industrial classifications, while many large companies now straddle industrial boundaries. The flexibility of the open technique of organisation makes it possible for trade unions to adapt more easily to industrial change, while industrial unions are able to compensate elsewhere for a secular decline in membership and are perhaps more ready to adopt a more defensive stance. Their fluid structure also enables these open unions to cater for the varied representa-tional needs (skill, occupational, industrial, regional, etc.) of their members more effectively. There is also much in Allan Flanders'

contention that 'the reluctance of the British trade unions to make
a fetish of any particular type of organisation has probably contributed to their strength and sense of common purpose'.[5] It is
certainly unlikely that an insistence by the TUC on industrial
unionism would have increased the unity of a movement distinguished for its organisational diversity.

Critics of the movement have also made much of the apparent
proliferation of British trade unions. Yet, in fact, the number of
trade unions has fallen considerably. In 1900, there were 1,323
unions with a total membership of a little over 2 million. In 1960
there were 664 unions with a total membership of over 10 million.
In 1974 there were 488 unions, with a total membership of just
under 12 million. It is true that there are about 250 small trade
unions, but they account for only 0·6 per cent of total membership.
Not only do the combined membership of the twenty-five largest
unions add up to more than three-quarters of total union membership; the nine largest unions organise over half and the big three
(the TGWU, the AUEW, and the GMWU) actually organise about
a third.[6] So British trade unionism is characterised by a high concentration of union membership in a small number of unions – a
concentration, which with amalgamation (see below), is bound to
become greater. As for the small unions, if they continue to survive
(despite the demands of trade union members generally for a higher
quality service and despite rising administrative costs) then who is to
say there is not a case for their continued existence? Quite often
small unions, highly geographically concentrated and operating
in restricted and limited fields, have given and may possibly go on
giving a reasonable service to their members.

HOW TO REFORM 'COMPETITIVE' UNIONISM

The real structural problem is not so much the excessive number of
trade unions but the consequences of the overlapping membership
interest of the major unions. It is, however, important to be clear
that some aspects of multi-unionism are not necessarily harmful.
It is possible to have a factory in which, though there are a number
of different unions, each recruits only among a particular group of
workers. Thus one union represents supervisors, another clerical
groups, a third craftsmen, and the fourth unskilled and so on. This
type of multiple representation need not lead to inter-union friction.
Even when unions are competing for the same class of membership,
this may not be disadvantageous provided they do not organise in

the same factory. The workers' side of joint industrial councils often contains competing unions who have grown accustomed over the years to putting forward joint policies, while, on a wider basis, federations, like the Confederation of Shipbuilding and Engineering Unions, have performed a similar function. However there is little to be said in favour of multi-unionism which involves competition within a plant for the same kind of membership.

This type of multi-unionism is not in the best interests of the trade union movement. It can lead to disputes which are caused not by the needs of the workforce but by the persistent and almost neurotic organisational self-assertion of rival unions. Even where some sort of *modus vivendi* is patched together, it is usually chronically difficult to achieve any kind of long term policy co-ordination and inevitably a system of double servicing grows up which is extremely wasteful of scarce union resources. It is a reflection on the disadvantages of this kind of multi-unionism that when the need arises shop stewards of different unions often have to meet together unofficially. The futility of such competition, which affects large numbers of mainly unskilled workers, is already highlighted by existing bargaining structures and will be accentuated by the introduction of boardroom representation. It will be difficult enough to build up an effective system of employee directors without having also to cope with jurisdictional and other kinds of sectional disputes.

The onus is, therefore, on the trade union movement to tackle the competitive aspect of the multi-union problem more effectively than in the past. In 1968 the Donovan Commission made a number of suggestions, including an increase in the number of trade union amalgamations, more closer-working arrangements between unions, and the adoption by the TUC of the principle of 'one union for one grade of work within one factory' as a guide for future structural development.[7] However, partly because of the diversion of trade union thought and energy caused by the Industrial Relations Act, the affiliated trade unions did not respond as vigorously as they ought to have done to the 1970 TUC interim report on structure.[8]

Amalgamation has an extremely important part to play in reducing inter-union rivalry. Indeed, as the history of British trade unionism illustrates, competing unions have quite often ended their rivalry by combining. During the 1960s, partly as a result of the Amalgamation Act of 1964, the pace of trade union amalgamations increased. Some major mergers took place, including the creation of the Amalgamated Society of Boilermakers, Shipwrights and Blacksmiths, the Society of Graphical and Allied Trades, the merging of the Foundry Workers and the Draughtsmen with the Engineers, and in the white collar field, the emergence of the Association of Scientific, Technical and Managerial Staffs. In the 1970s, however, though a number of smaller unions have been swallowed up by the major unions, there have not been any really large scale amalgamations. Discussions took place between the EETU-PTU and the GMWU, and between the EETU-PTU and the AUEW but they came to nothing. Certainly, there are many obstacles in the way of successful amalgamations, including conflicting union structures, the attitudes of activists, and the ambitions of trade union leaders. And sometimes mergers, while resolving old inter-union disputes, can open up fresh ones. But there is now an overwhelming argument for a fresh initiative by the TUC, not so much to encourage amalgamation for its own sake, but to see how far and in what sectors it is possible, by amalgamation, to eliminate wasteful and unhealthy inter-union competition. If a merger between two or more of the competing open giants could be achieved, the gains in terms of better union co-ordination, more effective servicing and a higher standard of representation would be immense.[9]

However, amalgamation negotiations take time. There are more immediate advantages to be secured from developing a systematic set of closer-working arrangements between unions. Over the years a number of such agreements have been signed; the most important is the one between the Transport and General Workers and the General and Municipal Workers which provides for the transfer of members without loss of their accumulated rights. Under this agreement, the two great general unions have negotiated 'spheres of influence' deals, including one, in 1974, dividing up recruitment in the hotel industry. There should now be an examination of all those industries and sectors in which unions compete for the same grade of membership to see where closer-working and spheres of influence agreements should be made, and more effective co-ordinating machinery set up, and between which unions. If four major competing unions in engineering – the AUEW, the EETU-PTU, TGWU and the GMWU – could arrive at a really effective co-ordinating arrangement (including the setting up of joint representation committees to direct company level bargaining and boardroom representation), it would do much to overcome one of the main structural flaws in British trade unionism. A similar deal in the public services between the unions representing local authority manual workers and hospital staff would be almost equally advantageous. And, if wasteful inter-union warfare is to be averted, similar agreements should be rapidly made in the white collar field. As well as these kind of arrangements, direct exchange of memberships, particularly between the two great general unions is also desirable. In 1964, a joint working party of the two unions discussed the possibility of the GMWU leaving municipal transport entirely to the TGWU, in return for the withdrawal of the TGWU from the gas industry in favour of the GMWU. In 1976, discussions on closer-working between the two unions were re-started which could lead to action in a number of cases. It would be good for trade unionism if other competing unions also became involved.

In overcoming the difficulties which arise from multi-unionism, the TUC ought to play a major part. The principles of the TUC 'Bridlington agreement' and the revised version of rule 12 of congress have helped the movement in dealing with some of the more blatant consequences of inter-union rivalry. But as the TUC itself has admitted, they represent 'at best ways of solving problems that should never have arisen'.[10] The time has come when the TUC must claim for itself a more positive role. If individual unions continue to drag their feet, the TUC must take the initiative in bringing them together on a systematic and regular basis. As a first step, all unions should be asked to examine their closer-working arrangements. This ought to lead to a whole spate of new spheres of influence agreements and more effective co-ordination, including the setting up of joint representation committees where appropriate. Then, there should be further discussion to see where membership exchanges can be made, both on a company and industrial basis. In a number of cases such negotiations could pave the way to amalgamation, or in other cases lead to looser arrangements such as federations or 'dual membership' deals. The TUC might issue guidelines for these more ambitious agreements. In particular, they should point out the importance of building up internal groupings (such as trade groups and industrial conferences) not only from the democratic viewpoint (as described in the last chapter) but also as a means of persuading unions to join together. Unions are far more likely to agree to amalgamation or federation if they can retain some form of identity within the larger unit.

THE NEED FOR BETTER SERVICES

There is already an increasing and persistent call, from the shop-floor and from trade union officials themselves, for more and better trade union services. If trade unions are to extend collective bargaining to seek representation at boardroom level and to develop a wider role, the argument for the expansion of trade union services will be even more compelling – as will be the case for a radical increase in the financial resources of trade unions.

As far as shop stewards are concerned, they are convinced of the need for better servicing. It is true that, in one sense, their power depends largely on organisation. But they are also well aware that their position as representatives is immeasurably strengthened if they are technically equipped to bargain on something like equal terms with management and, where necessary, to call on the services of skilled full-time officials, backed by union specialist departments. At the very least, they need some countervailing power to the immense resources available to the management of the larger corporation, which are likely to include industrial and personnel specialists, experts in work study, productivity and job evaluation, economists and accountants, lawyers and publicists. Full-time officials, faced by demands from the shopfloor for better quality and more frequent advice, the increasing complexity of negotiations, and a growing involvement in the interpretation of industrial and social legislation as well as in the manning of various governmental and non-governmental bodies, are almost unanimous in the view that they need more and better support services.

A big increase in trade union functions will make existing trade union services seem even more inadequate. At shopfloor level, it has been argued that there should be an extension in the scope of collective bargaining to cover manpower planning, training and work design as well as the universalisation and codification of the more advanced shopfloor agreements. The development of a system of employee boardroom representatives will also have profound implications for trade union servicing. It will be necessary not only to train and service the boardroom representatives but also to ensure that their constituents are in a position to make an informed appraisal of company performance as well. In addition, trade union involvement in the shaping and implementation of industrial economic and social policy at all levels is likely to grow.

Perhaps the first priority is an expansion of training. When management introduces a job evaluation scheme or claims that company results do not justify a wage increase, shop stewards must be trained to challenge management's assumptions or use of facts. And if shop stewards are to become concerned in manpower planning and work design, then they must at least understand the basic principles of these subjects. In addition, there will be the requirements of boardroom level representation. Between 6,000 and 11,000 employee representatives will have to be equipped to carry out their new functions,[11] while shop stewards, particularly those on the joint representation committees, must at least be in a position to carry on a constructive dialogue with them. The Donovan Commission found that only a third of shop stewards received any kind of training.[12] Since then, there has undoubtedly been an increase in training. A number of unions, including the TGWU, the GMWU, ASTMS, the NUR have either expanded or have plans to expand their educational facilities. The GMWU, which now has two residential colleges as well as a developed system of regional courses, have places for over 8,000 students in a year. This means that it should soon be in a position to provide some kind of training for the vast majority of its 26,000 shop stewards and full-time officials. But at least some part of the overall expansion of training has come from an increase in training courses run by employers.[13] And there are still many unions, including the AUEW, which give their shop stewards and officials little training at all. The TUC, which in 1974, despite improvements, arranged for only about 10,500 student places, does not fill the gap. Indeed, the judgement that 'our unions have by far the worst education services of any union movement in the western world'[14] is probably an accurate one. Their inadequacy will be further exposed if the trade union movement adopts new functions.

What is required is an educational development plan for the trade union movement, under the auspices of the TUC. The TUC has already produced reports on training which have shown that it is fully aware of the need.[15] But, partly because of conservatism and partly because of financial considerations, response has been very limited. The role of the TUC must be primarily a directing one, though it should also continue to provide, though on a larger scale, a supplementary service, both nationally and regionally, for those unions without the resources for their own educational programmes. The main effort must, however, come from individual unions. All major unions must give adequate training to their shop stewards. In addition, they must provide more advanced training to their full-time officials. Though there are advantages in residential courses in trade union schools, both for reasons of space and of finance the majority of programmes will have to be day-release and run by local educational establishments, though with overall union guidance. It will mean a very large increase in union expenditure on education, though it will be possible to defray some of the cost through grants from the Department of Education and through payments from employers to stewards attending courses. There may also be a case for government assistance to help employee representatives at boardroom level.

An essential element of trade union servicing is provided by full-time officers. Traditionally, the British trade union movement has always had a relatively lower proportion of full-time officials to members compared with those in other countries; and the Donovan Commission recommended that the number of officials ought to be substantially increased.[16] However, the total of full-time officers (roughly 3,000) must be considered alongside the hundreds of thousands of shop stewards (the TUC claims over 300,000) whose number and power is far greater than in other comparable countries. The existence of a large army of shopfloor bargainers is bound to take some of the burden off full-time officials, particularly if the former are adequately trained for the job. Indeed, in many industries, particularly, those in which domestic bargaining is important, the role of full-time officials is likely to resemble more and more that of consultant, who is called in either to provide specialist advice or to solve difficult shopfloor problems. Even so, the heavy existing workloads of most full-time officials, particularly in relation to plant-level issues, and the feeling of many shop stewards that they would like to see their officers more often is strong evidence of the need for more full-time officials.[17] That need will be increased if trade unions take on further functions. The extension of shopfloor negotiations and the creation of a corporate bargaining structure will inevitably add to existing pressures, while the introduction of employee representation at boardroom level, will certainly require that officials learn new skills, even if these new representatives will usually be drawn from the shopfloor. The impact of industrial planning developments and further legislation has also to be considered, as does the requirement to recruit more trade union members.

But if there are overwhelming arguments for increasing the number of full-time officials, trade unions will have to take care that the best use is made of additional resources. There are two main areas in which the number of officials needs strengthening. The first is those directly servicing the plant, both in terms of general advice and also of organisational responsibilities. The second is the supply of specialist officers on which shopfloor representatives and more generalist full-time officials can call. It will be important to ensure that, attached to every regional headquarters, there are enough officials with the relevant skills (for example in work study, job evaluation, work design, agreement analysis), as well as officials who have built up a specialist knowledge in a particular industry.

Trade unions must also develop adequate service departments to assist their officials. In the past decade, most have built up research departments, staffed, in the main, by graduates or trained personnel. The functions of these departments vary but they include the provision of information and arguments for wage claims at both national and local level, the preparation of policy statements, speech material and guides and briefs for full-time officials and shop stewards, and general servicing of national and regional officials in their many activities, and in one or two cases, a role in the union's longer term thinking on its own future.[18]

Yet, despite the growth in trade union research, it is clear that trade union officials and shopfloor representatives need a higher standard of servicing.[19] In particular, they require more detailed information on company finance for bargaining purposes and access to a comprehensive agreements library which would instantly provide an up-to-date guide of developments in particular fields. In the near future, boardroom representatives will also need assistance on a wide range of financial subjects. In order to give an effective service on these lines, trade unions will not only have to build up their headquarters' departments but also attach research staff to their regional offices. There is also an argument for more co-ordination of union research. With respect to the major unions, particularly the big three, there is often unnecessary duplication, while some of the smaller unions cannot afford to give their officials adequate research facilities. The TUC already has its own research and economic staff to service its committees. But, apart from the small Ruskin Research Unit which has done valuable work for some unions, there is no trade union movement research centre which can supply all unions, perhaps on a computerised basis, with the basic background information on company finance and agreements. If one was created (perhaps building on the work of the Ruskin Unit) the research departments of the affiliated unions could then concentrate on providing the specialised information appropriate to their own particular circumstances. They should also be involved, as a matter of course, in the longer term strategic planning which is so vital to the future of the unions but which in the pressure of events is too frequently neglected.

There are also other areas, apart from research and education, in which there should be an expansion of trade union services. Officials, shop stewards and boardroom representatives must be able to call upon experts in management techniques (including work study, job evaluation, productivity bargaining, work design, manpower planning, industrial training and information and control systems). With the development of a union role under the Social Security Act of 1975, trade unions badly need advice on occupational pensions. Yet only one union (the GMWU) has actually set up a pensions department. Publicity also has a vital part to play in trade union affairs. Officials and shop stewards often require the support of the public if they are to create the right atmosphere for their negotiations. They must also inform their members of union policies. Equally important, a more favourable climate of opinion for trade unionism needs to be developed if it is to prosper and expand. Trade unions must learn to explain their actions better and to put their case more effectively. Their public relations is too often grossly inadequate. This means training in media techniques; it means an effective union journal, supported by a good internal communications system; and it means effective union publicity departments. Lastly, with the growth in industrial and social legislation, trade unionists will need more help on legal matters. Already most of the major unions have legal departments. But it is important that these should have both a monitoring and advisory role at headquarters and a strong local presence, so that availability can be combined with central direction. It is also essential that there should be overall co-ordination of the unions' service function, if the most effective use is to be made of those additional facilities. Unions should, therefore, consider either appointing a services director or assigning overall direction to an assistant general secretary.

The expansion of services argued for above raises tricky personnel management issues. The employment of trained, sometimes graduate staff, which is an inevitable consequence of service growth, can create some difficulties in a largely working class organisation, run on democratic lines. The ability to collect, sift and analyse material quickly usually also implies a certain independence of mind which can sometimes be awkward to work alongside but which, if adequately utilised, can also be invaluable to the union. These 'irregulars' have to learn to present their material in a readable form, to establish a good working relationship with union officials and to remember that, whatever their paper qualifications, they are only servants of the union. But union leaders, in their turn, have to allow their central departments some latitude to come forward with ideas, which, if properly sifted, can be extremely useful to the union.

HOW TO PAY FOR THESE SERVICES

The appointment of specialist staff calls into question the general level of union salaries. Unions have to compete with government, industry and the universities for the services of graduates and other trained personnel. So they cannot afford to offer pay levels which are wildly uncompetitive. The problem is to offer enough to attract the right recruit without damaging the union salary structure. Traditionally, many unions have not believed it right to pay their officials much more than their members' average wage. However, in the 1970s trade unionists' wages increased extremely fast, while union officials found that they were, themselves, part of a steadily growing labour market. Many firms, including management consultancies, were prepared to pay highly for the services of experienced trade union negotiators. Thus trade unions had increasingly to protect themselves against marauding industrialists by increasing the salaries of their officials. As a consequence, and also because of the increasingly limited job opportunities generally available, it became less difficult to attract trained staff to join union service departments.

However, if union services are to expand sufficiently, there must be an increase in union resources. There may be room for some retrenchment on expenditure. Traditionally, trade unions, particularly craft unions, have provided a wide range of benefits, including unemployment, sickness, accident, funeral and superannuation. Though these account for a declining proportion of expenditure, there may be a case for scaling them down further in some areas, particularly where they coincide with state benefits. However, many trade union activists believe that these benefits are useful both for recruitment and membership retention purposes. As far as income is concerned, during the last decade there has been a large expansion in contributions deducted at source. In some unions, this has gone further than others. The GMWU estimates that over 80 per cent of its members are now covered by 'check off' arrangements. These have the advantage of ensuring a steady income as well as helping with the retention of membership. Over a number of years, many unions have also invested their income sensibly, so much so that there is a tendency for the major unions to derive a large and growing proportion of their income from investments.

However, contributions still remain the major source of union income, and increases in union services can only be paid for by increases in contributions. There is little doubt that British employees get their trade unionism on the cheap. Even taking into account the differences in standards of living, the American worker is paying twice as much in contributions, and most European workers pay more than the British worker. In 1975, contributions had declined as a proportion of average weekly earnings to less than a third of the 1939 levels.[20] If union services are to match up to what is needed, then trade unions will have to ask their members for very substantial increases. Fortunately, there is considerable evidence that trade unionists would be prepared to pay, provided they knew they were getting worthwhile services in return.[21] The biggest obstacle is not so much the attitude of members but the fear of individual unions that their rivals will use their own contribution increase as a recruiting weapon. So it is unlikely that a major individual union will ever summon up the courage to increase contributions by the amount required unless there is a major TUC initiative. The TUC must, therefore, persuade its affiliates to agree to a common level of increase and, thereafter, to link further increases to a proportion of average weekly earnings – say 1 per cent. Only thus will the trade union movement acquire enough resources for its needs.

This chapter has argued that, if industrial democracy is to become a reality, there must be reforms in trade union structure and a big increase in trade union services. The solution to the structural problem of British trade unions lies not in the pursuit of an unobtainable industrial unionism but in a TUC-directed strategy (including amalgamations and federation, dual membership deals and membership exchanges, and multilateral closer-working and spheres of influence agreements) to eliminate the destructive and wasteful side of multi-unionism, which remains such a barrier to the development of effective representation, particularly at company and boardroom level. With respect to services, what is required is an expansion in training, more officials and further back-up services, financed by a substantial increase in trade union contributions.

REFERENCES

1 *Trade unions* p. 31.
2 *Will Thorne* chp. 3.
3 *Royal Commission Research Paper no. 5* Part 1 para. 40.
4 *Royal Commission on Trade Unions and Employers' Associations* paras. 677–78.
5 *Trade unions* p. 39.
6 Figures derived from the *Report of the Committee of Inquiry on Industrial Democracy* pp. 16–19.
7 *Royal Commission on Trade Unions and Employers' Associations* paras. 679–95.
8 *Structure and development* TUC Interim Report 1970.
9 See H. A. Turner 'British trade union structure: a new approach' *British Journal of Industrial Relations* July 1964 for a discussion of the beneficial effects of a merger between the Engineers, the Transport and General Workers, and the General and Municipal Workers.
10 See *Structure and development* para. 17.
11 *Report of the Committee of Inquiry on Industrial Democracy* p. 156.
12 *Royal Commission on Trade Unions and Employers' Associations* para. 712.
13 See *Workplace industrial relations 1972* Table 32.
14 Robert Taylor 'Schooling the unions' *New Society* 4 September 1975.
15 For example *Training full-time officers* TUC 1972.
16 *Royal Commission on Trade Unions and Employers' Associations* paras. 701–05.
17 See *GMWU Congress report* 1976 pp. 555–58 for a union reaction.
18 See 'Trade union research departments' Young Fabian evidence to the *Royal Commission on Trade Unions and Employers' Associations*, and Giles Radice 'Research and the unions' *Management Today* November 1971.
19 For example, see William Brown and Margaret Lawson *The training of trade union officers* University of Warwick Industrial Relations Research Unit Discussion Paper 1972 pp. 39–41.
20 See *Labour Research* July 1975.
21 *Royal Commission on Trade Unions and Employers' Associations* para. 717.

Chapter 11

The TUC and the Labour Party

The TUC and the Labour Party are highly relevant to the central arguments of this book. The TUC not only has the crucial part to play in the co-ordination and monitoring of a common approach to industrial democracy; it also has the responsibility for seeing that its affiliated unions make the changes (in recruitment and internal democracy, in structure, services and contributions) that are needed if industrial democracy is to become a reality. And if trade unions are to exercise the political role which should be theirs, they require both a strong TUC and effective Labour Party.

THEIR DIFFERENT ROLES

In a previous chapter, it was pointed out that, for a number of reasons, the trade unions must be involved in politics. But, though they have a political function, their main task is industrial. Their social and political involvement derives from and must, in the end, remain subsidiary to their primary objective of democraticising and humanising industry. In order to preserve the delicate balance between, on the one hand, developing a worthwhile political role and, on the other, retaining the independence necessary for effective industrial representation, they require organisations which will act on their behalf. Hence their creation and support of the TUC and the Labour Party. The formation of the Labour Party was not inevitable. It might have been possible for the trade unions to have adopted a more independent stance. However the low priority that the Conservative and Liberal Parties gave to trade union interests and the ferocity of the employers' offensive at the turn of the century finally convinced trade unions that they needed their own political representation in parliament. And, though the Labour Party has become far more than a trade union pressure group the benefits derived from the connection have kept the unions faithful to the Labour Party.

Without the existence of the Labour Party, the position of the trade unions would be far weaker. One authority, writing in 1960, commented that 'it is doubtful whether the unions appreciate the advantages of having a government which is basically sympathetic until they have to cope with a hostile one'.[1] Faced by the Heath administration in the 1970s, trade union leaders, despite their disenchantments with the Labour governments of the 1960s, saw only too clearly the advantages of the Labour connection – both as an ally in their opposition to the Industrial Relations Act and as an alternative government committed to its repeal.

However, the Labour Party is more than a purely defensive weapon. The alliance also provides the trade unions with positive advantages. Thus the Labour administrations of 1945–51 initiated many of the improvements for which trade unionists had fought, while the Labour governments of the 1970s implemented measures which had been previously jointly agreed by the TUC and the Labour Party when in opposition. These reforms can be divided into two kinds. The first were derived directly from the trade unions' industrial functions; the Attlee administration repealed the 1927 Trade Disputes and Trade Union Act, and the Wilson administration of the 1970s repealed the 1971 Industrial Relations Act and also legislated to extend collective bargaining rights. The second kind were concerned with the wider aspirations of trade unionists; the Attlee Government established the National Health Service and nationalised some of the basic industries, and in 1974 the Labour Government carried out its obligations under the social contract, to increase old age pensions substantially and to repeal the Housing Finance Act.

The association of the trade unions with Labour's economic and social policies highlights a further benefit of the alliance. By reminding the trade unions of their obligations to the community, it is a powerful barrier against them becoming merely another powerful sectional group. Traditionally, the British trade unions have been representative of all parts of the labour force, including the underdog and the weak. If they cut themselves off from the old, the sick, and the low paid, they would still be powerful but would lose their moral right to call themselves a movement. Looked at in this light, trade union participation in the work of the Labour Party contributes to their vitality and ensures that they remain socially concerned.

The authority and strength of the TUC – the second great instrument of the trade union movement – makes a Labour strategy the more feasible. For, when Labour is in opposition, even right-wing Conservative governments have to take note of the TUC. It is instructive to consider what happened to the Heath Government's hard-line policy of abandoning the practice, generally followed by previous post-war Conservative administrations, of listening to the trade unions. After refusing to consult the TUC over the principles of its industrial relations legislation, it later discovered that, in order to operate an incomes policy, it had to seek the co-operation of the TUC. When Labour is in power, a strong TUC is not only able to influence the development of implementation of policy; it can also prevent a Labour Government from becoming too remote from the views of the trade union movement. In 1969, when the Labour administration introduced the short Industrial Relations Bill, part of which the trade unions rejected, the TUC became the focal point for opposition and, with the help of Labour MPs, particularly trade union sponsored members, forced the government to back down. So the Labour Party and the TUC are *complementary*. Through the Labour Party, the trade unions can seek to change society. In the TUC, the trade union movement has an instrument which can influence governments of either party. In a sense, British trade unions get the best of two worlds. They obtain the advantages of commitment, while retaining the benefits of independence.

THE NATURE OF TUC AUTHORITY

This chapter argues for an increase in the authority of the TUC. It is, however, important to be clear about the nature of this authority. The TUC itself pointed out that its authority 'must, with clearly specified and justified exceptions, be defined in terms of influence, not of power',[2] while Allan Flanders argued that 'any further strengthening of the general council's position . . . is much more likely to come from an increase in its influence rather than its powers'.[3]

The limits on TUC prerogative are partly explained by its history. Though it was founded in 1868, it only became a real co-ordinating centre in the 1920s with the establishment of the general council and the introduction of rules 11, 12 and 13; these rules gave the council powers to intervene in industrial and inter-union disputes, and to suspend and recommend to congress the expulsion of any union which it considered to be acting in a manner 'detrimental to the interests of the trade union movement or contrary to the declared principles of Congress'. By then, most of today's major unions had either already emerged or were in process of emergence. So they had little incentive to create a body which would usurp their own individual function or powers. Rather they wished to provide a means by which they could achieve collectively industrial and political objectives which were either impossible or difficult to achieve separately. Their jealous regard for their autonomy was reinforced by the diversity of their needs. Given the different types of trade union structures it was difficult for the national centre to lay down any uniform pattern of development. In addition, the TUC had no really effective way of imposing its will on recalcitrant affiliates. In the case of large unions, expulsion harmed the TUC as much, if not more, than the individual union. The expelled union could normally be expected to survive without the TUC. On the other hand, the TUC was always conscious that its authority derived from its ability to represent trade unions collectively, and that the loss of a big union could detract substantially from its authority as the body representing, in contrast to most other national trade union centres, all major unions, both white collar and blue collar. It is both a strength and a weakness that very few unions have ever been expelled from the TUC.

It follows from this description of its authority that the TUC should not be expected to act as a kind of trade union overlord, intervening in union affairs at will – still less as industry's 'super-policeman'. Its strength should be measured by how far its affiliates are prepared to accept its views on matters both external and internal as their own and by how successful it is in persuading outsiders (primarily the government) to agree with its case. However, a recognition of the limits of TUC power does not imply that it has no authority. On the contrary, it already has a great deal and could and should have more.

As was pointed out in chapter 8, the social contract approach certainly led to an increase in the political influence of the trade union movement, in that the TUC was able to play a major role in the shaping of economic and social policy. But potentially, at least, it also represented a modification of what most affiliated trade unions believed to be the main *raison d'être* of trade unionism; for implicitly it involved an acceptance that wage bargaining could not be considered in isolation from the wider concerns of trade unionists or from its impact on the community as a whole. The difficulties which the TUC experienced, particularly during 1977, in persuading trade unionists of the need for a continuing pay policy show how big an education job has still to be done before the TUC's authority on this issue is accepted on a longer term basis by the movement.

The crucial importance of industrial democracy as a trade union objective has been emphasised throughout this book; while the implications of such a democratic strategy for trade union recruitment and internal democracy, for services, structure and contributions have also been pointed out. However, once again the affiliated unions have not been prepared to give the TUC full authority. Whatever the merits of the argument it is certainly the case that the TUC's bargaining position with government was considerably weakened by the refusal of major unions to accept TUC policy on industrial democracy. Industrial democracy illustrates the difficulties facing the TUC when it tries to intervene in areas which its affiliates consider to be their preserve. The TUC has stated that its job is to identify 'things which unions should be doing, but which for one reason or another they are not doing' and to stimulate them 'to take the necessary action'; it has also defined its role *vis à vis* its affiliates as establishing 'standards of good trade union practice'. It has been argued that if the trade unions are to adopt a more positive ambitious democratic approach, then higher standards of good trade union practice will be needed – in recruitment and internal democracy, in trade union structure, services and finance. It follows that TUC intervention in these matters is urgently required, not to bolster up TUC authority for its own sake, but to point to the direction in which the trade unions should be going.

STRENGTHENING THE TUC

The truth is that extensions of TUC authority are only likely to be approved if they are seen by a majority of affiliates, including an overwhelming proportion of the major unions, to be essential for trade unionism. Chapter 5 described how eager trade unions are to build up the position of the TUC when, as over *In place of strife* and the Industrial Relations Act, they feel they are under direct attack but how when it comes to a more positive initiative they are usually far less eager to support the TUC. The TUC has to show that, without a sustained strategy of the kind outlined in these pages, even the biggest unions will find themselves under such pressure from their members, from management, and from government that they will be under threat. In short, a stronger TUC is not a marginal issue but fundamental for trade union survival and development.

It has sometimes been suggested that the TUC would find it easier to increase its authority if there was a full-time general council. In reality, such a change would probably weaken rather than strengthen its position. A full-time general council, which, by definition, would no longer be composed, as it is now, of the leaders of most of the major unions, would be treated with suspicion, particularly if it attempted to increase its powers at the expense of TUC affiliates. But if the TUC secretariat is able to persuade the present part-time general council of the need for TUC intervention, it has gained the support of most of the powerful trade union general secretaries – and the battle is at least partially won.

What is needed, however, is for the TUC general secretary to play a more dynamic leadership role than in the past. The last three TUC general secretaries (George Woodcock, Victor Feather and Lionel Murray) have all, in their different ways, tried, with some success, to build up the authority of the TUC. TUC policies must, of course, still be based on a consensus of trade union opinion – but it should be a consensus for action rather than for the *status quo*. The TUC report on structure noted that 'a propensity not to offend and not to appear to be interfering with union autonomy has historically often led the TUC to eschew taking initiatives'.[4] Now, more than ever, it is the TUC general secretary's task to make its affiliates face up to the pressures facing the movement and develop an appropriate strategy.

Though the main responsibility for change must lie with individual unions, the TUC can help to shift the climate of trade union opinion. The general secretary should ask why it is that the trade unions which so persistently ask for the planning of industrial and economic affairs are so reluctant to formulate a strategy for themselves. He should take every opportunity to bring home to officials the critical nature of the situation and the necessity for a coordinated trade union response. It would greatly assist if the general council made a practice of presenting policy statements to congress, if regular use was made of the device of holding conferences of executives between congresses, and if the TUC regional councils and, in particular, the 500 trade councils devoted more time and resources to propagating TUC policies. In addition, individual unions, through their own communications system, ought to give wider coverage to TUC activities. In short, the TUC, led by its general secretary and general council members, must exhort, stimulate and cajole its affiliates to reform themselves.

If the TUC is to intervene effectively, a number of changes in the

TUC's own structure will be required. Some unions have argued for reform of the general council trade group structure. Though this is more of an electoral device than a method of industrial representation, it does at least have the merit of ensuring that most of the leaders of major unions are members of the general council. There should be some revision so that *every* union with 100,000 members or more is directly represented.[5]

It is, however, much more important to expand the system of industrial committees. These committees, which include members of the general council as well as representatives of all the unions concerned, already cover construction, fuel and power, transport, textiles and clothing, hotel and catering, printing, steel, local government and the health service. They should be extended to embrace all the main industrial sectors.

The TUC's industrial committees have already proved themselves more effective than the trade union side of joint industrial councils in dealing with industrial problems. Both the construction and textiles committees, for example, have responded to the difficulties facing their respective industries by successfully seeking general council support for changes in government policy. It would, therefore, be entirely appropriate for these committees to discuss the major issues facing unions in their industrial sectors and to devise a co-ordinated response which would include the extension of power-sharing to all levels of decision-making. They would also have to consider the implications of a power-sharing strategy for trade union representation, recruitment, servicing and so on. An expanded system of industrial committees could also provide the TUC's functional committees, such as the organisation, education and economic committees, both with the detailed information on which to base decisions and with an additional means of implementation.

Some of the functional sub-committees will need strengthening. For example, the organisation sub-committee must assume a greater role. Its most immediate task should be to secure agreement on a general increase in union contributions. Given the part that contribution levels play in inter-union competition, only the TUC can provide the impetus required to raise contributions really substantially and then to link them to, say, 1 per cent of average earnings in order to provide, on a permanent basis, the resources needed for a modern trade union movement. In conjunction with the industrial committees, the organisation committee must also intervene more effectively to persuade unions to tackle the problems arising out of multi-unionism. It should set in motion a whole series of inter-union

discussions with a view to promoting amalgamations, membership exchanges, and closer-working and spheres of influence agreements. In addition, the organisation committee must expand its role
in safeguarding internal union democracy and individual membership rights. Mention was made in chapter 9 of the need for an
effective appeals system, both within individual unions and at TUC
level. There is also a case for the circulation of internal democratic
guidelines to unions, stressing the necessity of involving shop
stewards in trade union government and of legitimising combine
committees of shop stewards representing different unions. In other
words, the organisation committee must act as the *engine* of trade
union reform.

The setting up of a TUC services committee should also be
seriously considered. The need for a big improvement in trade union
services has been emphasised in the last chapter. The TUC requires
a powerful committee which can stimulate the necessary expansion
in trade union education, in the number of officials, and in trade
union specialist servicing including research. The TUC education
committee could be linked to this new committee, which would also
oversee the work of the TUC research centre (which, as advocated
in the previous chapter, would provide all unions with basic information on agreements and company finance). The services committee would have to work closely with the industrial committees,
as the latter would be in a good position to discover the deficiencies
of trade union servicing at sectional and corporate level.

If the TUC is to carry out successfully its new responsibilities, then
its own manpower must be greatly increased. Despite some improvements, John Hughes' comment that 'the TUC's work is handled by
departments that are under-staffed, over-worked, under-paid, and
with access to too few secretarial and technical resources' still
remains substantially true.[6] The TUC is fortunate that it is served
by a dedicated, and in many cases, high quality staff. The main
problem is that there are not enough of them – and a bigger TUC
role will mean an even greater burden. This is not an argument for
indiscriminate bureaucratic expansion. It is, however, essential that
the extended system of industrial committees and the more powerful
functional committees are adequately staffed.

The TUC will also need to have much larger financial resources
at its disposal. At the moment, the services it can provide to individual unions are severely limited by its income which represents
only 1·5 per cent of total union income and is far lower than most
other national trade union centres. Most trade union activities will

of course continue to be carried out by individual unions. But the TUC must be able to staff its more powerful committee structure and to finance those services which, like some aspects of trade union education and information provision, are best provided on a common basis. Once individual unions have decided to put their own finances on a more realistic footing by raising radically the level of contributions, they will find it more difficult to resist a TUC request for a substantial increase in affiliations, particularly if it is made clear to them that it is essential for the health of the trade union movement.

REFORMING LABOUR PARTY INSTITUTIONS

Trade union involvement in the Labour Party has increased considerably in recent years. Trade union responsibility for ensuring that the party is an effective political organisation is therefore, all the greater. The classic description of the different roles played within the alliance was made by Frank Cousins, the general secretary of the Transport & General Workers Union, to the 1956 Labour Party conference. He explained to delegates in characteristically blunt terms 'I told you last year not to tell the unions how to do their job, and I am certainly not going to tell the Labour Party how to do its job'.[7] Broadly speaking, the contention was that the politicians should be left to get on with leading the party when in opposition and, in power, with running the country; in return they were expected not to meddle in trade union affairs. Since then, however, there has been a modification of the traditional roles. Labour governments have been forced to intervene in collective bargaining. It is true that, after the 1970 election defeat, Labour leaders publicly admitted that the *In place of strife* approach was mistaken. But, in government they have insisted – and are likely to continue to insist – that some limitations should be placed on the level of wage settlements. In their turn, trade unions wanted greater influence on Labour governments than in the past. They, of course, accepted that a Labour government, elected by the people, had to represent the interests of the community as a whole. They also believed rightly that the primary trade union function was industrial – and it would, therefore, be inappropriate for them to try and dictate to the Labour Party in political matters. But they felt that, if they were to represent their members effectively in modern conditions, they needed to be more politically active than in the past.

This shift in trade union attitudes took shape after Labour's 1970 election defeat and was symbolised by the setting up in 1972 of the TUC-Labour Party Liaison Committee and the publication in February 1973 by this committee of *Economic policy and the cost of living*, which first introduced the social contract. The background to and the implications of the social contract for trade unions have already been discussed.

With respect to trade union involvement in the Labour Party, acceptance of the social contract also represented a significant departure. Before 1970, such a detailed and far-reaching pact with the Labour Party would have been considered unnecessary – and probably undesirable as well. After all, in theory, at least, the overwhelming union majority at party conference, their substantial presence on the National Executive Committee (NEC) of the party, and their sponsorship of a third of the parliamentary Labour Party, gave them considerable power. In addition, the TUC normally liked to feel free to bargain with a Tory government. The hostility of the Conservative administration under Heath was one obvious explanation for the change in trade union views. A further reason was a belated recognition that Labour had become, if not the natural party of government, then at least as likely to be in power as the Conservatives. If a Conservative administration could pass the Industrial Relations Act, a Labour administration could repeal it. And whereas a Conservative government was not prepared to give the trade unions anything very much in return for their support for an incomes policy, Labour was likely to be far more sympathetic to their aspirations. There was also the need to tie Labour's hands on certain issues, while the party was still in opposition. The strange episode of *In place of strife* was still fresh in trade union memories. In addition the pressures of the late 1960s and early 1970s had convinced many trade union leaders of the need for a more coherent trade union view on social and economic matters. It was no longer enough to leave it to the politicians. So it was on the basis not so much of traditional loyalty but, for the first time, of a specific and wide-ranging agreement that the trade unions gave Labour their backing. But if their support was more conditional, it was also more emphatic than it had been for many years – as the union effort in the 1974 election campaigns and subsequent underpinning of the Labour Government showed. Within the limits prescribed by their basic industrial purpose, the trade unions had assumed a more vigorous political role.

One effect of greater trade union involvement was to highlight the shortcomings of the Labour Party's governing institutions. These cannot be understood without reference to their origins. When some trade unions and various socialist societies met at the Memorial Hall, Farringdon Street, London in February 1900, they set up an extra-parliamentary association – the Labour Representation Committee (LRC). Though twenty-nine LRC candidates were returned at the 1906 general election, a number subsequently increased by the adherence of most of the miners' MPs, until 1914 the group was little more than a trade union adjunct of the Liberal Party.[8] The outside activities of the party – the passing of resolutions at annual conference and the building up of electoral organisations – was at least as important as what went on inside parliament. Even when Labour's political prospects were transformed, first by the 1914–18 war and then more profoundly by the 1939–45 war, its structure remained more appropriate to a party in permanent opposition than to a party of government.

Constitutionally, the annual conference is the supreme authority within the party. Obviously, as with trade union conferences, there is a sense in which it is not really possible for a body of men and women meeting only once a year to control the parliamentary leaders. The election of the NEC by conference to act on its behalf is an implicit admission of this. But when Labour is in opposition, the support of the party outside parliament is crucial for the leadership. In government, however, the NEC and party conference become less central. This is not to say that, in opposition Labour leaders can ever afford to ignore the electorate as a whole or that, in power, it is not essential for a Labour administration to retain the support of its activists. But a Labour government has other 'constituencies' to satisfy, including opinion both at home and abroad; it has also to face up to the realities which are only too easy to neglect out of office. Inevitably there are occasions when a Labour government has to disappoint the aspirations of party members, even though these are embodied in a conference resolution. The tragedy is that as things are now arranged, all too often the deliberations of conference and the NEC produce public clashes with a Labour government, without leading to any greater party influence over it.

It was in part because they felt the need to create a more effective forum of discussion and influence that the trade union movement agreed in 1972 to the establishment of the TUC-Labour Party Liaison Committee, made up of representatives of the parliamentary leadership, the NEC, and the TUC. It is true that the trade unions already had a powerful voice in the existing Labour Party institu-

tions. The affiliated unions, if they act together, can always dominate conference and they also have a considerable position on the
NEC. In addition, usually about a third of the parliamentary Labour
Party are union sponsored (that is to say, their constituency parties
receive regular trade union financial support). However, the shortcomings of conference as a means of control have been discussed
above. In any case, the trade unions have for long believed that,
even if they always voted the same way on issues (which they do
not), it would be impolitic for them to be seen to be dominating
conference in too overt a fashion. As far as the NEC is concerned,
the trade union section only elects twelve out of the twenty-nine
seats. In addition, the major trade union figures opt for membership of the TUC general council. As a result, the trade unions view
the NEC as a useful but secondary body. The trade union group
of the parliamentary Labour Party certainly remains, as their
virtual veto of Labour's industrial relations legislation in 1969
showed an important 'reserve army'.[9] But here again the most
prominent trade union leaders are no longer members of parliament.
What was required was an additional institution which would enable
the trade union leadership to meet the political leaders on a regular
basis, and, where necesary, to reach agreement on policy matters.
Hence trade union support for the TUC-Labour Party Liaison
Committee.

It was the Liaison Committee which was the architect of the social
contract, one of the main planks of Labour's 1974 election campaigns. After Labour achieved an overall majority in October of
that year, the body continued to play a significant role. At its
meetings, the government was able to discuss in a realistic fashion
the problems it faced, including inflation, the depreciation of sterling, public expenditure cuts and the referendum on continued
membership of the European Economic Community. In their turn,
the trade unions were able to put pressure on government ministers
over unemployment, prices and pay policy, industrial relations and
social legislation. In this way, the committee made an important
contribution to the solution of a number of economic and social
policies facing the Labour Government. At the same time, it provided the trade union movement with a means of carrying its political function in a more vigorous and creative way.

But, if the TUC-Labour Party Liaison Committee has now become
an indispensable part of the Labour Party's governing structure, the
trade unions cannot afford to ignore the defects in Labour's own
institutions. At conference, there will always be tension in a left-

wing party between party activists and the leadership. What is needed is some form of arrangement which, at least, acknowledges the special position of senior ministers when Labour is in government. At the 1976 party conference, the Chancellor of the Exchequer, Denis Healey, was allowed only the regulation five minutes allocated to speakers from the floor, despite the fact that conference took place against the background of a sterling crisis.[10] Leading cabinet ministers must be given the opportunity of explaining government policy. In the past, much has been made of the 'block vote' and of the dominant part played by trade union delegations at conference, particularly by the left of the party. However, in view of the split in union voting patterns during the 1960s and early 1970s, little more has been heard of this particular criticism. In any case, the trade unions need to retain, through their conference vote, a veto on party policy which, though it must only be used in the last resort, remains one of the guarantees of the Labour alliance.

There is also a strong argument for reforming the NEC to make it more representative of the party as a whole.[11] It would probably be unwise for the unions to press for an increase in their own representation, though they need to see that their representatives play an effective part. But there is a case for including a limited number of parliamentary spokesmen (nominated by the party leaders) and for allowing the parliamentary Labour Party to elect some representatives to the NEC, as well as establishing a local government section elected from the annual local government conference; the constituency section should be represented not by MPs but by party activists. Such changes would involve leading Labour ministers, parliamentarians and local councillors in the work of the NEC and also give the party opportunities to influence government decisions in other than confrontation situations. Both party and government would benefit.

With respect to their relationship with the parliamentary Labour Party, the trade unions need to reconsider their sponsorship strategy. The Labour Party was originally created to ensure that the trade union viewpoint was heard in parliament. However, a Fabian study concluded that the post–1945 era has 'brought about a major contradiction in the sponsorship policy of the unions: on the one hand they have needed the trade union group less than ever before, on the other they have had to make greater sacrifices (in personnel and principle) than ever before to maintain it'.[12] It is certainly the case that direct union access to government and to party leaders makes parliamentary representation less of a priority. However, when Labour is in power, a well briefed trade union MP can make a significant impact on legislation which affects trade union interests, particularly at committee stage. More generally, a powerful trade union presence in parliament ensures that the parliamentary Labour Party remains sensitive to trade union views and interests. If the trade union movement allowed the number of trade union MPs to decline dramatically, there would be a danger that the Labour alliance would be gradually undermined. Yet since 1945 trade unions have had to struggle to preserve their one-third proportion of the parliamentary Labour Party; most of the able union officials have opted for industrial rather than political careers at a time when constituency parties are increasingly choosing candidates for their parliamentary potential. In some cases, unions have responded by selecting candidates with graduate backgrounds for their parliamentary panels. There is nothing necessarily wrong about that. With the development of white collar unionism and of specialist union departments, there is a growing body of men and women of middle class backgrounds with real knowledge of the trade union movement who would make good trade union MPs. However, such a policy must remain supplementary to finding prospective members of parliament from amongst trade union officials and shop stewards. Here, most unions have been slow to react to the rejection of their candidates by constituency parties. More ought to follow the example of the AUEW which has a competitive examination procedure for its budding parliamentarians, which not only means that only the best go forward but also provides some training in political skills. Positive encouragement to potential MPs should be given by running regular courses for interested shop stewards at union schools. In addition, trade unions should consider earmarking one or two of their most able officials for parliament. For it is essential not only that there should be trade union MPs but also that Labour cabinets should continue to include trade unionists.

TOWARDS A MASS PARTY

One of the greatest threats to the Labour alliance – and to the long term future of the Labour Party – is the erosion of the party in the constitutencies. Though it is possible to exaggerate the extent to which any of the British political parties has ever been a mass party in the continental sense, at its zenith in the early 1950s the Labour Party probably had over 1 million individual members. Although on the basis of official Labour Party figures total individual membership in 1975 was nearly 700,000 this was a big overestimate as all constituency parties now affiliate on the basis of 1,000 members. The best guess is that individual Labour Party membership is no more than 300,000.[13] In many constituencies, including those which return Labour members of parliament there are fewer than 500 individual members.

This decay has serious implications. The small number of activists in some constituencies makes it far easier for these constituencies to be taken over by extremist groups who are totally unrepresentative either of trade unionists or of Labour voters as a whole. In the longer term, this could have a disastrous effect on Labour's electoral prospects. The decline of membership also makes it more difficult for the Labour Party to run an effective election campaign. The superiority of the Conservative electoral machine is at least in part due to the much larger membership of that party. More fundamentally, in many constituencies political education and propaganda between elections is almost nil. Although the Labour Party has equal access to the mass media, it also depends on word of mouth contact on the doorstep, in the factories, and in the pubs and clubs. Unless there is an active political organisation on the ground, the Labour case will go largely by default.

As the GMWU recognized in its motion at the 1977 Labour Party conference, the trade union movement cannot allow this state of affairs to continue. It is not enough for trade unions to be involved centrally. They must also play a more active part in the constituencies. Of course, in many constituencies, particularly in Labour strongholds in the North of England, Wales and Scotland, there is a large trade union financial affiliation and individual trade unionists participate in the local party. However, far too few trade union activists do party work on a continuous basis. Trade unions affiliated to the Labour Party could do much more to encourage their members to joint constituency parties. They should also carry out political campaigns on the shopfloor in conjunction with local Labour Party organisations. Trade unions should also be putting pressure on the Labour Party to involve individual members in the government of constituency party affairs. There is a strong case for a system of 'closed' primaries, in which *all* party members in a constituency could vote for the main constituency offices, members of the NEC, and candidates for parliamentary and local elections. In short, if trade unions care about the future of the Labour Party and parliamentary democracy, they should give a much greater priority to grassroots political activity.

Political activity cannot be divorced from financial considerations. The Labour Party is in deep financial trouble. It told the Houghton Committee on state aid to political parties that it was doubtful how far it would be able to maintain even the existing level of activities, inadequate though these were (only a quarter of Labour constituency parties now have paid agents).[14] The Labour Party is already heavily dependent, both locally and nationally, on the affiliations and donations which trade unions make from their political funds. If trade unions raise their contributions substantially, they may be able to increase the political levy proportionately.[15] But though such an increase is desirable, it is unlikely to be forthcoming in the near future. There is, therefore, a strong case, as some unions have argued, for the introduction of state aid to political parties (there is already some support for the parties in parliament). This should be used by the Labour Party primarily to increase substantially the number of full-time agents. These must act as spearheads of a membership drive in the constituences.

A strong TUC and an effective Labour Party are essential to modern trade unionism. The TUC has a crucial part to play in the creation of a democratic industry and the reform of the trade unions; and, if the trade unions are to assume the political role which, in an industrial democracy, is theirs by right, then the authority of the TUC must be strengthened and the Labour Party reformed. Given the nature of TUC authority, its impact on its affiliates will mainly depend on the persuasive abilities of its general secretary and general council members, rather than on any additional powers. But there must be an extension of its industrial committees and a strengthening of its functional committees, as well as an expansion of the manpower and financial resources available to the TUC. In these ways, the TUC will be better able to give the lead that is so urgently required. The creation of the TUC-Labour Party Liaison Committee has led to a more active trade union involvement in the work of the party at national level. But reforms are required in Labour Party structure and organisation if the party is to come to terms with its emergence as a party of government and to become more representative not only of all aspects of party activity but also of the views of trade unionists and Labour activists and voters. Above all the decline of the party at the grass-roots must be reversed. If the Labour Party is to survive and expand, the trade unions will have to play a more active role.

REFERENCES

1 Martin Harrison *Trade unions and the Labour Party since 1945* Allen and Unwin 1960 p. 349.
2 *Structure and development* para. 6.
3 *Trade unions* p. 165.
4 *Structure and development* para. 5.
5 John Hughes *The TUC: a plan for the 1970s* Fabian Tract 1969 p. 29.
6 *The TUC: a plan for the 1970s* p. 34.
7 *Labour Party Conference Report* 1956 p. 82 (quoted in *Trade unions and the Labour Party since 1945* p. 342).
8 See Henry Pelling *A short history of the Labour Party* Macmillan 1961 chp. 2.
9 J. Ellis and R. W. Johnson *Members from the unions* Fabian Research Series 1974 p. 29.
10 At the 1977 conference, Denis Healey was allowed ten minutes to explain his policies.
11 See Dianna Hayter *The Labour Party: crisis and prospects* Fabian Tract 1977 p. 23, and John Cartwright 'Labour Party Structure in a Changing World' *Socialist Commentary* October 1976.
12 *Members from the unions* p. 28.
13 *Report of the Committee on Financial Aid to Political Parties* paras. 5–10.
14 *Report of the Committee on Financial Aid to Political Parties* paras. 5–16.
15 Political funds are derived from the political levy, paid under the 1913 Trade Union Act, by members who have not 'contracted out'.

Chapter 12

The impact on the community

This book has advocated trade union involvement in the running of industry *and* a full recognition by government of the crucial role of the trade unions in economic and social affairs. But it has also emphasised that, as well as rights, trade unionists have obligations not only to other trade unionists and their families but also the wider community. This chapter considers the impact on the rest of society of the changes proposed in this book. It examines the effect on management, discusses what safeguards are needed against abuses of trade union power, and explains the consequences for British democracy.

THE ROLE OF MANAGEMENT

The contribution of management will be crucial to the success of the democratic enterprise. As was pointed out in chapter 7, whatever the system of policy control, the management function remains vital to modern industry. And, as the British Institute of management (BIM) comments, managers have a special position within the enterprise: 'Most managers are in the position of representing the interests of employees while at the same time being employers themselves. From this position, they can help weld together complementary aspirations for the good of the shareholders and employees.'[1]

It is natural that many managers should be suspicious of proposals for democratic change. In the uneasy and highly competitive world of today, they face formidable external pressures; it is therefore hardly surprising that they should view the concept of industrial democracy as an added burden rather than a constructive approach to one of their main difficulties. But what managers must understand is that the challenge from the shopfloor will not go away; on the contrary it is more likely to intensify. So whether management likes it or not, moves towards more industrial democracy are now permanently on the agenda of British industrial relations and politics. The Bullock Committee rightly concluded: 'Sooner or later, we believe, this is a decision which will have to be taken, whatever government is in power.'[2]

Of course, the proposals outlined in this book will involve some managements in substantial changes of attitude. They will have to learn how to justify policies, how to demonstrate consistency between one set of policies and another, and how to listen to points of view other than their own. As the BIM says, 'they will need to develop their skills as leaders, arbiters and conciliators, and to improve their ability to convey ideas and make rational explanations'.[3] It is arguable that such changes are overdue; a professional approach to human problems is just as important to the enterprise as expertise in other fields. Managements which have already adopted more participative and open systems of management should find the transition to a more structured system of industrial democracy less difficult. Indeed, in some cases, what is required is the spread and adaptation of the best practice. In any case, the phased and flexible introduction proposed in chapter 7 should allow enough time for learning and experiment.

More generally, managers should not forget that the advantages to be gained from an effective democratic system are potentially very great indeed. It is not claimed that industrial democracy is a magic formula that will immediately bring sweetness and light to industrial relations. There will always be conflicts in any system, however democratic; people at different levels will always tend to see things differently, whilst there will continue to be differences of view even amongst those at the same level. More industrial democracy should, however, help to reduce that feeling of alienation so characteristic of British industry and increase the sense of commitment to the enterprise which is so necessary to our economic recovery. It should also provide a framework within which it should be possible to minimise the areas of conflict and maximise the areas of co-operation. In these ways, those energies of both managers and trade unionists which are now used up in dealing with the difficulties which arise from an authoritarian system should be freed for more productive purposes. It should become easier to remedy some of the main faults of British industry – a resistance to change and an ineffective use of investment, including manpower. And, with the new basis of consent, it will become possible to carry through the programmes of investment and reorganisation which are so vital to the recovery of the British economy. In short, despite the difficulties, the democratic changes proposed are very much in the long term interests of management.

TRADE UNION RESPONSIBILITY

The changes proposed in this book will give trade unions more power. Trade unionists and their representatives would have a far bigger say at the level of the enterprise, while, in the wider community, a trade union movement fully recognised by government would have won considerable leverage in policy formulation. What will be the consequences of this increase in trade union power for the community?

It is partly a question of how this increase in power is exercised. As was pointed out in the opening chapter, charges of trade union irresponsibility in relation to strikes, inflation or productivity are much exaggerated. And a trade union movement which is more closely involved with the running of industry and in the nation's affairs is likely to act in a more and not less responsible fashion. However, the community has a right to expect that the trade unions exercise their new power with a proper regard to their effect on the rest of society.

At corporate level, employees and their representatives must accept new responsibilities; in return for a shift of power within the company, they should be prepared to give a greater commitment to it. The beneficial consequences of such a commitment have been examined above. As far as their wider role is concerned, the trade union demand for full recognition by government carries with it corresponding obligations. Governments attempting to combine differing economic objectives, will inevitably intervene to influence the level of pay settlements. Trade unionists will have to accept once and for all that their actions have wider consequences and draw the appropriate conclusions. They must recognise that, if it was possible to create an enduring incomes policy which was clear, flexible and fair, then it would be good not only for the community but for their members as well. A system of unregulated collective bargaining which pushes up prices, threatens employment and favours the strong at the expense of the weak cannot be in the long term interests of the trade union movement. So, in return for a more influential involvement in determining economic and social policy and for a shift of power within the enterprise, they must help to create a permanent incomes policy.

With respect to participation in economic and social policy, trade union leaders have to point out to their members the implications of their demands. They have to see that objectives are mutually consistent. And they have to ensure that trade union policies take account of realities. If trade unions put forward their views in a rational way, they are not only acting in the interests of their members; but, given Britain's economic weakness, they also make a significant contribution to national welfare. So responsible trade union involvement is in the interests of the wider community.

It is not solely a question of ensuring that trade unions exercise their power responsibly. There must also be safeguards to protect the interests of individuals and of the community as a whole.

Previous chapters have described how legislation during the 1970s extended individual rights at work and also recommended further extensions. The Health and Safety Act of 1974 covered safety rights, while the Sex Discrimination Act of 1975 followed the example of the Race Relations Act of 1968 in matters of race and outlawed discrimination on grounds of sex in the employment field. The Employment Protection Act of 1975 increased rights at work in a number of areas, including unfair dismissal, redundancy, guarantee payments, maternity, insolvency of the firm, and time off work. It has also been suggested earlier that a right to training should be established, so that all citizens over the age of sixteen should either be in a job or, if they so wish it, in training, and that, within a company, directors should have regard for employee interests.

But, a number of rights derived from existing legislation are confined to trade unionists or trade unions. For example, the Employment Protection Act gave trade unions rights of recognition and disclosure of information for collective bargaining purposes, while, under the Industry Act of 1975, trade unions are entitled to further information rights about the enterprise. It has also been argued in chapter 6 that legislation may be needed to set up statutory joint shop steward-management committees at shopfloor level, while, if there is to be effective employee representation at board room level, strong trade union participation will certainly be required; hence the case for a trade union trigger mechanism (see chapter 7).

There are strong reasons why, in the examples quoted above, rights have to be granted to trade unions or trade unionists.

Employees derive power from acting collectively, and, if their collective power is to be strengthened, rights have to be given to the organisation. The case for representation at boardroom level being mainly through trade unions has been made earlier. Trade unions provide the most effective means of linking boardroom representation with the shopfloor and they also act as an insurance against the system being exploited by management for their own purposes. There is also the practical argument that, unless the trade unions are involved in the democratic reforms, these are unlikely to be successful.

However, giving special rights or a special position to trade unions undoubtedly raises the question as to whether additional safeguards are needed either for individuals or for the community as a whole. The closed shop, which highlights the potential clash between the rights of individuals and trade unions, was discussed in chapter 4 in the context of the provisions of the 1971 Industrial Relations Act. It was pointed out (in chapter 4) that a closed shop helps trade unions to build up an effective countervailing power to management, this giving protection to its members; that, in satisfying the trade union's organisational requirements, it also removes one potential source of industrial conflict; and that it accords with the belief of most trade unionists that those who benefit from trade union action ought at least to join the union and give support when required. However, there *is* a strong case for protection of individuals. That does not mean outlawing the closed shop – even if that was possible. It is significant that the Donovan Commission came down against banning the closed shops and concluded that it was 'better to recognise that under proper safeguards a closed shop can serve a useful purpose and to devise alternative means of overcoming the disadvantages'.[4] As a result of the two statutes repealing the Industrial Relations Act, of 1974 and 1976, it became legal again for an employer who was party to a closed shop agreement to refuse to employ and to dismiss employees who refused to join a trade union, except on grounds of religious conviction. But, as was described in chapter 9, the government decided against the Donovan recommendation of a statutory procedure to protect individuals against arbitrary exclusion or unjust disciplinary proceedings by trade unions. Instead, it encouraged the TUC to set up an independent review body, under the chairmanship of Professor Wedderburn, to consider complaints by trade unionists or potential trade unionists against unreasonable trade union behaviour where a closed shop existed. In addition, individuals are also protected by common law rights. It is arguable that at a time when, partly because of the impact of the recognition provisions of the Employment Protection Act, closed shop arrangements are likely to increase, some further protection for individuals is required. However, before legislating (perhaps on the lines suggested by the Donovan Commission) it would be sensible to see whether or not the TUC review body proved effective.

Before, during, and after the passage of the 1976 Trade Union and Labour Relations (Amendment) Act, fears were expressed that its closed shop provisions could threaten press freedom.[5] The new legislation had coincided with efforts by NUJ chapels to impose the closed shop in a number of newspapers and, in some cases, to freeze out the union's smaller rival, the Institute of Journalists. Editors of a number of newspapers, including *The Times,* the *Guardian* and the *Financial Times* became concerned at possible threats to their own independence and their freedom to ask outsiders to write for their columns. As a result of pressure from backbench Labour MPs, the legislation in its final form included a clause which made provision for a charter which would lay down guidance on these issues. It is to be hoped that the charter proves effective, as it is essential that the justifiable NUJ demand for closed shop arrangements does not lead to undesirable pressures on newspaper editors.

Protection of individual rights will become even more important if employee representation at boardroom level is mainly through the trade union channel. The onus will be on the TUC and its affiliates to review the effectiveness of their own democratic machinery and to ensure that the independent review body's terms of reference are widened to deal with issues arising out from the new democratic system. Otherwise the pressure for some form of statutory protection will become irresistible.

The most obvious area of potential conflict between the interests of the community and those of trade unions is that of industrial disputes. Although the British strike problem has often been exaggerated, it is undeniable that strikes in major industries, particularly in those industries which provide vital community services, can seriously disrupt the lives of many thousands of people. It is, therefore, essential that trade union officials and shop stewards should continue to regard the strike as a weapon of last resort. There are also powerful arguments for really effective conciliation and arbitration machinery and, more fundamentally, for a strategy to tackle the underlying causes of strikes.

However, anti-strike legislation is likely to prove counter-productive. Sanctions against unions to discipline their members are far more likely to lead to internal union disruption than to a reduction in strikes. Sanctions against shopfloor representatives, who are usually less militant than members, are liable to increase conflict rather than lessen it. More generally, sanctions tend to sour the industrial relations atmosphere without doing anything to tackle the causes of conflict. The setting up of ACAS (the Advisory Conciliation and Arbitration Service) an independent but statutory service, to provide conciliation and arbitration advice and investigation as a means of avoiding industrial disputes, has already proved a far more successful approach. There has been a big expansion in conciliation and arbitration and, at the same time, a stimulation of improvements in collective bargaining procedure.[6] These hopeful developments should be taken further. The democratic reforms recommended in this book should also help to improve industrial relations, and in the long term, make a significant contribution to reducing the number of disputes.

TRADE UNIONS AND PARLIAMENTARY DEMOCRACY

The charge that a more powerful trade union movement is a threat to parliamentary democracy ignores the classic democratic argument that an independent trade union acts as a check on the arbitrary exercise of power by government. It was an early trade union leader, Frederick Rogers of the Bookbinders, who pointed out that, although it was essential to increase the power of the state to prevent capitalist exploitation, 'there must be an independent life within the state to prevent government becoming tyranny, and the trade unions will be chief among those who shall call that independent life into being'.[7] Certainly, after seizing power, totalitarian governments of both right and left have quickly crushed trade union movements which they have seen as a potential threat to their rule, while, in parliamentary democracies, the continued existence of trade unions ensures that governments cannot ignore the voice of labour. So the trade unions already play an important role in making democracy work more effectively.

The development of a more democratic industry should serve to reinforce parliamentary democracy. The British political system is superimposed on an industrial structure which remains, in many respects, profoundly authoritarian. If employees were prepared to go on accepting this state of affairs, this might be a matter of concern for idealists alone. But, the lack of commitment and alienation from the industrial system, (whether it is expressed in strikes, high turn-over or resistance to technological change) could have disturbing political implications. The stability of parliamentary democracy in this country has been at least partially sustained by the ability of industry to provide increases in living standards. The growing lack of consensus at shopfloor level could not only weaken still further an industry which in many areas has fallen behind our main rivals; it might also eventually undermine the wider democratic consensus. In this context, the significance of industrial democracy is that, by giving employees more influence at all levels, it is likely not only to increase commitment to the enterprise (and thus substantially improve the performance of British industry), but also ensure continuing support for parliamentary institutions.

There is another sense in which an increase in industrial demo-cracy could assist the workings of political democracy. The aliena-tion which is so widely felt at shopfloor level is also a feature of the wider democracy. The decline in Labour Party membership was noted in the last chapter, while the proportion of those who vote at general elections – and for the two major parties – has fallen considerably since the early 1950s. At the very least, a more democratic industry would not be a discentive to participation in political activity. In the longer run, by stimulating involvement at the level which is of the most immediate importance to the majority of citizens, it could create a better climate for a genuinely partici-pative democracy.

With respect to the trade union demand for an equal status with management in relationships with government, this is sometimes denounced as anti-democratic.[8] If it meant governments becoming trade union puppets, there would be justice in the charge. The truth is that the British trade union movement has, for at least 50 years, fully accepted a democratic government's right to govern. But what they ask for is the right to be heard and for their view to be taken into account by government.

There is nothing particularly sinister about this claim. Democratic governments, above all, must rule with the consent of the governed. In a modern society, this means that they have to pay particular attention to the powerful industrial interest groups, especially the employers and trade unions. The new factor – and it is often deeply resented by the critics – is that, for the first time in peace-time, the trade unions have been fully accepted into the charmed circle of the powerful. During both world wars, the leading politi-cians realised that they had to have the support of the trade unions.

In this sense, Lloyd George's 1915 'Treasury' agreement and Ernest Bevin's initiative as Churchill's Minister of Labour were forerunners of the social contract. But until the 1970s, governments, even Labour ones, were reluctant to accept the full implication of the growth in trade union power. The development of the close relationship with the TUC after 1974 can hardly be described as shackling government. On the contrary, the support of the trade union movement sustained and gave strength to an administration which had at best a slim parliamentary majority, at a time of high inflation and world recession. Although a future Conservative government could not expect to have such a close arrangement with the trade union movement, the Tories would be well advised if they learnt the lesson of the Heath administration – namely that the government of a modern industrial democracy must keep on reasonable terms with the trade unions.

However, the development of a bargaining relationship between government and the great industrial interest groups of management and trade unions raises the crucial issue of democratic control. While it is entirely right and indeed part of the democratic process that governments should seek to secure the support of these groups, it is also essential that, in any arrangement, the community interest should not only be served but be seen to be served. It is a legitimate criticism of this process of bargaining between government and the industrial groups that it has so far largely escaped public scrutiny. When the Prime Minister and leading members of his cabinet meet the CBI or the TUC, the proceedings are entirely private although leaks to the media sometimes reveal at least part of what went on. If it may be desirable that the actual process of bargaining should take place off-stage, there is a strong case for more public surveillance of the relationship.

During the October 1974 election campaign, Mr Heath, then still Conservative leader, suggested that the proceedings of the National Economic Development Council (NEDC), the tripartite body in which government, management and trade unions are represented, might be televised. By bringing the policies of government and interest groups under public gaze, he hoped not only to contribute to popular education but also to influence the attitudes of the interest groups.[9] There is certainly an argument for more publicity for the proceeding of NEDC (including the publication of all its documents). But such a development would hardly add up to the rigorous examination of the participants which is required for meaningful democratic control.

The obvious body for public investigation should be parliament. However, its power and influence has declined sharply over the last fifty years. The rise of disciplined mass parties (which has reduced the role of the individual MP) and the growth in the powers of government (which has increased the role of the executive and the bureaucracy) have both contributed to the down grading of parliament. The powerful interest groups have largely by-passed parliament and dealt direct with government. The elected representatives of the people (apart from government ministers) play almost no part in the vital bargaining process between government and interest groups.

John Mackintosh has proposed a new second chamber in place of the House of Lords in which, as in mediaeval parliaments, the interest groups would be directly represented. 'Few now think the votes of MPs indicate the positive assent of those they are held to represent which is why the acceptance of a law by the House of Commons is not now regarded as carrying sufficient legitimacy by itself. But it is of considerable help to the government if the contemporary equivalent of the barons give their assent – if the CBI, the unions or professional associations indicate their agreement – since they can then be held to account and can be expected to secure the co-operation of their members.'[10] Though the suggestion has the merit of bringing the main industrial protagonists to Westminster, it still does not ensure that their views are exposed to inquiry by elected democratic representatives.

What is needed is reform of the House of Commons.[11] The Commons provides an excellent arena for the confrontation between the main political parties. It is less good at other functions – particularly the detailed scrutiny of policy and legislation. If the elected representatives of the community are to increase their influence over government policy, including its relationship with the industrial interest groups, then it is essential to build up the committee structure. For though the chamber is an admirable forum for debate, only strong committees, with powers to question witnesses in detail, can effectively probe the policy makers.

Though, since the middle of the 1960s, there has been a growth in the influence of the House of Commons select committees, they still lack the scope, authority and resources either to challenge the executive or to increase democratic control over the executive's dealing with outside interest groups. There is now an overwhelming argument for the establishment of subject committees to cover each major government department. Such a system already exists in embryo; the sub-committees of the expenditure committee in practice act very much as subject committees. These sub-committees should become fully fledged departmental committees, while the general sub-committee, which, in any case, spends most of its time examining the assumptions behind government spending plans, is well equipped to become the budget committee, investigating not only the activities of the Treasury, but also the role of trade unions and employers in the national policy-making process. Leading CBI and TUC spokesmen would, as a matter of course, go in front of the budget committee for detailed questioning by members of parliament on their policies and assumptions. The meetings of these committees should be televised and on radio, as well as reported in the press. In this way, the process of interest group bargaining would be subject to public scrutiny, and justice for the community would not only be done but be seen to be done.

This chapter has argued that the extensions to trade union power proposed in this book would be in the long term interests of management and strengthen rather than weaken democracy. It is, however, essential that trade unions use their new rights responsibly, that there should be protection against abuse of that power, and that the process of interest group bargaining with government be brought under parliamentary scrutiny. These safeguards should ensure that more industrial democracy will be to the benefit of the whole community.

REFERENCES

1 *Employee participation* p. 29.
2 *Report of the Committee of Inquiry on Industrial Democracy* p. 161.
3 *Employee participation* p. 26.
4 *Royal Commission on Trade Unions and Employers' Associations* para. 602.
5 See, for example, *Press freedom* pamphlet published by Westminster Press.
6 See the annual reports of the Advisory Conciliation and Arbitration Service.
7 Quoted in Henry Pelling *A history of British trade unionism* Penguin edition 1971 p. 178.
8 For example, Paul Johnson 'Farewell to the Labour Party' *New Statesman* 9 September 1977, and *The Times* leading article of 14 September 1977.
9 See the article by David Wood in *The Times* 7 October 1974.
10 *Reshaping Britain* PEP Broadsheet December 1974 p. 91.
11 See Lisanne Radice *Reforming the House of Commons* Fabian Tract 1977.

Conclusion

The main themes of this book are the need for trade union involvement in the running of industry and for a full recognition of their wider role.

In today's uncertain world, trade unions are more than ever necessary. But they face three serious challenges. Employees, particularly those of a younger generation, are beginning to reject an industrial system in which human needs are still given too low a priority. They are demanding not only more satisfying work but also a greater say in the running of enterprises. Yet, despite the increase in the number of issues negotiated at plant level, these kind of issues are still largely decided by management prerogative.

Meanwhile, there are developments on the management side which have disturbing implications. The pace of technological change threatens jobs, disturbs pay structures, and undermines existing work patterns. The growing predominance of the large firm, with its impact on the lives of employees, its capacity to draw on vast resources, and its ability to centralise certain types of decision-making, also requires a trade union response; while the rise of the multinational company, with its ability to move profits around and to switch production and investment, creates additional problems.

At the same time, governments, trying to combine different and sometimes conflicting economic objectives, have intervened – and will continue to intervene – to try and influence collective bargaining. This means more difficulties for trade unions, whose traditional functions appear threatened by incomes policy. What is now needed is a positive trade union strategy which remains closely linked to existing trade union purpose and functions but which takes account of the developments mentioned above.

Trade unions have considerable power. But, in the main, it is power of a reactive rather than of an initiating kind. If, in modern conditions, they are to fulfil their purpose (which has always been a democratic one) then they will need new powers.

Trade unions should now seek a share in all industrial decisions which affect their members (including work design, production, investment, marketing, the question of corporate strategy) and at all levels. This will require a linked system of representation, organisation, and services all the way up from shop floor to boardroom. In a modern democracy, trade unions also have a right to be heard on the wider economic and general issues which are of importance to their members. This implies that they should seek a continuing dialogue with government on economic and social priorities.

A strategy which was based on these separate but interlocking objectives could receive substantial support from trade union members. It should also match up to the challenge posed by changes in the industrial environment and the propensity of governments to intervene in collective bargaining. A more positive trade unionism is also likely to be to the benefit not only of management but the community as a whole.

There should be an extension of both the coverage and scope of collective bargaining. Trade unions will need to give a greater commitment and adopt a more specialised approach to recruitment. They must take full advantage of the recognition provisions of the 1975 Employment Protection Act (though these will need to be strengthened) and press for further changes in wages council procedures. At plant level, the most advanced bargaining practice should be formalised and extended to other plants by a trade union campaign for written agreements. The scope of joint regulation should be widened to include manpower policy, training and work design. There should be a development of bargaining arrangements at corporate level, to fill the gap between shopfloor and industry-wide negotiations. To cover the operations of multinationals, trade unions must build up their co-operation across national frontiers by exchange of information, by international arrangements and, where appropriate, by the development of international councils.

If employees are to influence strategic decisions, there must be a right to representation in the boardroom. What is needed is a flexible, non-mandatory and multi-dimensional system which operates at all levels and takes account of different needs and views. There is a strong case for a phased introduction. The first phase, which would come into operation with the assistance of enabling legislation to permit the appointment of employee representatives at boardroom level and to extend company directors' obligations to take account of employee interests, would allow time for management and unions to agree on participation arrangements covering strategic issues. These arrangements could cover extensions of collective bargaining as well as boardroom representation. The second phase, establishing a right to boardroom representation, would come into force later. An effective system of employee directors will require a co-ordinated and strong representative structure (with a joint representative council of shopfloor representatives at corporate level, and a build-up towards parity between employee and other representatives of boardroom level) and a powerful trade union involvement (which an exclusive control of the initial triggering mechanism should guarantee). The adoption of a two-tier structure, with a supervisory board overseeing a smaller executive board, should be considered; there is also much to be said for a chairman or additional directors elected by both sides to provide a means of resolving deadlocks.

In a modern industrial society, trade unions are inevitably involved in a relationship with government. Governments need the co-operation of trade unions over incomes policy, while trade unions must seek to persuade government to adopt industrial, economic and social policies which will benefit trade unionists. To carry conviction, both with government and their own members, the trade union movement must have realistic and coherent objectives. These should include a sensible approach to industrial relations legislation, including support for changes in the law relating to picketing, extension of rights in the manpower, training and work design areas, and a phased introduction of industrial democracy. As far as economic and industrial policy is concerned, trade unions need a continuing commitment to sustained economic growth. There must also be an effective system of economic and industrial planning supported by a planning unit within government and adequate powers of intervention. A manpower strategy which both matches men to jobs and monitors the job potential of different sectors of the economy will also be required. Trade unions can make a major contribution to the success of their policies by their support for incomes policy, for measures to improve productivity, and for involvement in the running of industry. With respect to social policies, the trade unions should press for a fairer distribution of wealth and incomes. They need, however, to ensure that public spending programmes are effective both in terms of value for money and of redistribution. Lastly, trade unions cannot ignore the international dimension; in particular, they must play a constructive role within the EEC and lend their support to those who argue that world problems (such as the recession in world trade, the divide between rich and poor nations, and the possible energy gap) can only be solved on an international basis.

The adoption of the objectives outlined above implies substantial change. Though power within trade unions is, in a very real sense, diffused and decentralised, trade unions must improve their own internal democracy. All union chief executives should be elected and, when they are not subject to re-election, should retire at sixty. Though there are arguments for and against the re-election of other full-time officials, there is a strong case for postal ballots where there are elections and for government assistance in meeting their cost. Lay members should be in a majority on trade union executives and trade union conferences should fully represent all groups of employees, including female and younger workers. Special attention should be given to shop stewards, the direct representatives of the shop floor; in particular, there should be shop steward representation on negotiating bodies, the new joint representative committees at company level should be composed of shop stewards, and more emphasis should be given to regular industrial conferences of shop stewards. Where appropriate, ballots and reference-back arrangements should be used to stimulate participation by the membership, whilst every effort should be made to improve communications by more effective branch structure, factory meetings, and a lively union journal.

There must also be reforms in trade union structure and a substantial growth in trade union services. The solution to the structural problems of British trade unions will be found not in the pursuit of an unobtainable industrial unionism, but rather in the elimination of the destructive and wasteful side of competitive multi-unionism, which remains such an obstacle to the development of effective representation, at plant, company and boardroom level. What is required is a TUC-directed strategy of amalgamation and federation, of dual membership deals and membership exchanges, and of multilateral closer-working and spheres of influence agreements. If trade unions are to extend collective bargaining, to seek representation at boardroom level, and to develop successfully their wider role, then the argument for an increase in trade union services will become even more compelling than it is now. There must be a major expansion of training for shop stewards and officials. More officials are required to service the shopfloor and to provide specialist advice. In addition, there should be a further development in trade union back-up services. More research facilities are needed both at headquarters and regional level, as well as better co-ordination between union research departments; trade union officials also need more advice on management techniques, pensions, policy and legal matters. These improvements in services imply a big increase in trade union resources which are still far too small. There is now an overwhelming case for linking union contributions to a proportion of average weekly earnings.

A strong TUC and Labour Party are essential to modern trade unionism. Given the nature of TUC authority, its impact on its affiliates will depend mainly on the persuasive abilities of its general secretary and general council members rather than on any additional powers. But there must be an extension of its industrial committees and a strengthening of its functional committees, as well as an expansion of the manpower and financial resources available to the TUC. With respect to the Labour Party, the creation of the TUC – Labour Party Liaison Committee has led to a more active trade union involvement in the work of the party at national level. However, reforms are required in Labour Party structure to make it more representative not only of all aspects of party activity but also of the views of trade unionists and of Labour activists and voters. Trade unions need also to review the effectiveness of their sponsorship strategies for MPs. Above all, the trade unions must see that the decline of the party at the grass-roots is reversed by ensuring that their members participate more vigorously in constituency parties.

It is vital to ensure that the increase in trade union power summarised above benefits the community as a whole. Society is entitled to expect a greater trade union commitment to the success of the enterprise and to the creation of a long term incomes policy. Safeguards are needed to protect individuals against arbitrary behaviour by trade unions in closed shop situations and in the new system of employee representation. A voluntary appeals system run by the TUC is preferable; but if that is ineffective it will be hard to resist those who argue for statutory protection. A further development of conciliation and arbitration is required so that strikes become increasingly rare. Finally, while it is an integral part of a modern industrial democracy that government should seek to secure the support of the industrial interest groups (including the trade unions), it is essential that in this bargaining process the community interest should not only be served but be seen to be served. There is therefore a strong case for the development of strong House of Commons' committees covering the departments of central government, equipped to investigate the relationship between government and interest groups as well as the workings of government.

These proposals will mean radical change. There will have to be far-reaching modifications in existing trade unions attitudes and practice. Management will have to accustom itself to a different way of doing things, and governments – of all parties – will have to get used, as a matter of course, to taking trade union views into account.

Naturally, it is the trade unions who face the biggest test. It is they who will have to agree on the objectives and then will the means. The achievement of such a programme may take as much as a decade or more but, despite the difficulties, it is essential that the trade unions now move forward. For the costs of standing still could be extremely heavy, while the benefits of even limited success will be high.

If trade unions continue as they are, it is likely that their traditional collective bargaining role will be at least partially undermined by developments on the managerial side, the challenge from the shopfloor, and by the propensity of governments to intervene. They may even find themselves drawn into unwanted industrial conflict, which would be extremely damaging for all concerned. Above all, they are likely to find that there will be growing support for anti-union legislation.

If, however, they succeed in creating a system of participation and power-sharing from shopfloor to boardroom, this will help substantially in reducing the sense of alienation felt by too many British employees. An increased commitment to the democratic firm should also substantially assist our economic recovery, as well as providing a firm basis for a permanent incomes policy. In addition, such a development will give the unions a new and more constructive role. In the longer term, an industry with greater worker participation should strengthen democracy as a whole.

In the past, British trade unions have shown considerable ability to adapt. They now have the possibility of participating with management in the running of industry and, on a wider stage, in the national decision-making process. The question, which the trade unions alone can answer, is whether they have the imagination and determination to grasp this opportunity. What is certain, however, is that a trade union decision in favour of industrial democracy would be immensely beneficial to employees, managers, and the community at large.

A note on the 1978 industrial democracy White Paper

This book would be incomplete without some reference to the government White Paper on industrial democracy, which was published in late spring 1978, after more than a year's consultation and debate. Its main recommendations are the establishment of the right to discuss strategic issues in companies employing more than 500 people, followed later by the introduction of an additional right to employee representation on supervisory boards of companies employing more than 2,000 workers.

Its emphasis on a flexible and phased introduction of industrial democracy is very much in line with the proposals contained in this book. The White Paper envisages most arrangements being worked out by those involved, with statutory rights only being invoked as a last resort. In the private sector, there would be no question of any imposed boardroom representation for three or four years, which should give management – and trade unions – sufficient time to adapt. In any case, some unions will prefer to take up the strategic bargaining option which would come into force immediately. In the public sector, there is likely to be a swifter advance towards boardroom representation, as the government has asked the heads of nationalised industries to start discussions with the appropriate unions.

The White Paper provides ingenious answers to two questions discussed in Chapter 7. With respect to the single channel of representation, it proposes that in both forms of industrial democracy (extension of collective bargaining and employee representation at boardroom level) the joint representation committee (JRC) of the appropriate unions should represent the employees. However, the White Paper suggests that any homogeneous group of a hundred or more employees should have a right of appeal to ACAS.

On the issue of 'parity' between employee and shareholders' representatives, the White Paper expresses the argument for and against, and comes down in favour of the employee representatives having a third of the seats on the supervisory board as a 'reasonable first step'. Provided this is seen as a step towards parity rather than a final limit, then some caution, given managerial misgiving, is understandable.

Judged as a whole, the White Paper should be welcomed by both management and trade unions. It could well provide the basis for a decisive move towards industrial democracy.

INDEX

Acton Society Trust 39
Advisory Conciliation and Arbitration Service 77, 102, 107, 142, 219
Alfred Herbert 29, 151
Allen, V. L. 5
Allis Chalmers 119
Amalgamated Society of Carpenters and Joiners 182
Amalgamated Society of Boilermakers, Shipwrights and Blacksmiths 185
Amalgamated Society of Engineers 182–3
Amalgamated Society of Railways Servants 61
Amalgamated Union of Engineering Workers
  formation of 186
  and industrial democracy 120, 128, 130
  internal democracy of 167–8, 172, 173, 174, 176
  and National Industrial Relations Court 74, 76
  'open' structure of 183
  relations with other unions 186
  Roberts Arundel strike (1967) 43
  services of 189
  share of total union membership 184
  sponsoring of MPs 209
  white collar membership 99, 183
Amalgamation Act (1964) 185
Anderson, Perry 10
Association of Professional Executive Clerical and Computer Staff 99
Association of Scientific, Technical and Managerial Staffs 99, 186, 189
Attlee, Clement 89, 197

Basnett, David 168, 176
Batstone, Eric 127
Bevin, Ernest 85, 142, 221
Biedenkopf Commission 128
British Institute of Management (BM) 116, 213, 214

British Leyland 29, 56, 119, 151
British Petroleum 42
British Steel Corporation 124, 131
Brown, George 64, 152
Brown, William 104
Butler, David 57

Carr, Robert 72
Casserini, Karl 44
Central Arbitration Committee 77, 107
Chrysler 44, 56, 110
Churchill, Winston 64, 142–3, 221
Clegg, Hugh 167
Collective bargaining
  challenges to 10, 85–7, 97
  company-level 86–7, 97, 109, 225
  and comparability 63
  and 'competitive' unionism 185
  and the community 143, 199
  and 'custom and practice' 81, 85, 86, 104–5
  and employees 54, 97
  and Employment Protection Act (1975) 77
  government intervention in 3, 4, 61, 62, 63–4, 67, 94, 111, 113, 215, 224, 225
  information for 107–8
  impact of 62, 143
  and industrial democracy 103–4, 109, 115, 117–18, 120, 123, 126, 129, 134, 135
  and Industrial Relations Act (1971) 75–6
  industry-wide 16, 68, 85–97, 108–9
  international co-ordination of 87, 97, 109–11, 225
  and joint industrial councils (JICs) 83, 108
  limitations of 9–10, 30–2, 117, 119
  and management 85–7, 97
  and multi-national firms 43, 86–7, 97
  and manpower policy 105, 225
  plant 16, 68, 85–7, 97, 104–8, 109, 117, 118, 122, 124, 171, 190, 225
  and Royal Commission on Trade Unions and Employers' Associa-

in West Germany 21
Industrial Relations Act (1971) 71–5
  assumptions of 13
  and closed shop 72–3, 75, 217
  and collective bargaining 75–6
  and industrial disputes 73, 76
  and industrial relations 76–7
  and industrial tribunals 143
  and Labour party 196
  and management 75–6
  on recognition of trade unions 74–5, 101–2
  repeal of 144, 146, 197, 217
  and Royal Commission on trade unions and employers' associations 71–2
  and trade unions 19, 21, 71–7, 78, 138, 139, 140, 185, 196
  and trade union rules 173
  and TUC 90, 92, 140, 143
Industrial Training Act (1964) 105–6
Industrial Training Boards 106, 142
Industries
  hotel and catering 15, 100–1
  construction 15
  distribution 15, 100, 102
  engineering 16
  mining 17, 34, 35, 36, 51–7, 118
  gas 17
  electricity 17
  newspaper 17
  docks 17, 50, 57, 69
  motor 17, 34, 69
  capital intensive 17, 23, 36, 37
  chemicals 17, 23, 34
  oil-refining 17, 23, 34
  cotton 34, 36
  agriculture 3, 35
  shipbuilding 34, 35, 36, 50, 57, 151
  railways 34, 36
  synthetic fibres 34
  service 34, 35, 100, 102
  public administration 34, 35
  iron and steel 35
  marine engineering 35
  transport 35
  manufacturing 15, 35, 155
  shipping 69
  motor repair 100
  clothing 102
  aircraft 151
  banking 155
  insurance 155
  tourism 155
Industry, Department of 147, 153
Industry Act (1972) 147

Industry Act (1975) 107, 146, 216
Inflation
  causes of 21–4, 65
  and full employment 62–3
  and employees 20
  and government 22–3
  and incomes policy 23, 87–8
  and investment 23
  and management 14
  and multinational firms 23
  and taxation 22, 65
  and trade unions 21–4, 98
  and unemployment 87–8
  and wages 23, 87, 111
  of the 1970s 2, 87, 139
Inquiry on industrial democracy (Bullock Committee)
  criticisms of 121, 123, 124, 134
  and CBI 121
  and directors' responsibilities 129
  and German co-determination system 124–5
  and the Liberal Party 121
  and libertarian argument 127
  main recommendations of 120–1, 214
  membership of 116
  origins of 116
  and 'parity' representation on boards 126–7
  and trade unions 128
  and TUC 120
Institute of Journalists 218
International Business Machines (IBM) 43
International computers (ICL) 151
International Confederation of Free Trade Unions (ICFTU) 109
International Federation of General Workers 23, 100
International Federation of Chemical and General Workers 23, 100
International Federation of Commercial, Clerical and Technical Employees 110
International Metal Workers Federation 44, 110
International Telephone and Telegraph Corporation (ITT) 45
Italy 109

Jackson, D. 22
Japan 148, 152
Jenkins, Clive 120
Joint representation committees 121, 132, 177, 187, 227

and multi-national firms 40, 42
and multi-unionism 187, 194, 202–3
and National Economic Development Council 143, 153
and National Incomes Commission 143
and public expenditure 156–9
and recruitment 99, 133
representative nature of 89
and government 199, 200, 221
and research 191, 203
review body of 217, 219, 228
and select committees 223
staff of 203, 228
structure of 202–4
and trade union contributions 194, 202
and trade union rules 173, 203
and trade union structure 185
and training 189, 203
Trade Union and Labour Relations (Amendment) Act (1976) 218,
TUC Labour party liaison committee 92, 205, 206–7, 211
Training Service Agency 106
Transport and General Workers Union
formation of 182
internal democracy of 168–9, 176, 177
and National Industrial Relations Court 76
open structure of 183
and recruitment 99–101
relations with other unions 186–7
services of 189
share of total union membership 184

and white-collar membership 99, 183
Turkey 148
Turner, H. A. 22, 53–4, 81

Union of Construction and Allied Trades 182
Unemployment
and collective bargaining 105
and Conservative government (1970–74) 65–6
and investment 31, 155
and marketing 32
regional 16, 35, 155
and technology 34–6
and the 1970s 15–16, 35, 139, 154–5
and trade unions 16, 98
youth 155
Unilever 42
Union of Shop Distributive and Allied Workers 167, 176–7
United States 109, 148, 168
Upper Clyde Shipbuilders 119

Voltaire 5

Webbs, Sidney and Beatrice 9
Wedderburn, K. W. 62, 217
Western Germany 49, 109, 124–5, 127, 129, 131, 148
Whitley Committee 85
Wilkinson, F. 22
Wilson, Harold 44, 197
Woodcock, George 201

Yugoslavia 130

Zweig, Ferdinand 56